"Griffin Dix's book is highly readable, heart-rending, engrossing and suspenseful.
It is not a novel, or a fictionalized version of a true story. It is the true story."
—**David Hemenway**, Ph.D., Professor of Health Policy, Harvard T.H. Chan School of Public Health,
and Co-Director of the Harvard Injury Control Research Center

# WHO KILLED KENZO?

## The Loss of a Son and the Ongoing Battle for Gun Safety

# GRIFFIN DIX

# WHO KILLED KENZO?

## The Loss of a Son and the Ongoing Battle for Gun Safety

## GRIFFIN DIX

woodhall press

Woodhall Press | Norwalk, CT

woodhall press

Woodhall Press, 81 Old Saugatuck Road, Norwalk, CT 06855
WoodhallPress.com

Cover design: Jessica Dionne
Layout artist: L.J. Mucci

**Library of Congress Cataloging-in-Publication Data available**

ISBN 978-1-954907-62-1        (paper: alk paper)
ISBN 978-1-954907-63-8        (electronic)

First Edition
Distributed by Independent Publishers Group
(800) 888-4741

Printed in the United States of America

This is a work of creative nonfiction. All of the events in this memoir are true to the best of the author's memory. Some names and identifying features have been changed to protect the identity of certain parties. The author in no way represents any company, corporation, or brand, mentioned herein.

# CONTENTS

## Appendices

For Lynn and Kalani

# INTRODUCTION

## By David Hemenway

David Hemenway, Ph.D. is Professor of Health Policy at the Harvard T.H. Chan School of Public Health, and Co-Director of the Harvard Injury Control Research Center

When I was growing up, I implicitly believed that the job of grownups was to help keep me safe. I was raised by a wonderful family, and the many adults with whom I came in contract seemed honest and honorable and would never try to hurt me. But I slowly realized that I was, unfortunately, quite mistaken. Though none ever tried to injure me personally, many adults acted in ways that could injure anonymous children, of which I might be one.

As a teenager I remember seeing a smart child interviewed on TV, and they were asked what they learned from television advertisements. They thought about it for a moment and responded: "That adults will lie for money." When I became an adult, my career in public health taught me, over and over, that many seemingly respectable adults will act in ways that may result in thousands of children dying so they can become a little more successful, make a little more money.

Kenzo is one of the children who died needlessly. He did nothing wrong. He was responsible and he chose a responsible best friend. But like Kenzo, that friend was a teenager, and teenagers—like adults, but more so—do not behave perfectly 100 percent of the time.

This book is an autobiography of the life of a survivor—Kenzo's father, who has devoted his life to ensure that other children will not meet a similar fate.

A dozen years ago I wrote a book with 64 documented success stories in injury and violence prevention—how the world has been safer, so fewer people die or become seriously injured. Sadly, there were always individuals and institutions trying to prevent these

1

advances. I also described some public health activists who worked successfully, without fame or fortune, to help make your life longer and healthier. Griffin Dix is a public health activist.

His book is highly readable, suspenseful, engrossing, and often heart-rending. It tells about the common (we know a lot of teens will die the way Kenzo did, we just don't know whom), heart-rending events of the day of the "accident." It depicts the trauma, often life-long, to so many.

In my academic work, I have analyzed firearms data for more than three decades. I have read thousands of synopses of fatal firearm events from both the police and medical/examiner coroner reports. Among unintentional firearm injury deaths, a common scenario is a teenage boy accessing a semi-automatic pistol, taking out the magazine, thinking it unloaded, and pulling the trigger. Probably nothing terrible happens. But sometimes he shoots and kills his younger sibling—or his best friend. The easy way to prevent most of these tragedies is to make small, inexpensive changes to the firearm (e.g., magazine safeties and noticeable chamber-loaded indicators).

In the United States, guns have created a major public health problem. Compared to children in other high-income countries, an American child has a higher chance of being killed by a firearm. Not 20 percent higher, or 50 percent higher or twice as high, or 10 times as high, but 20 times higher. And our relative problem has gotten worse over time. Currently, for example, more US children die from firearms than from motor vehicles.

I have sponsored surveys of large numbers of high school students in cities across the United States. The students say how easy it is to obtain guns. Why do so many carry guns? Because they are afraid. Why are they afraid? Because so many other teens are carrying guns. We ask them—what kind of world would you like to live in, one where it is easy (their world), difficult or impossible for teens to get guns? The large majority want it to be impossible, including the majority of those who have already carried guns illegally. That is the world which adults in every other high-income country have created for their children.

I teach at a public health school with large numbers of international students. They cannot understand the United States. Why don't American adults do something more to protect their children? Why do we allow these deaths to happen?

In the United States, the overwhelming majority of adults want universal background checks, and a sizeable majority want limits on the ready availability of military weapons. This has been true for decades. We live in a democracy. Why don't our elected representatives heed our desires?

Griffin Dix's book is a personal history. It is not focused on answering these questions, but the answers are right there in the story of his life and are probably better illuminated and remembered than if they were in a scientific tome.

Much of the book is about the civil trial with the family as plaintiff and the gun manufacturer as defendant. That story is engrossing, suspenseful, and revealing of how the real-world justice system works—not always to the benefit of society.

This book is not a novel, or a fictionalized version of a true story. It is the true story. It is a case exemplar of many of the lessons I have been teaching for four decades in Injury Prevention 101.

The first and most fundamental lesson of Injury Prevention is that, for any injury, there are a host of things that had to have occurred, the absence of any one would have prevented the injury from happening. The lay public tends to focus on the exact moment of the event itself, but it is almost always true that changing things upstream is more effective, and more cost-effective, for preventing the injury. Typically, that means changing the product or the environment rather than focusing solely on changing human nature. Unfortunately, many industries are making profits from making products that are killing us and don't want to make any changes.

Motor vehicle manufacturers, for example, advertised freedom, adventure, power, and prestige, and, historically, did not want motorists to think about the dangers of motoring. They refused to compete on safety. They had to be forced to put seat belts and collapsible steering columns in their vehicles, and for two decades fought against adding air bags. Today, largely because of the vehicle safety testing and data analyses conducted by the federal government and a non-profit insurance institute, consumers know which vehicles are safer, and companies compete on safety. While virtually every motor vehicle collision requires some sort of human error or bad behavior, and drivers today are no better than they were a half century ago, deaths per mile driven have fallen more than 80 percent.

Tort suits against the tobacco industry provided evidence that the industry was knowingly lying about the science relating smoking to chronic diseases and was trying to hook children on nicotine to turn them into lifetime cigarette consumers. The tobacco industry has been labelled a rogue industry by public health, but the firearms industry appears to be no better.

Decades ago, the gun industry was in a difficult situation. Its product—firearms—lasts a long time, and the main demand—for hunting and sports shooting—was decreasing. The industry decided to change directions, to start selling (hand)guns for protection. To do this it had to start selling fear—of armed criminals and the "other." Unlike the motor vehicle and cigarette industries which were worse off if their products led to harm, that wasn't the case for firearms. More firearm homicides, especially mass shootings, can lead to more fear and more firearm sales. That type of profit motive is not good for public health.

Cigarette companies did their own research on the effects of tobacco and hid or misled about the findings. The gun industry seemingly does almost no research on the effects of its product, and incredibly, has been quite successful in limiting the research of others. For a quarter century, it wielded enough political power to prevent the CDC from conducting firearms research. Its allies in Congress gave the industry other unprecedented protections—it seems to be the only industry not subject to any federal safety oversight, and, as discussed at some length in this book, it has been given unique protections against civil lawsuits. At the state level, it has succeeded in preventing most municipalities from passing firearm laws to protect their constituents against gun violence.

Finally, what also differentiates the gun industry from other industries is that it has been able to openly and successfully prevent virtually anyone in the industry from effectively breaking ranks in ways that would reduce firearm injury and death. As this book discusses, when the CEO of the gun company Colt's tried to encourage the industry to act to help reduce firearm violence he was quickly replaced, and subsequently when the CEO of Smith & Wesson began to take actions in that direction, an industry boycott led to his resignation.

Before his sudden death, the teenaged Kenzo Dix, for a homework assignment, wrote that when he died in old age, what he hoped to leave his own children were the lessons he would have learned about the nature of the world and human beings. He never lived long enough to have children or to learn many of the world's lessons. But if he has been watching from heaven, I think he might conclude that there are some bad guys and some good guys in the world. The bad guys put profits, position, and power first, and are willing to let tens of thousands of people die as a consequence. Indeed, the worst are those who also prevent others from effectively addressing the problem. The good guys—like his father—try to prevent others from experiencing the type of tragedy his family endured. I think that Kenzo would be quite proud that due to the actions of his dad, and of many other California residents, his state now has the strongest gun laws in America and has experienced a dramatic reduction in firearm deaths.

David Hemenway

# PART I

# Kenzo

# 1

## How Could This Happen?

It was a bright Sunday afternoon in May 1994. I'd done some all-too-rare yard work, and had just stretched out on the couch to relax and read when the doorbell rang.

Two strangers, a young woman and a slightly older man, were on my front porch. When I opened the door, the woman, who was holding a folder, said, "We're here to help, if you'd like to talk about what happened."

Before I could respond, the phone in the kitchen rang.

My wife, Lynn, answered, and I heard, "Yes?...What?" She sounded puzzled, her voice strained and high. "Can't you tell me more than that?"

I asked the strangers to come in and wait while I went to the kitchen. Lynn was just hanging up.

"Kenzo is at Oakland Children's Hospital," she said, heading for the door. "He's been in some kind of an accident. They said to go there immediately. They wouldn't tell me more."

Lynn and I were out the door in seconds, shouting an apology as we rushed past the man and woman still waiting inside the front door. We raced past the kitchen bulletin board and out the door, passing by an odd snapshot I had taken of Kenzo not long ago.

———

It's suppertime on a weekday evening in April—already seven p.m. and cool, the peak of the glowing evening hours, the best time of the day. I can almost feel the sun hesitate on the horizon, pushing back the night and holding onto the daylight just a bit longer.

Lynn is cooking, and the spicy smell of a green Indian curry floats through the house. I'm setting the table. Kenzo and his older brother, Kalani, have just come in from shooting baskets outside. A pulsing hip-hop beat blares through Kenzo's bedroom door.

"Dinner's ready!" Lynn shouts. No response. She has to push open Kenzo's door and yell again for the boys to hear.

As pots bubble on the stove, Lynn scoops mounds of rice into a Hawaiian koa wood bowl. Short, poised, and efficient, she quickly tosses the salad.

Kenzo bounds in, his dirty feet slapping the linoleum. They are long and slender, having outgrown the rest of his body, which is racing to catch up. He is already tall, especially for a half-Japanese kid. He is wearing baggy "jams" he bought on our last trip to see Lynn's family in Hawaii. A faded Day-Glo gecko is peeling off the front of his T-shirt.

"Dinner's not even ready yet!" he gripes after a quick look around. As if in reply, gasps of curry-scented steam burst from the pots on the stove.

10

"Oh, you twerp," Lynn laughs. "You can help your dad set the table." Her arm darts out, and she tickles him below the ribs. He jumps back, grinning. His braces glint in the evening light. She gives him a big hug that tips his head back, then squeezes her nose between her thumb and forefinger, "Whew, Kenzo, you need a bath!"

Looking up, he spots the few wine bottles in a plastic rack above the kitchen cabinet, pulls a chair up, and jumps onto the countertop. He stretches high to grab a bottle of red wine.

"Hey, Kenzo, get down from there with your filthy feet!" Lynn complains.

Kenzo pays no attention. "This wine's from Bordeaux. Isn't that where we went last summer?"

Without answering, Lynn grabs the camera and hands it to me with a shrug and a grin. I frame Kenzo in portrait mode as he stands on the counter, balancing jauntily on one leg. His head almost touches the ceiling as he steadies the bottle against his tummy to examine the label. His lower lip protrudes as he puzzles over the French.

Snap!

———

When we raced out of the house, Lynn got behind the wheel and we made our way through Berkeley to Oakland Children's Hospital, trying to figure out what was going on. Lynn's lips were pursed tight. "I don't like this," she said. "I think Kenzo must be hurt badly. Why wouldn't they tell us how he is?"

"I'm sure he's in good hands. He'll be okay," I answered. But I wasn't so sure.

At the hospital, we were pointed to a cold white waiting room and told to sit down. We fidgeted. Occasionally, we tried to say something, but there was nothing to say.

Finally, a doctor came in. "Are you the Dixes?"

We nodded.

He took a deep breath and sat down.

"I'm Dr. Steven Yedlin," he began. "Your son was with his friend when the boy got a gun in his house and accidentally shot your son. Apparently, he didn't realize the gun was still loaded. The bullet went through the shoulder and into his heart. They called 911. When your son got here, we did everything we could, but we couldn't save him."

I didn't believe him. *Isn't there something this doctor should be doing, right now?*

Lynn asked, "Can we see Kenzo?"

"No. He's been taken out of the emergency room. You can't see him. I'm sorry. It's hospital policy."

Kenzo was gone.

Kenzo had died.

We couldn't see him.

The doctor left and reentered a minute later with a young woman.

"I have to go now," he said. "I'm very sorry for your loss. This is Isabel Rodriguez. She's a clinical social worker who'll help you."

The woman told us there were psychological counseling services we could use and gave us the names of two people to call. She explained, "They were notified to go and help you, but I guess they got to your house too early. They thought you'd already been notified."

There was nothing left to do but drive home, mostly in silence, passing by the Ashby BART station and Berkeley High School.

I was too shocked to say anything. I couldn't help wondering what Kenzo looked like. Where was he now? Did he suffer? We were not prepared for this.

My thoughts were everywhere, and now I thought about Kalani. He was almost eighteen, ready for college. What would this mean for him? He and his brother were so close.

When we got home, Lynn called Kalani into the living room. He looked at us, wary.

I plunged in, suddenly able to speak. "Sit down," I said, motioning to a chair. "We just got back from the hospital. Kenzo was over at Mark's and there was an accident. Kenzo was shot. They tried to save him at the hospital, but they couldn't. He was killed."

"He was killed? Kenzo?" Kalani stared at us, shocked. "How did it happen?"

"Mark got his father's gun and shot Kenzo by mistake. They called 911. There was nothing they could do."

None of us could believe it. We all sat there, unable to help each other. There was nothing that could help.

Before long, a tired-looking man walked up the stairs to our front door and introduced himself as a police detective. He'd already spoken with everyone at Mark's house, and now he had come to tell us what happened. We pointed him to the blue couch and switched on the lamp next to it.

He sat on the edge, his back straight, and we pulled up chairs.

"Your son was at Mark's when Mark decided he would go get his father's gun." He told the story slowly and professionally, watching our faces. Why was he looking at us like that? With a shock, I realized that his job was to see if we might get so angry we'd retaliate.

Eventually, he finished his story. We didn't doubt it was an accident. We knew Mark. He was a good kid, one of Kenzo's best friends since they'd met at Berkeley Arts Magnet School.

We thanked the officer, and he left us alone in silence.

Before we went to bed that night, Lynn said, "We should go to Mark's house tomorrow to tell him we know he didn't mean to shoot Kenzo."

I didn't want to face it, but I knew she was right.

We soon learned that when he was taken to the police station that first evening, Mark was asked to explain in writing what had happened. He wrote his story on six pages of lined paper, in his kid's printing, like a school assignment.

When we got to my house we went to my room and sat in there for a couple of minutes and listened to one of my tapes....Kenzo loaded and shot the Sheridan BB gun at some birds. I loaded it and shot it once....

I went downstairs alone to my dad's and mom's room. I unzipped the bag that carries his Beretta, released the clip, unzipped a second compartment of the bag, and took an empty clip out, ran upstairs to my bedroom, put the empty clip in.

Kenzo turned around with the Sheridan in his hand. He said something. I flicked the safety up and Bam! He was shot in the arm, with his face in my futon on his knees. I tried to pick him up to take him to the living room. I left him.

My mother ran to see what happened while my sister was in her bedroom and my grandfather in his, right next to mine. I screamed, "Help, I shot Kenzo" (not exactly sure).

My mother said, "What? What?"

"I shot Kenzo—hurry, call 911!" I ran around.

She said, "Calm down" (she said that repeatedly).

I ran to Kenzo. My mom gave me a towel. I tied it around his shoulder, picked his head up, tried to open his mouth. My mom said, "Do that CPR." I plugged his nose and blew in his mouth. He gasped for air. I pushed his chest in like I've seen on TV. I got up and looked to see if the 911 operator was still on the line.

I ran back to Kenzo and said, "Look at me, open your mouth." He did slightly. I put my finger in his mouth to move his tongue so he did not choke. I blew into his mouth again, pumping his chest. I then pushed his eyelids so he would keep his attention on me. (I forgot. After I picked him up, I ran downstairs and put the gun back in the bag.)

Then the cops came in and told me get out. I did. Another officer said, "Slowly, show me where the gun is." I showed him with my hands in the air so nothing would happen. I backed away and pointed at the gun in the bag next to the bed.

14

—

That first night I lay in bed squirming, sweating, and sleepless. My body wanted to defend itself; it wanted to protect Kenzo.

In the morning, we drove to Mark's house.

A woman I had never met answered the door and said she was Mark's stepmother. Her face was chalk-white and puffy, her swollen eyes bleary and tearful. She brought us into the living room and asked us to sit.

We couldn't sit.

Mark's father, Clifford, came in, his eyes red. I had met him only once, briefly, when I had dropped Kenzo off there. He ran his palm over his crew cut and told us how sorry he was for what had happened.

Then Mark staggered into the living room, head down. I barely recognized him as the good-looking kid I knew. His sallow face was streaked with tears. His shirt, drenched in sweat, stuck to his back. Lynn blurted, "Mark," and put her arms around him. He embraced her and broke down, his shoulders heaving as he gasped between loud sobs. Over and over, he cried, "I'm sorry. I'm sorry. I love Kenzo. I'm sorry." Then I hugged Mark, too. His muscular body dripped sweat and tears. He wailed, "I'm sorry. I'm sorry."

"Mark," Lynn asked gently, "can we see where it happened?"

None of this seemed real.

Mark led us down a dark narrow hall, up a flight of stairs, and into his room, messy with clothes, dumbbells, and other sports equipment. On the beige carpet a small spot of dried, brown blood screamed for attention—Kenzo's blood. This is where Kenzo lay in pain.

We could not bear to stay there.

When we got back from Mark's, Lynn told a neighbor what had happened to Kenzo. Our neighbor couldn't believe it. She asked what she could do to help.

"I don't know," said Lynn. She felt trapped in agony. "I guess maybe we could take a walk this evening, before the sun goes down."

At 6:30, we went outside. From our front porch we were looking down on a crowd of about thirty people standing on the sidewalk and out in the street. Normally I might have felt shy or embarrassed, but I was too dazed to feel anything. Our neighbors hugged and consoled us, and then we all took a walk together through the tree-lined streets of the neighborhood, around a few blocks, and past Great Stoneface Park, with its big rock that the kids liked to climb on. People who happened to look out their windows curiously watched a strange, quiet crowd walk slowly by.

Our neighbors helped us get through the first blurred, numb days. Without asking us, they each volunteered to deliver dinner to our house every night for weeks. One night, someone would arrive with a favorite meal of polenta and a salad, home-baked bread, and pie for dessert. The next night someone else would show up with a wicker basket filled with ribs, corn on the cob, and asparagus with shaved almonds. The next evening the doorbell would ring and a vase of flowers would be sitting next to a pot of delicious soup with challah made from an old family recipe.

One of Kenzo's friends told us that if they could just see Kenzo once more, it might help them. So we held a viewing. It was the only time I saw Kenzo again after he left home that Sunday morning.

He lay in his casket at the mortuary, pale, pasty, somber, and still. His friends filed past, hanging onto each other for support and crying softly. As they walked by his casket, they saw the small basketball, the teddy bear wearing Kenzo's old T-shirt, and a few other mementos Lynn had placed next to him. One of his friends pulled his Berkeley High School ID card out of his wallet and placed it next to Kenzo. Soon dozens of cards, hats, and other impromptu personal offerings lined the sides of his casket, to be sent off with him.

Later, at the funeral, we put up a large poster board covered with pictures of Kenzo, his friends, and our family in the atrium of the chapel at the Northbrae Community Church. We wanted to celebrate his short but happy life.

There was a picture of chubby little Kenzo, a tot holding his older brother's hand as they stepped carefully through the patch of strawberries we grew when we lived in San Jose and I taught cultural anthropology at Santa Clara University.

There was my favorite picture of Kalani and Kenzo, taken when Kenzo was about seven. They sit side by side on the small deck off our kitchen. Kalani playfully mugs for the camera, and Kenzo's arm is draped gently around his brother's shoulder, his head thrown back in easy abandon. The evening light bathes his smooth skin, highlighting a smile of utter contentment. Kenzo offered joyful affection to all of us.

Next to the pictures we had pinned a poem Kenzo wrote for a high school assignment, prompted by the title, which his English teacher gave.

*I Believe*
*I believe in the mind and its unknown wonders,*
*The lifelong friendship,*
*The drive to the basket,*
*The importance of humor,*
*The midnight snack.*
*But I don't believe in the economy, and working only for the money.*
*I believe in seizing the day.*
*I believe in a good night's sleep.*
*I believe in relaxation and meditation.*
*And I believe in random sibling playful fights that bring people closer,*
*And the importance of sister/brotherhood in family and throughout life.*

And there was that odd picture of Kenzo balancing on one bare foot on the top of the kitchen counter, a bottle of French wine in his hand.

During the funeral, a friend sang a ballad in pitch-perfect voice, in Kenzo's memory. At the reception, another friend of Kenzo's played jazz piano.

At the grave site, I remember being a little surprised to see Mark's father, and mostly avoiding him—not knowing how to deal with my feelings toward him. There was anger and confusion, but also somewhere in my mind, sympathy as well, albeit unexpressed.

And there were other strong emotions I could not name—new, raw, jumbled, potent.

After the funeral, we kept the pictures of Kenzo in our dining room for visitors to see.

Whenever I walked by them, I felt as if I were looking through a dim window at someone else's happy life, although it had been my life only yesterday.

I took some time off from my research and consulting business. As time passed, gradually, fewer friends came to visit, and one day no sympathy cards arrived in the mail. People seemed to expect us to put our lives back together. We were alone again.

I was exhausted from sleepless nights, stunned by the physical attack grief made on my body. My mind refused to give in. I was still waiting for Kenzo to come back where he belonged. When I went out, I often saw him out of the corner of my eye, a tall, handsome, Asian-looking kid. I looked again; it wasn't him.

I could not stop looking for the boy who had walked out the front door one Sunday morning and disappeared through a hole in the universe. I could not stop looking for that hole, waiting for him to walk back through it, to reappear suddenly as if nothing had happened.

This was a colossal practical joke we'd laugh at together when things got back to the way they should be.

We left Kenzo's room as it was, as if by leaving it we might somehow prevent his disappearance from our lives. His school books—math, history—sat on his desk on a pile of homework papers, where his hand had left them. His pens stuck upright in the holes of his ceramic basketball pen holder, ready for his hand to grab. His drum set remained just to the left of his bedroom door, waiting for him to come back and practice complex rhythms, to make a great noise. The poster he had taped above his window still cried out, "No Justice, No Peace."

I listened for his music coming from his room.

Every time I walked by, I expected to see him. But he wasn't there. And every day I asked, "How could this happen?"

# 2

## After

On Christmas Day in 1994, six months after Kenzo's death, Lynn and I walked up the small hill to Kenzo's grave in Sunset Cemetery, just north of Berkeley. As we approached, we saw a piece of white paper flutter in the wind as if someone were waving it at us. It was stuffed into the metal flower container in front of the gravestone.

Lynn picked it up. The weathered sheet crinkled in her hand as she unfolded it. A message printed in large script was still legible, though the ink had been blurred by the night's dew.

*Kenzo, how are you? I still am hella missing you, bro. You must not be too lonely with all of your friends coming by + visiting you. I think of you every day + think of what it would be like if you were still around. Anyways, I go with*

21

*Wendy now. I don't think you know her. She's beautiful. Sam goes with Susie + Jimmy with JoAnna. I wish I could talk to you face to face. I miss you, my friend. I wish we could have grown up to be old and gray + to talk about all our good childhood memories together. I thought about the secret rock you only showed to Sam and me. He has it now. I love to think how I became your friend. I miss you + I can't wait till we see each other again. Merry Christmas—I hope you read this note whenever you are lonely + I hope it will cheer you up. Much love to you, brother. I love you, homie!!!!*

A shiver of regret and affection for these sweet kids ran through me. I would still be seeing them often if Kenzo were alive.

I knew Kenzo had died, but I did not *know* it. I was still trying to refuse it. As though I were some dark tree deep in a foggy forest filmed in time-lapse, wisps of life's winds rushed past me but I remained closed down, numb.

I could not help but keep Kenzo a part of my daily routine, as he had been since he was born. At night when I went to bed, I often lay awake for hours thinking of him as if he were in the next room. When sleep finally came, I wrestled fitfully with demons I could not identify.

Sometimes when I woke up in the morning, I wondered what Kenzo and Kalani had going on that day, and if there was something I should remind them of—until I realized. As I struggled off to breakfast, my body ached and felt drained of energy. The kitchen was painfully quiet and somber.

The days crawled past. In fits and starts old habits reasserted themselves, only to be shattered by the new reality. It's hard to say which was worse: briefly falling back into a comfortable routine that included Kenzo and then suddenly being jolted out of it when

I realized his absence, or steadily missing him, aware that he would never be with us again.

Somewhere I had gotten the idea that grief was psychological, but this was physical. I always felt beat-up, in a state of exhaustion somewhere between wakefulness and sleep. Lynn felt the same.

Looking back, our sufferings must have felt so personal to each of us—almost like bodily functions—that we hardly spoke to each other about them. We had little energy left over for more than just getting by.

Lynn had always been known for her vitality, humor, and adventurousness. As a French major at the University of Hawaii, she had transferred to the far-off, frigid University of Wisconsin for something different. When she graduated, she won a Fulbright and lived in France, coming back to UH for her master's in teaching English as a second language.

After I had served in the Peace Corps in South Korea, I had become a graduate student at the University of Hawaii, where a Peace Corps friend in Lynn's department had introduced us. After a whirlwind courtship, we had married and gone to Southern California, where I studied for my PhD in cultural anthropology at the University of California, San Diego, while she worked. When I was ready to go back to South Korea to do fieldwork in a rural village, she was eager to go, despite never having been there and knowing no Korean.

But now, after Kenzo's death, her adventurousness and humor had evaporated. Like me, she struggled through the days, hoping only that eventually this would pass.

I can see now that we should have sought counseling early on, before patterns set in. But we were completely unprepared for what was happening, and felt entirely alone, despite the support of well-meaning friends. Through our inaction, by default, we chose merely to wait out our grief in the hope that it would eventually pass.

In this I was particularly guilty. It seems a male strategy: to hunker down and wait—stubborn and dogged. I may have tried to put a good face on it, thinking that being patient and stoic was in some odd way manly, or "responsible." But now I can see that I was detached, impassive, and withdrawn when others in my family whom I loved were suffering.

Kenzo died at the end of May. Soon the school year was over and the students were set free. Without Kenzo, Kalani was spending hours alone in his room, with his friends more than ever before. But they didn't know what he was experiencing, or whether they should ask him about it. He told me he had one conversation with a group of his friends about what he was going through, but in general, none of them seemed comfortable talking about it. Soon they all fell back into old routines.

They weren't the only ones acting this way. Lynn and I had tried to talk with Kalani about his feelings, but it seemed as difficult for us as it was for him.

A few months after Kenzo died, Kalani went on a two-week Outward Bound trip in the High Sierra that we had scheduled before Kenzo's death. When Kalani got back, we sat him down at the kitchen table to hear about it. Mellow light from the long summer evening floated in through French doors from the small deck behind our house. Looking dirty, tanned, and fit, Kalani seemed to have recovered his old energy. He told us the group of teenagers set daily hiking goals for themselves of many miles. We could see from his face how proud they all became that they had helped each other achieve them.

He became more animated, telling us how the counselors had taught them wilderness survival skills, even showing them how to catch fish with their bare hands. He said he'd peeked over the bank of a stream into a dark pool where a counselor thought a fish might be. Something was moving there. Demonstrating for us, he said he'd reached down into the cold water, felt around, and touched the

24

bottom of a fish's belly. It didn't move, and he'd plucked it out of the water. Everyone spent at least one night alone or with a friend, away from the group, taking almost no food with them. Kalani told us he went alone, and thought about Kenzo the whole time.

When their excursion was over, Kalani exchanged phone numbers and promised to keep in close touch with these new friends from all over the country. But during the whole trip he never once told any of them what was uppermost on his mind: that he had just lost his brother.

For a while after Kalani had returned from his trip with such energy, it seemed as if things were getting better. But gradually, back at home—unable to pop into Kenzo's room and lonely without him—Kalani withdrew once again into his own sorrow and confusion. And struggling with our own grief, we were powerless to help him, or each other.

Our sorrow and loss also introduced a wedge between us and our friends. Many of them thought it polite to avoid the subject of Kenzo, his death and our grief, and to pretend that everything was back to normal. A few friends were able to go beyond quick expressions of sympathy, to ask us how we were and listen for an answer. But we didn't know how we were or what we were feeling; it changed from moment to moment.

Questions about our future lurked. How would Kenzo's death affect us? What would we do now? We were unable to take such questions on yet. When you have fallen off a cliff, on the way down it's hard to think about what you'll do once you hit the ground.

Those first months after Kenzo died are still a blur of pain. Fortunately, a couple of wise and generous therapists who lived on our street offered to help us, and they did. Lynn and Kalani each met with Danny Goldstine several times. Every week for quite a while, I would go and sit down with Hilary Goldstine in her office. She would push her glasses back on her head and in a soft voice say, "Well...," and we would begin talking. Soon we'd be crying together, and she would gently guide me toward ways I could help Kalani through this.

On the occasions—too rare—when I went into his room, planning on an intimate father-son soul-baring talk, Kalani and I found it easier to get diverted to other topics, and so we somehow never got around to asking each other about our feelings, taking the time to listen or express our private thoughts to each other.

Soon the summer ended, and Kalani went away to Humboldt State University in Northern California, to face all of these difficult issues on his own. He had friends there from Berkeley High. Most of them seemed more excited by the freedom from parental oversight than by academics.

In those first months, I thought constantly about the circumstances of Kenzo's death—although *thought* might be too logical, too conscious a term. I mulled over Kenzo's death; I ruminated about it; I tried to let go of it. But I could not avoid it.

Kenzo's death yanked open a door to a room full of questions about agency, cause, and responsibility. We had been shocked; his death seemed so senseless. One question in particular began to needle me: Was Kenzo's death just a bizarre accident, or could it somehow have been prevented—and, if so, by whom?

The question was inseparable from our process of grieving because of the particular way he had died. His death was not like one caused by a disease.

But how to find answers?

We each felt utterly alone those first months after Kenzo died.

Then we discovered that we were not alone at all.

# 3

## The Reluctant Club

A few months after Kenzo's death, Lynn said that someone at her office in legal information at San Francisco's Pillsbury, Madison & Sutro law firm had given her the name of a highly respected man who was a leader at preventing injuries to children.

We made an appointment to meet with Andrew McGuire and his wife, Kae, who had founded the Trauma Foundation at San Francisco General Hospital. Over lunch in a restaurant on Market Street, we told them what had happened to Kenzo.

They listened carefully. That day, for the first time, we heard about the public health effort to prevent gun violence.

Andrew suggested several conferences I might go to, and soon, I began occasionally traveling to conferences of the Coalition to Stop Gun Violence and other groups, such as the HELP Network, an organization of physicians and public health researchers trying to prevent gun deaths and injuries. The faux-opulent hotels, with their rooms for nonsmokers that smelled of stale smoke, and their little refrigerators filled with tempting but costly treats, were like those at any other convention. But the people I met at those conferences were an odd mix of remarkable professionals and brave victims.

Some were doctors and academic public health experts. A few of the physicians were emergency trauma surgeons, among the first to touch the victims of gruesome gunshot wounds. Researchers, many from university schools of public health, came to explain their pains-taking studies in a language of specific methodologies and necessary caveats. I remember Dr. Christine Cassel reporting on a national poll that indicated 84 percent of Americans wanted handguns registered in the same way we register automobiles. I wondered why Congress would not pass or even discuss the registration of firearms. In fact, it explicitly outlawed the practice.

Victims of gun violence, like me, were there searching for answers. I was something of a hybrid, a former social science researcher and college professor, now a victim of gun violence.

Many of the grieving survivors I met had started their own local nonprofit organizations. At several conferences, I got to know Karen Dickson, whose teenage son Andrew Papen had wanted to be a marine but was suddenly shot in Toledo, Ohio. She stood all day at her elaborate traveling exhibit, covered with worn and creased pictures of her dead son and of the marches she had organized. She never tired of talking with strangers who stopped to ask her what had happened. She would talk about her local group, ANDREW, named in honor of her handsome son, now gone.

There were many other small survivors' organizations: SOSAD (Save Our Sons and Daughters), MAD DADS, Mothers Against Violence, Drop the Gun Try the Son, Illinois Council Against Hand-gun Violence, CAVEAT (Canadians Against Violence Everywhere

Advocating Its Termination), and more. Each survivor was dedicated to saving other parents from the misery that she or he had endured.

During breaks, we stood in small circles, told our stories, shook our heads, and hugged. We were each shocked, yet also relieved, to find others like us. We were discovering an American reality that we had always assumed had nothing to do with us.

Survivors could identify others by the pictures of smiling lost children pinned to our shirts. We could not be more diverse. Black, white, Hispanic, rural, urban, educated or not, Republican, Democrat. We formed small circles at cocktail receptions and bonded. We asked each other what happened to each other's child. How did the killer get the gun? Did they catch him? What was your experience with the police, with the courts?

We told each other how we sought relief from grief, the ways our lost children came back to us in beautiful dreams and wrenching nightmares, how we seemed to have lived two lives—one before, and one after we heard the phone ring or the knock on the door. Soon I began to hear of deaths like Kenzo's, that happened because someone took a loaded magazine out of a semiautomatic handgun and thought the gun was unloaded.

I came back home from these conferences energized but still confused about what to do. As Lynn and I mulled over what had happened, we realized there was more behind Kenzo's death than we had originally thought. But what actions should we take? To start, we had to find help. We needed models.

Then, during the winter after Kenzo died, we happened upon a flyer for a rally in support of a bill in the California legislature to strengthen the state's assault weapons ban. We had read in the papers that its impetus had been the horrendous 101 California Street massacre perpetrated by a paranoid, failed businessman with a misplaced grudge against a law firm. He had attacked it with military-style assault weapons, killing nine people and wounding six.

When Lynn called the number on the flyer, Michelle Scully picked up the phone. She was organizing the rally. Lynn was surprised to hear Michelle's name; everyone in the Bay Area knew her story.

———

On July 1, 1993, eleven months before Kenzo was shot, Michelle Scully had been working at an empty desk on the thirty-third floor of the gleaming new 101 California Street office building. Not yet thirty, she was a recent law school graduate who hoped to use her skills to improve the lives of children. She was there to be near her husband, Mark Scully, twenty-eight, and already a lawyer at Pettit & Martin.

The firm-wide meeting scheduled for that day had been canceled, so Mark was working on a lawsuit at his desk on the thirty-fourth floor. Suddenly he heard gunfire. He thought of Michelle, and ran down the staircase to the thirty-third floor. He burst into the room where she sat and shouted that they had to get out fast. They raced down the hallway.

"Suddenly this guy walked around the corner and shot a man dead in front of us," Michelle later told a reporter. "We ran into someone's office and tried to barricade the door with a filing cabinet and hide, but he found us."

As the man raised his gun, Mark threw his body in front of Michelle's. In an instant, the rapid-fire assault weapon had blasted six bullets into Mark's side. Michelle watched the shooter's eyes as he pulled the trigger again and again.

When the gunman finally moved on, Michelle frantically called 911, then tried to help Mark survive. He lay in her arms for a half-hour as they waited for help. She begged him to hold on as his blood spurted across the floor. Eventually he said, "Michelle, I'm dying. I love you."

30

Mark Scully died a few hours later at San Francisco General Hospital. He had never met his killer before that day. He had saved Michelle's life, though she was badly wounded in one arm.

The gunman had continued through the building randomly murdering people who happened to be in the same office building as Pettit & Martin. Finally, he went back to the stairwell and headed down. When he saw two police officers coming toward him, he pointed one of his guns up under his chin and fired a bullet through his head.

Three floors of the tall, gleaming building looked like a war zone. The assault weapons had shot through glass walls and wooden doors. Bullet casings littered the halls. Bodies lay on the cold floor. The wounded writhed and moaned.

To commit his mass murder-suicide, the shooter had carted especially lethal weapons into the building. His two Intratec TEC-9 assault pistols were fitted with Hell-Fire triggers for rapid shooting, and they accommodated magazines holding 50 rounds each. He'd brought 250 rounds of 9mm Black Talon bullets made to expand on impact, as well as .45 caliber ammunition for his pistol.

His name was Gian Luigi Ferri. An obsessed fifty-five-year-old former client of Pettit & Martin, he thought he'd been given bad advice in the 1980s that had caused him to lose his real estate holdings. He owed almost nine million dollars to creditors, and the landlord of his ritzy Woodland Hills apartment had recently served him an eviction notice.

But money was not his only problem; he was paranoid and delusional. He believed there was a plot to lace his food with too much MSG. On his body police found a four-page typed letter headed, "LIST OF CRIMINALS, RAPISTS, RACKETEERES, LOBBYISTS." One of the thirty people listed was a former Pettit & Martin lawyer who had helped him buy a mobile home park in the early 1980s. Ferri was apparently a satisfied customer at the time. Only later did his extravagant life as a millionaire real estate developer crash.

31

A year after the shooting, Michelle Scully, who suffered permanent nerve damage to her right arm, still had nightmares almost every night. She'd see a gunman chasing her down a corridor. "I try to run away but it's hopeless, and then suddenly I wake up sweating. The dream happens a lot," she said. "I would see the whole thing happening again and again. It would always end with Mark's face, very bloody, with the blood coming out of his nose and his mouth, just like it was that day."

The life that Michelle and Mark had built was gone. She doesn't practice law anymore. For a time, she had trouble concentrating; sometimes she forgot to do basic things, like paying her bills. She never once returned to their apartment, nor to their favorite hole-in-the-wall Chinese restaurant. To enter those places would have drowned her in bittersweet memories.

"I ask, 'Why me?' a lot," she said. "It's unfair. I feel really cheated out of a wonderful person and a very wonderful life."

I know just what she meant.

———

Lynn and I attended the rally and got to know Michelle Scully. She told us about the lawsuit that the 101 California Street victims' families and the Center to Prevent Handgun Violence had filed against Navegar, maker of the assault pistol Ferri had used. Their complaint argued that the gun maker negligently contributed to the illegal use of its product.

Lynn asked Michelle if there might be some kind of action we could take to force gun makers to change the design of their semiautomatic handguns and help prevent what happened to Kenzo from happening to other kids. I don't think Lynn was even thinking of a lawsuit, just something—*anything*—we might be able to do.

Michelle suggested we call Dennis Henigan, the lawyer for the 101 California Street victims' families, who worked for the Center to Prevent Handgun Violence.

I might have found a way to put off calling some stranger big-shot lawyer out of the blue, but before I even had time to think about procrastinating, Lynn called Henigan. He did not seem like a DC big shot at all; he was friendly and helpful—just not very encouraging. He said the Center carefully selected only cutting-edge cases that might set new legal precedents or reform the gun industry. Still, he asked us to send him information about our case.

We mailed him newspaper articles, the police reports, and Mark's handwritten description of what had happened that Sunday afternoon.

When Henigan called us back, he said he thought our case might have some potential—in part because California has good product liability laws—but he couldn't be sure. He promised to contact us when he next came to San Francisco to meet with the 101 California Street victims.

While we waited, we attended gun-violence-prevention events in San Francisco, where we got to know some of the 101 California Street victims' family members. One night we had dinner with their small, informal group. Marilyn Merrill, Carol Kingsley, and Steve Sposato were already in the San Francisco restaurant when we got there. The spouses of all three had been killed in the shooting.

They greeted us warmly, and we launched into the many things we had to talk about—experiences that most people are fortunate not to have. After we ordered, Lynn brought up our son, Kalani, and asked them how they had helped their children cope with grief.

Marilyn Merrill, a soft-spoken, down-to-earth mother whom I had watched on TV and seen quoted in the newspapers, began telling us how close her young daughter had been to her dad. "Kristen kept asking, 'What do you mean, Daddy is no more?'" Marilyn's voice rose and cracked in a sort of plea. "She was still waiting for him to come home. Eventually I made myself take the kids back to that building and show them Mike's empty office. They'd been there often when we did things together in the city after work. They had loved seeing that he'd put the pictures they'd drawn for him on the walls around his desk. We stayed in his office a whole hour, opening the drawers of his emptied-out desk and talking about him."

Marilyn looked kindly at us. "No one else out there really knows what you're going through." She paused, then asked, "Has your son seen a therapist?"

I said our neighbor, a psychologist, had seen him for a short time, but like most teenagers, Kalani was reluctant to talk about his emotions, so he'd quit going after a few sessions. "Kalani doesn't talk about losing Kenzo," I told her, "but I know he's suffering. He keeps his grief bottled up."

The waiter put beautiful platters of food in front of us. Some ordered a second glass of wine. Our conversation turned to how long to hold on to the memory of the person you loved by keeping their room as it was—and when to give in to the inevitable, remove their clothes from their closet, redecorate, and face the fact that they are slipping away.

In a surprisingly dispassionate way—since by now, she'd said this many times before—Carol Kingsley, a tall, dark-haired lawyer whose husband Jack Berman had died that day, told us how Ferri had planned his delusional "revenge" around the capabilities of the concealable assault pistols and the large-capacity ammunition clips, made to spray bullets into killing fields.

"Without them," she said, "he couldn't have planned a mass murder like that. And if the staff meeting scheduled for that day hadn't been canceled, he would've killed a lot more people."

She told us that when the 101 California Street victims' families learned about these weapons, they were outraged. Why were weapons like that so easily available, and, in fact, advertised to criminals as fingerprint-resistant?

We agreed completely. I found it enormously comforting to find other people who understood our shock, bewilderment, and despair, and who had struggled with the same issues. Even though outwardly our tragedies were very different, I felt that I could have been them, and they could have been me. Part of the same reluctant club, we intuitively understood each other.

Eventually it was time to go. Lynn and I thanked them for being so helpful. We all said good night, then she and I made our way back home to Berkeley and went to bed exhausted.

As I lay looking at the dark ceiling, I recalled turning on the TV the evening of the 101 California Street tragedy. Red and blue emergency lights had flashed across my living room. I had seen the limp bodies of strangers—perhaps my new friends' spouses—lying on gurneys as medics shoved them into emergency vehicles. I remembered watching cameramen run in circles to catch glimpses of the ashen faces of the wounded. At the time, I had no interest in gun policy and, even in my worst nightmares, never would have dreamed that before long I would be reliving traumas with the same strangers that I watched that day in TV news land.

When Lynn and I next met with the 101 California Street victims, we listened in awe at everything they had already accomplished.

Not long after the massacre they learned that California's assault weapons ban had worked—within California—but that Ferri had circumvented the state assault weapons ban; because federal gun laws were so lax, he was able to obtain his arsenal at a gun shop in Nevada. The victims' families began working to get Congress to pass a national assault weapons ban.

With a wry smile, Steve Sposato told us about testifying before a US Senate committee with his daughter, Meghan, asleep in a child carrier on his back. Steve, a Pacific Bell executive and self-described lifelong Republican, whose wife happened to have been in the 101 California Street building that day, had suddenly become Meghan's sole caretaker.

His efforts paid off. On September 13, 1994, after a year of persistent work by many of the 101 California Street victims, Steve stood beside President Bill Clinton as he signed the federal assault weapons ban and dedicated it to Steve's deceased wife, Jody Jones Sposato.

In addition, in 1993 the grieving families of the 101 California Street victims and many of their San Francisco lawyer friends created the Legal Community Against Violence (LCAV). Later, the group changed its name to the Law Center to Prevent Gun Violence, and then to the Giffords Law Center to Prevent Gun Violence, in 2017. (Former congresswoman Gabrielle Giffords is married to retired NASA astronaut, Senator Mark Kelly. On January 8, 2011, while speaking to constituents in Tucson, Arizona, Gabby Giffords was shot in the head by a gunman who killed six people and injured twelve others. She resigned from Congress to recover, and became an inspiration to advocates of evidence-based gun laws. (You can learn more about this by visiting https://giffords.org/about/gabbys-story/).

At events that LCAV and the Center to Prevent Gun Violence sponsored, Lynn and I got to know Michelle Scully and the other survivors better. We learned how much we had in common—the preventable nature of our losses; our certain knowledge that *this should not happen.*

During that first year after Kenzo died, one nightmare—the same nightmare—began to descend on me almost every night. There were no people in this dream, only an urgent, irresistible imperative. It began with a vague awareness of some place or goal across the room that I had to get to—a spot or objective over there that I had to reach or intervene in, *somehow*. But I couldn't. I felt trapped; I could not move. Despite my violent attempts to intercede, this vague goal always eluded me. My failure drove me into a panic. Lynn told me that while asleep I would thrash around wildly, pounding my open hands or fists into the bed over and over. I often sat up or lunged, waking only when my head hit a wall, the floor, or a lamp.

My torment kept Lynn awake. This was one of many problems plaguing us. Despite the steps we had taken together to support other victims of gun violence, our marriage was slipping away. Much of our focus had always been on our children, but now Kalani was away at college and Kenzo was gone. Our home—only recently bursting with the joyful chaos and enthusiasm of two active children and their friends—had become empty and lifeless. All the happiness had evaporated, blown away on a May wind.

They say people grieve differently. I guess this is true. Now, at dinnertime, Lynn and I hunched at the kitchen table that Kalani had made for the family. We spooned our soup softly into downturned mouths—exhausted from sleeplessness, seldom speaking. Each of us remained imprisoned within our own private ruminations. We conducted the old ritual dinners together at that family table as painlessly as possible, then escaped to sit in separate rooms, staring into separate voids. The things that needed to be said were not. Held hostage by our individual turmoil and grief, we each turned inward, with no energy left to comfort each other. Kalani, the son we each loved so dearly, was up at Humboldt State, left on his own, too.

After seeing one marriage counselor, then another, Lynn and I came to understand each other's problems with our marriage. But, still struggling with the loss of Kenzo, neither of us was able to change our behavior toward the other. We did not argue. In fact, we loved and respected each other, but it was no longer a marriage. It was as if we were separated from each other by thick Plexiglas so scuffed it had become opaque. Even when together, we were not really together. There was no more analyzing it. There seemed to be nothing more we could do to change it.

Nine months after Kenzo died, I found an apartment to rent and moved out. I always remember that it was nine months, because that's how long it takes to *make* a child. Within a year Lynn and I divorced. Apparently, that often happens to parents who lose a child. We had joined yet another reluctant club.

# 4

## The Public Safety Committee

After Lynn and I separated, I rented the small downstairs unit in a home in Berkeley. After a while, I began dating, without much interest. I had been singing in a jazz choir, but I'd never played jazz before. I took some jazz piano lessons. Nights—with Kenzo in mind—I mentally repurposed beautifully heartbreaking old ballads to my own emotional needs and clumsily tried to play them:

"Spring is here, why doesn't my heart go dancing?"
"The way your smile just beams, the way you sing off key, the way you haunt my dreams, no, no, they can't take that away from me."
"Don't know why, there's no sun up in the sky, stormy weather."

"Missed the Saturday dance. Heard they crowded the floor. Couldn't bear it without you. Don't get around much anymore."

After a while, my jazz piano teacher fired me. She complained that I wasn't practicing real jazz, such as the Thelonious Monk and Dizzy Gillespie she wanted to teach me (partly true); that I didn't like real jazz (some of it); and that she didn't like the sentimental old ballads I was playing—so maudlin, so old-fashioned (beautiful to me).

As I waited impatiently to hear whether the Center to Prevent Handgun Violence would file our lawsuit against Beretta, I got a call from Barrie Becker, who had replaced Michelle Scully in managing the tiny, shared San Francisco office of the Legal Community Against Violence (LCAV) and Handgun Control, Inc., the precursor to the Brady Campaign to Prevent Gun Violence. Barrie asked me if I would be willing to come with her to Sacramento to testify before the California Assembly Public Safety Committee in favor of Assembly Bill 630, a bill to promote safe gun storage.

"Of course, I would," I told her with a thumping heart. I was about to dip a toe into the strange world of gun politics. And so, ten months after Kenzo died, I argued face-to-face with the California leaders of the gun lobby about a gun safe-storage bill.

When I awoke the morning I was to testify, I felt hopeful. It was a clear and sunny day as I looked out across the San Francisco Bay. The rare fogless morning made the city's skyline sparkle in the distance. I got ready quickly, stuffing a folder with stats, studies about unsafe gun storage, and notes for my testimony into my bulging briefcase. I joined the early-morning commuters on the drive across the Bay Bridge to meet Barrie Becker in San Francisco and hitch a ride to Sacramento. I was eager to confront the lions of the legislature in their den.

When I strode into the empty lobby of the old office building where Barrie worked, the musty smell of ancient dust hit me. Aside from a few halfhearted art deco flourishes, it had nothing to recommend it except for the faded mystique of a 1940s film noir. Searching the framed listing of offices, I found neither the Legal Community Against Violence nor Handgun Control, Inc. I double-checked the address, and the list again. Not there. What was going on?

Rummaging through my briefcase, I found the room number that Barrie had given me, took the elevator to the eighth floor, and walked down the hall to a nondescript door with the number but no sign. I knocked, wondering what sort of a situation we have in this country when people like these, working for public safety, are afraid to put a sign on their door.

A woman yelled through the locked door, "Who is it?"

"Griffin Dix!" I shouted.

That did the trick. A harried woman let me in with a quick nod and dashed back to her phone call. I stood just inside the door, wondering what to do next.

Around me was a scene of controlled chaos: a hurricane of papers piled on two small desks, pages taped to walls and stuck to bulletin boards, overflowing the edges. I took a step in. Three bulletin boards were bursting with curled lists of legislators, their phone and fax numbers, names of committee members, schedules of upcoming bills in Senate and Assembly committees, volunteers' schedules, sheets of stats, and talking points.

Posh it wasn't. The only decorations were a few posters stuck onto the smoke-stained walls. One showed a couple in the midst of an argument, a man leaning toward a woman, yelling and pointing an angry finger. The panel below showed the couple in the same pose, but now instead of his finger, he was pointing a gun. At the bottom, in thin dark letters: "A handgun can turn an argument into a funeral."

I took a few more steps to examine another poster. A "Saturday Night Special" revolver was painted like an American flag under the words, "Last year handguns killed 48 people in Japan, 8 in Great

Britain, 34 in Switzerland, 52 in Canada, 58 in Israel, 21 in Sweden, 42 in West Germany, 10,728 in the United States. God Bless America."

I could see into two tiny offices in the back. There was barely enough room to squeeze past the desks and bookshelves to get to them. A contrasting photo I'd recently seen crossed my mind: the National Rifle Association's huge, gleaming corporate headquarters outside Washington, DC.

From all three tiny rooms, volunteers offered hasty smiles in my direction before continuing their work. I spotted Barrie, a short, thirtyish bundle of energy, chattering into her phone. Finally, she looked up, nodded my way, but continued speaking nonstop.

I walked toward her office, wondering what she was so worked up about. It was something about the specifics of an upcoming bill to ban Saturday Night Specials. As she ticked through the details of the bill, I stood outside her office, shifting from one foot to the other, watching the three-ring circus.

Pattie, the volunteer who had let me in, was faxing something with one hand and answering the phone with the other. She put another call on hold for Barrie. I looked at my watch.

I knew Barrie from a few meetings and press conferences I'd attended. Despite the regular losses she and her cause suffered, she was relentlessly upbeat and on the move. She worked more than half-time for Handgun Control, Inc., helping organize local chapters, and more than half-time for LCAV, providing information about local gun safety ordinances to city councils all over the Bay Area. Evenings, she attended meetings of local groups. One night she'd go east to Contra Costa County, another night, south to Los Altos, driving forty miles each way. She'd show up at small meetings in someone's home to provide the latest update on the gun bills she was trying to negotiate over each hurdle in the legislative process.

Finally, Barrie finished her call, took a deep breath, gave me a smile, glanced at the clock on the wall, frowned, and quipped, "Let's go before the phone rings again." She jammed a few papers into her briefcase, and we rushed out the door.

As we drove out of San Francisco in her beat-up sedan, we made polite conversation. She'd made the trip dozens of times and seemed glad to have company. But as we passed Davis and approached Sacramento, I began to tense up.

I was reluctant to testify for this bill. I had studied the text of AB 630 the night before. I thought it was too weak, filled with gaping loopholes and compromises. It took only small steps toward safe gun storage, personal accountability, and responsibility. Prosecutors had a choice of bringing either misdemeanor or felony charges against the gun's owner, if a child or teenager *under age fourteen* got his unlocked gun and killed or "caused great bodily harm" with it. The "under age fourteen" limit was too low. Mark had been fourteen, so this law would still not allow criminal charges against his father, Clifford, for leaving his gun loaded and unlocked. But Mark was still just a kid who should not have had access to a loaded handgun in his home.

What prosecutor would bring felony charges if a gun owner left his gun accessible to a child under fourteen who killed someone with it? Prosecutors were likely to feel that the family had suffered enough. I could certainly understand that, given the trauma that I had seen Mark suffer. But without any enforcement teeth, the law would be unlikely to convince gun owners that they need to lock up their guns when "left unattended in a dwelling."

The other option for a prosecutor was to charge the gun owner with a misdemeanor. But as we sped along I-80, I played that scenario out in my mind. *If* a father kept his gun unlocked, and *if* his child killed someone with it, and *if* the father was prosecuted, and *if* he was found guilty of a *misdemeanor*, the *maximum* fine the bill mentioned was $500. Quite a long string of "iffy" occurrences, I thought—and at most, only a $500 fine for causing a death? With such a low maximum fine, why would a prosecutor even bother taking such a misdemeanor case to court? If the law would not be enforced, it would probably not have the preventive effect it was supposed to have.[1]

Barrie and I were still just making conversation as all these questions rattled around in my brain. Finally, I cut in. "This is a pretty weak bill, you know. It's riddled with loopholes!"

"You're right," she said, glancing my way. To my surprise, she acknowledged every weakness I mentioned. Then she explained gently that lots of compromises had to be made in the hope of persuading just one Republican on the Public Safety Committee to vote for the bill.

"A better bill would never pass," she said. "The Public Safety Committee is equally divided between Republicans and Democrats. We're hoping that Assemblyman Richard Rainey might break ranks and vote for it. He's a moderate Republican from Contra Costa County."

She looked my way again. "At least the bill is an improvement over existing law." She went over several good provisions. In general, the bill would tighten accountability for guns stored at home and at gun shops by encouraging people to lock up unattended guns. That could reduce the number of guns being stolen and getting into criminal hands.

Okay. I was convinced. I asked Barrie, "Who could be against that?"

"You'll see," she said, with a bit of a smile.

Finally, we crossed the drawbridge over the Sacramento River. As we made our way up Capitol Avenue, the Capitol building was an impressive sight, standing in the middle of its own block at the center of the city, where many roads converged. The building's expansive columns and dome announce America's Manifest Destiny with the confident grandeur of the state's nineteenth-century empire builders.

Barrie and I climbed the Capitol's wide steps and walked past massive stone columns worthy of the Acropolis. I could open the huge bronze door only by setting my feet and pulling on it with the entire weight of my body. Metal detectors were a thing of the future. The marble floors and high domed ceiling echoed the slightest sound.

My eyes were drawn up several stories, past the granite statues of legendary California politicians, to the arched, painted ceiling that glowed with celestial light from a ring of windows. Paintings of vast, wondrous California valleys surrounded us.

No one can enter this temple without being in awe of those who wield its power. My misgivings—assuaged a bit after Barrie's pep talk—crept back.

Soon I saw that the grandeur was only a facade. Stitched to the grand old Capitol like an afterthought is a bland twentieth-century office building where most of the work is done. Legislators' reception rooms are cramped, allowing only enough space for a few citizens to wait patiently for a brief word with their legislator or a staff member.

The crowded, windowless hearing room for the Assembly Public Safety Committee was long and narrow. In the front, behind an enormous, semicircular dais, sat the committee members, protected from the public by a low wooden railing and a guard. Those he let in sat in the center at tables far below the legislators, as if under interrogation in a pit. Legislators peered down at them, with only their heads and shoulders showing. From the back of the room about twenty-five rows of seats sloped downward so all eyes could focus on the legislators.

The Assembly Public Safety Committee was considering more than twenty-five bills that day—so many that legislators could not possibly have read all of the laws on which they were to vote.

Barrie and I sat down and waited for AB 630 to come up.

Soon Barrie turned and looked toward the back of the room. "That's Steve Helsley," she whispered, pointing inconspicuously, "the NRA's chief California lobbyist. And that's Gerald Upholt, the lobbyist for the California Rifle and Pistol Association." Both were well-dressed white men, overweight, with graying hair. Helsley was a little taller, with a big jaw, but neither was unusual-looking. In fact, they looked like ordinary businessmen. Unlike everyone else, they stood and leaned against the back wall apart from everyone else, whispering.

Hour after hour as our bill approached, I became increasingly nervous. I kept looking down at the notes I held ready in my hand, rehearsing what I would say. Speaking for that bill was not like ordinary stage fright; it felt deeply personal to me. Finally, at about 2:30 p.m., the committee chair announced AB 630, the safe-storage bill authored by Assemblyman Antonio Villaraigosa from Los Angeles, an up-and-coming politician who would later be that city's mayor. With a serious look on their faces, Helsley and Upholt strode confidently up the aisle, sat down, and adjusted their microphones.

Helsley's manner was smooth and self-assured, his testimony brief. The bill was "flawed," he told the legislators. "This bill is a solution in search of a problem. Not many kids die from guns left unlocked."

I listened, tense, amazed, and increasingly angry. Helsley's testimony—given with a quiet, sensible-sounding demeanor and a straight face—mischaracterized the bill. He said it was a one-size-fits-all solution that requires all gun owners to keep their guns locked up; but in fact, the law only required gun owners to keep their "unattended" guns locked up if a child could get them. He failed to mention that no one could be prosecuted for this misdemeanor unless they left a gun "*unattended* in a dwelling."

When Helsley called the bill a solution in search of a problem, I thought certainly he and everyone else *knew* that was not true. He did not mention the recent rapid increase in California's number of gun deaths. He said nothing about the homicides, suicides, unintentional shootings, and school shootings that resulted from guns stored unsafely.

When Helsley said the law was an overly broad, one-size-fits-all solution and that many gun owners do not live in households with children, I thought of the many times I had told people about Kenzo's death. They had told me their own harrowing stories involving guns stored unsafely in homes. Some of the stories were about injuries or close calls involving children who were with their parents when they visited a relative—someone who had no children, but who stored his guns unsafely.[2]

By the time I was called to testify, a transformation had occurred in me. I was no longer nervous; I was mad. I said, "The spokesperson for the NRA just told you that the most probable cause of death of your child, which for anyone in California under age twenty-five is a gun, is not really a problem. He said that this bill is 'a solution in search of a problem.' But this bill would help prevent many of these deaths, because so many of them happen when a youth gets his father's unsafely stored gun, or a criminal steals it. These deaths are preventable. *They do not need to happen.*"

As I told them Kenzo's story, I felt my body go cold. I began to shake. My voice quivered and got husky with emotion. But they could hear me fine, and I had their attention.

"Parents in your districts have kids that visit their friends' homes, and about forty percent of American homes have guns. One in five gun owners stores a gun both loaded and unlocked. The results are tragic. Every year approximately seven percent of all teenage gun deaths are from unintentional shootings."

*How could this not make an impression on them?*

"Gun owners need to take responsibility for their guns," I concluded. "They need to be warned about the risks and told how to store their guns safely. If they know a child could get their gun, and they still do not store it safely, and then a child kills or injures someone with it, there should be consequences."

I glanced up, wondering how much of this the legislators were hearing.

"If guns aren't stored safely," I added, "they can easily be stolen. Every year, about half a million unlocked guns are stolen and in criminal hands. One-third of felons report that they stole the gun they most recently acquired. This bill will help prevent guns from getting into criminal hands."

I knew I had to finish my testimony quickly, or the chairman would cut me off.

I took a breath and looked Republican assemblyman Richard Rainey in the eye. His face was impassive, as if he were somewhere else. I was emotional, tearing up, my voice cracking as I spoke about Kenzo, and the many other lives up and down California that could be saved if this bill passed.

Finally, I looked directly at Rainey with a plea: "Your vote will either save lives or it will help kill innocent children. Please vote for this bill."

Rainey looked away. Then, in a moment, to my surprise, he responded. "There's already a law against an adult storing a gun where a child can get it and cause harm with it." That stopped me cold; I drew a blank. But a physician at the table who had testified with us pointed out that Rainey had it wrong. That law applied only if the child takes the gun *outside* his home. Assembly Bill 630 involved the use of a gun *inside* the home as well as outside.

I was relieved. Rainey's objection had been answered. Now that he knew this bill added something important, maybe he would change his opinion and vote for it. I looked hopefully up at him for a response. He was quiet, his face expressionless.

It took only moments for all the members of the Assembly Public Safety Committee to vote. I remained hopeful to the end. But when the chairperson looked at Assemblyman Richard Rainey and he said, "Nay," a shiver of disgust passed through my body.

All the Democrats voted for the safe-storage bill. All the Republicans voted against it. There were equal numbers of Democrats and Republicans, so the bill failed to pass out of committee. It would not make it to the Assembly for a floor vote. That meant Assembly members did not have to go on record voting against it. And with no media attention, it would remain below the public's radar. Even these legislators' constituents would never know how they had voted.

I was having an Orwellian moment. I couldn't get over the Public Safety Committee's disregard for public safety.

In fact, that day, Barrie and I watched as all Republicans voted against every gun bill before them. A bill requiring gun makers to build chamber-loaded indicators into all semiautomatic pistols was also defeated. I grew angrier and angrier. A prominent chamber-loaded indicator would have saved Kenzo's life.

The Public Safety Committee also rejected a bill requiring gun dealers to offer trigger locks for sale whenever they sell a gun. It was such a simple thing. When Helsley testified that the bill would ban the sale of many guns that had no trigger lock to fit them, Barrie whispered to me, "That is classic NRA. There is nothing in the bill about banning the sale of any guns."

"Why don't those gun manufacturers make trigger locks that fit their guns?" I asked. "What kind of excuse is that?" Barrie touched my arm, gave me a sympathetic smile and a gentle nod. I had so much to learn.

I was physically and emotionally drained, but Barrie was as energetic and determined as ever. She insisted we go directly to Rainey's office to talk with him. He was the last person I wanted to see at the moment, but I followed along.

To my surprise, we were immediately ushered in to see him. In contrast to the cramped reception room, his office was spacious and pleasant. Wood paneling warmed it. Bookshelves lined with leather-bound law books added a scholarly touch. Pictures of Rainey's family, photos of him with important dignitaries, and California and American flags were prominently displayed.

Rainey waited for us behind a desk so big, dark, and varnished that it seemed to embody political power. But the Assemblyman's face was still bland and expressionless. He stood up and I managed to shake hands with him politely. We sat down in overstuffed black leather chairs and Barrie got right to the point.

"We hoped you'd vote for AB 630, the safe-storage bill. Can you tell us why you voted against it?"

Rainey straightened up, put on his most official face, and said, "The bill was flawed."

I thought: How strange! Just the words that Helsley had used.

He would not give us any specific reasons why he voted against it and the other gun bills. He told us he used to be a police officer, and that the best way to reduce crime was to keep criminals behind bars longer.

Barrie said, "But how about all the lives lost—the lives like Kenzo's, the youth gun homicides and suicides. Kids get those guns in their homes where they're not locked up."

Rainey said nothing. He didn't deny it. He had no answer. His deadpan expression was an education in politics for me. I got the distinct impression he did not want to go into specifics because he was unfamiliar with the bills he'd voted against.

As we drove back home, I sat in sullen despair, shocked and angry.

Barrie, a seasoned veteran, regarded this as a predictable outcome. For her it was all in a day's work, nothing to slow her down for even a moment. She was already looking forward to finding ways to publicize the votes of these politicians.

I wasn't just disappointed; I was also puzzled. We drove in silence for a while. Finally, I asked, "So how does the gun lobby get so much influence over moderates like Rainey? I don't get it."

"They donate to his campaign, get some wealthy people to donate, run some ads, and maybe get some NRA supporters to walk door to door for him."[3]

"But people in Rainey's district say they want stronger gun laws," I said. "He knows that. Contra Costa County just voted overwhelmingly for strict regulation of handguns and for banning assault weapons. How can he keep voting this way and still get reelected?"

She glanced my way with another of her sympathetic smiles. "A few donations go a long way in a State Assembly race. And Rainey knows that if a politician crosses the NRA on just one vote, it can be relentless in finding and backing another candidate, even in the primary campaign when no one else is paying much attention."

The next day, frustrated and needing to complain to someone, I wrote a letter to the editor of the *Contra Costa Times*, the largest newspaper in Rainey's district. It was a rant:

> Assemblyman Dick Rainey, R–Walnut Creek, cast votes in Sacramento that endanger kids. He and other Republicans on the Public Safety Committee voted for the gun industry and against the safety of children....
>
> On April 4, I testified before the committee, and saw a disgusting disregard for public safety. More California kids die from guns than from auto accidents or anything else. Yet Rainey voted against commonsense gun regulations that would protect children from their greatest risk....On bill after bill the National Rifle Association told Rainey how to vote, and he sold his soul to the devil despite the risks to us all. Because of Rainey's votes, the bills were stopped in committee, and children are not safe when they visit homes with guns in them. How many more kids have to die before the Public Safety Committee acts for the public safety?

I was astonished when they published it.

I felt I had unfinished business with Assemblyman Richard Rainey and others like him. I was personally offended by the misstatements I had just heard from the gun lobby and the legislators who fed off of it.

From that day, a nagging little voice began to urge me forward—softly at first, then more insistently, as I discovered more new facts. Something was not right. Someone had to help Barrie narrow the gap between what the public wanted and what their legislators were actually doing.

Might I be someone for that job?

This was not my life. I did not want to do this. Just testifying in public about Kenzo was so emotionally wrenching that I wanted only to crawl into a hole and lick my wounds for days afterward. I was still deeply grieving. But after that day in Sacramento, the calculus of what was most meaningful to me began to shift.

Not long after my rude initiation testifying before the California Assembly Public Safety Committee, I received a call from Dennis Henigan.

The Center to Prevent Handgun Violence would help us bring a lawsuit against Beretta USA.

# PART II
# Legal Groundwork

# 5

## Our Lawyer, The Judge, The Rules

### *We Will Not Settle*

On May 4, 1998, nearly three years from the day Dennis Henigan had told me the Center to Prevent Handgun Violence would take our case, I got a call from Jon Lowy, the lawyer that Henigan had assigned us. He had disturbing news: Beretta had filed for summary judgment. The company was attempting to get our case thrown out of court.

"Could they do that?" I interrupted him.

"You never know what a judge will do," he said, and explained that our case was especially hard to predict since it was the first ever to demand that a gun manufacturer be held liable for not designing its guns with safety features, such as a built-in lock and a prominent chamber-loaded indicator, and for selling it without an adequate manual.

Jon said he was coming to California the following week and asked to meet with me to discuss the case, and separately, with Lynn. He was also meeting with Clifford, Mark's father. I thought that was probably to see how cooperative he'd be as a witness if the case made it to trial.

Jon asked if I could meet him for lunch on a street close to Clifford's house. I didn't like going anywhere near there—too many memories. But, calming my emotions, I agreed. Jon told me I couldn't miss him; he'd be carrying a square lawyer's briefcase.

As I stood on the noisy corner with cars rushing toward the I-80 freeway, I looked at the saris in the Indian shops and smelled the savory food roasting in tandoori ovens. This run-down neighborhood around the western part of University Avenue had become a Little India where entrepreneurial immigrants rented shops and put up signs in Hindi.

Soon I saw an energetic man striding toward me lugging his heavy briefcase. He was younger than I had expected. Thick black hair capped a high forehead. He was clean-shaven, but the shadow of dark whiskers covered his chin. As he walked, he seemed so deep in thought that I wondered if his talk with Clifford had discouraged him, but when our eyes met his mouth softened to a smile.

I had heard stories of "ambulance chasers" eager to use a tragedy to line their pockets; clearly, he was not one. In fact, I later learned that, win or lose, he would get no money from our case. He was on salary, working for a cause he believed in, though he could make far more by working in a corporate law firm. And, of course, he had not chased us; we had chased him.

We walked into an Indian restaurant painted in bright orange and pink with pictures of peasants, rajahs, and elephants marching along the walls. Sitting face-to-face in a booth, we sounded each other out.

He'd graduated from Harvard and then gone to University of Virginia Law School, where he'd met his wife, who was a law professor.

Jon had dark shadows under his eyes and began to sneeze and wipe his nose with a handkerchief. Soon, as if he couldn't hold it back any longer, he told me that only a few days before, his wife had given birth to twins, a boy and a girl, born prematurely and rushed into the intensive care unit. The judge assigned to our case had set an immediate date for us to argue against Beretta's motion for summary judgment. And so, surrounded by the noisy dramas of a bustling hospital waiting room, and gripped by fear for his wife and struggling twins, hour after hour through several nights Jon had typed our counterarguments into his laptop, frequently interrupted in mid-sentence by a nurse rushing out to tell him he was needed to guide his little family's critical care.

For days, he'd gotten only a few hours of sleep a night. Now, exhausted and three thousand miles from his wife, a cold was hitting him hard. But he was in good spirits, and told me the twins were doing well and had been released from intensive care. Eyes gleaming proudly, he pulled pictures from his wallet. Wrapped in soft hospital blankets, two tiny, pink, wrinkled heads crowned with a few strands of black hair lay side by side, squinting into the bright light.

New life—*a new beginning*, I thought.

I asked him whether Clifford had been cooperative. He said he wished he'd been more cooperative. As I wondered what that meant, he continued.

"Beretta's lawyers will try to set traps for Clifford that will make his testimony misleading. They'll try to get him to say he knew of the dangers, but, although he knew about firearms, he didn't know the risks of keeping a handgun accessible in his home. Beretta will argue that Clifford should have bought a trigger lock," he said, "but that's like automobile companies saying everyone should buy and install their own seat belts. The auto industry used to blame each driver every time someone was hurt in an accident, but now they *have* to design cars to be as safe as possible—even for people who drive over the speed limit. Gun makers try to hide information about the ways their guns keep getting into the hands of kids, untrained users, and criminals. There's always someone else conveniently to blame."

Then Jon leaned back and smiled.

"I remember when I first heard of seat belts in cars," he said. "I thought, 'Oh, no! Every time I come to a bridge I'll have to pull over and undo it, just in case my car goes over the railing. I thought the seat belt might trap me and I'd drown." He laughed, and added, "It's true."

"Actually," I said, "a lot of people felt that way. Me, too. It sounds so ridiculous now."

He nodded. "People resist new things. That's one reason prevention is so hard."

A young Indian waiter in sandals appeared at our table and handed us large menus. We glanced through the choices and ordered.

"What sort of documents are you getting from Beretta in discovery?" I asked, proud of the legalese I had learned.

Jon said he'd gotten a number of letters sent to Jeffrey Reh, Beretta USA's vice president, by gun experts and investors proposing locking devices that Beretta could incorporate into their guns. But Reh had sent them a form letter in reply, saying Beretta wasn't interested. He didn't forward the technical proposals to the engineers at the Beretta Italy headquarters, where the guns are designed.

Hoarse from exhaustion, Jon continued in a whisper, as if letting me in on a secret. "Beretta tries to sell guns to people exactly like Clifford. He's their market: people who are afraid, people Beretta can convince they need a gun instantly ready for protection." When he said "protection," Jon held up each hand and made two-finger quotation marks.

"But Beretta provides no means of storing a gun safely that will give their customers quick access to it. If Beretta's handguns had built-in locks, people could use them much more quickly than they could if they stored an unloaded gun in one place and the ammunition in another, as Beretta's manual tells them to. We will take them at their word and show that a built-in lock is a better design for exactly the emergency self-defense situations Beretta's ads tell their customers they are likely to face."

Jon settled back, resting his eyes on me. "You should be prepared that at some point Beretta could offer us an out-of-court settlement. They'll probably pick a time when you're most vulnerable and likely to settle in their favor."

I suddenly realized this must be one of the key issues he had come to discuss. He did not try to convince me not to take a settlement. The decision was completely up to Lynn and me. He acknowledged that he was our lawyer and would be working for us. But I knew that because the terms of settlements often have to be kept secret, they may have little influence on the gun industry or public opinion.

With a glance at the steaming rice and chicken masala the waiter put in front of us, Jon went on.

"If Beretta offers a large settlement *and* agrees to change the design of the gun *and* includes a time limit within which they would do that, then it could have a real impact on the entire industry. But they are not likely to do that." He told me that the company didn't want to build these types of safety features into their gun or take responsibility for the deaths that occur as a result of its design defects. They have money, and they think they can buy anyone with it.

"We're in this for the same reasons you are," I assured him. "To us this is not about money; it's about getting the gun industry to design safety features into handguns to save the lives of kids like Kenzo."

Jon leaned back, looking satisfied.

We served ourselves the hot Indian food and wolfed it down.

When we were done, I drove Jon back to San Francisco and dropped him off at City Lights Bookstore. Driving back to the East

Bay, I had a good feeling about Jon Lowy. He was soft-spoken, easygoing, and unassuming, but I thought he was brilliant, with a powerful craving for justice. I realized that I'd met not just a savvy lawyer, but also someone I could trust to work with us to right a wrong.

Several years before, when the Center to Prevent Handgun Violence had agreed to take our case, we had needed a good California product liability lawyer. A lawyer working at the Trauma Foundation in San Francisco had suggested Nancy Hersh, who had recently won damages for women who had used a diet drug that had horrible side effects. Lynn and I had gone to meet her, and found someone friendly, quick-witted, and energetic. When we told her about Kenzo's death and the Beretta's design, she was appalled at the behavior of the father and his son and the gun company. After asking us more questions, she seemed to think we had a case. Although we knew nothing about how to pick a lawyer, we felt she would be poised and articulate in front of a jury. By the time we walked out forty-five minutes later, we had chosen our California lawyer.

She sued Clifford. He settled immediately, and his homeowners' insurance (bodily injury) paid. Lynn and I each received $30,000, which we donated to help pay part of the expenses of our lawsuit against Beretta USA.[4]

Throughout the spring of 1998, the lawyers exchanged briefs regarding Beretta's motion to throw our case out of court. Jon sent me each set and I waded through the documents.

One of Beretta's arguments was that it is up to the legislature, not the courts, to decide whether handguns must include built-in safety features that would help make them less accessible to adolescents.[5]

Our briefs answered that courts often create duties that are laws. Moreover, California's existing product liability law already had this covered; there was no need for the courts to be making new "laws." Furthermore, our brief said Beretta USA "knew that children, adolescents, and adults would likely be killed as a result of its design and lack of warnings, in precisely the manner in which Kenzo was killed; and that Beretta could have prevented these deaths if it had utilized simple warnings and feasible safety features, some of which Beretta was specifically aware."

In support, we cited a well-known 1978 California Supreme Court decision that concluded that under California law, a product is defective if "the risk of danger inherent in the challenged design outweighs the benefits of such design," or if "the product failed to perform as safely as an ordinary consumer would expect when used in an intended or reasonably foreseeable manner." Certainly, there is foreseeable *misuse* of handguns by adolescents. Therefore, we argued that under California law, unless Beretta could prove that the benefits of its design outweigh the risks, it was required to design its product with the *foreseeable misuse* in mind.

Beretta countered that it was not liable, since Mark was not an intended user.

We answered that this design is unsafe for all users, and that Beretta was obligated by law to make its products safe for foreseeable *misuse*, even by "unintended" users. Unfortunately, kids get their hands on guns, often; Mark was a "reasonably foreseeable" user. Our trial was going to hinge on this abstract idea of foreseeable misuse.

Finally, we contended that this handgun had been sold without adequate warnings. Users were given no clear, prominent warnings that the gun should be locked away; there was no warning that thousands of children have died as a result of gaining access to unlocked guns in the home. This was the second major part of our case.

Beretta's lawyers hoped to have the case dismissed by relying on a special exclusion for firearms that the California legislature had passed back in 1983 at the behest of the gun lobby.[6] That law said that, unlike other products, firearms and ammunition could not be found defective on the basis that the risks outweigh the benefits. This was a unique exemption excluding firearms from the risk-benefit test that the California Supreme Court said could be applied in other strict product liability cases.

But that law allowed a crucial exception: If there had been "an improper selection of design alternatives," and therefore, the *design* of a gun was unsafe, then an injured party could bring a lawsuit against the manufacturer or distributor.

At the hearing on summary judgment, Judge Henry Needham denied every one of Beretta's issues. His decision said that we, the plaintiffs, raised several "triable" issues in regard to Beretta USA's responsibility for Kenzo's death.

### *The Media*

Meanwhile, the media noticed the trial and the issue of safer handguns. Jon Lowy told me Court TV was considering covering our trial. A producer of *60 Minutes* called me to see if I would be willing to go on camera if they broadcast a segment about our trial.

*U.S. News & World Report* ran a story headlined, "Childproofing Guns: A Novel Legal Strategy Focusing on Safety Poses a Threat to Manufacturers." It had a picture of Charlton Heston standing behind a National Rifle Association podium, his arm raised high, his mouth turned sharply downward in a dour grimace. On the next page, there was a picture of Lynn, arms folded, standing in front of the eight-foot-high mural of Kenzo's sweet face, painted by his art teacher in the no-longer-used outdoor handball court at Berkeley High School.

The June 22, 1998 article began, "Before he died, Kenzo Dix wrote an essay for his ninth-grade English class that said, 'When I pass away, I want to leave something that people will remember me by, a gift to the future from me.' Kenzo's mother, Lynn Dix, hopes that gift will be a safer gun, 'so there are no more victims.'"

The article suggested that the legal ground might be shifting in our favor. It quoted Stephen Teret, the leading expert on firearms at Johns

Hopkins Bloomberg School of Public Health, who predicted that at some point, a plaintiff was going to win a firearms liability lawsuit.

The *U.S. News* also quoted the president of Colt's Manufacturing Company, Ron Stewart, a relative newcomer to the gun industry, saying that the industry must change its outlook to survive. His article in *American Firearms Industry* magazine argued that gun makers' response to "the anti-gun lobby" was "pathetically inadequate." He said, "If we can send a motorized computer to Mars, then certainly we can advance our technology to be more childproof." The *U.S. News* article ended optimistically. "For sharply differing reasons then, both gun control advocates and gun makers appear at least momentarily to be pointed in the same direction: toward a safer gun."

But the many articles about our trial and the new push for safer gun designs were ignoring the power of the NRA and the National Shooting Sports Foundation. They opposed these attempts. Ron Stewart's article infuriated them. Even though in his two years as CEO of Colt's he had taken the company from bankruptcy to a profit of $10 million, within one year after he published his call for reform in the gun industry, he was no longer president of Colt's, or any other gun company.

Beretta USA took the highly unusual step of appealing the judge's decision on summary judgment. The company was going to fight us every step of the way. But Beretta's appeal was also denied. We were going to trial. Ours would be the first attempt to link an unintentional shooting that occurs when a child obtains his parent's gun to the design of the gun itself. Now the leading experts on opposite sides of one of America's most contentious issues would finally meet face-to-face before a jury to argue over the causes of a boy's death.

And that boy was my son, Kenzo.

## *The Trial Begins*

On Tuesday, October 13, 1998, Kalani and I picked up Lynn and we drove to the Alameda County courthouse. I had bought a house in Kensington, a small town just north of Berkeley. After two years at Humboldt State, Kalani was back home now, living with me and taking classes at a community college. We lived together as much like two bachelors as like father and son. We maintained a strong affection for each other as we struggled to overcome our grief and create new lives for ourselves. His daily presence brought me great comfort.

Kalani often had friends over to play music late into the night. The bachelor in me felt that the creative diversion of mixing music on his computer and learning to play electric bass and Kenzo's drums showed he was beginning to enjoy life again. The father in me hoped that he would get more interested in school and a career.

I maintained my research business and became secretary of a primarily California gun violence prevention group, the Bell Campaign, helping it organize to pass legislation. I also wrote a gun policy newsletter.

Now, on the way to the courthouse together, the three of us spoke hesitantly about what might happen in the trial. The atmosphere between us in the car was tense, yet familiar.

On top of the different ways we had each adjusted to the loss of Kenzo, Lynn and I were wary of signaling renewed intimacy—with all the potential pain any commitment might bring. Our separation and divorce had been excruciating. But now, we were going to the trial together with our beloved son. In recent months, despite the awkwardness, goodwill had gradually begun to reassert itself, and we'd started to feel almost like a family again. All three of us vehemently wanted the gun industry to change the design of its pistols; that would be our justice. Going into a strange courtroom where unpredictable people would make decisions according to rules unknown to us created an "us against the world" feeling.

We drove into downtown Oakland and parked near the legendary Alameda County superior courthouse, where US Supreme Court chief justice Earl Warren had first made a name for himself. The 1930s-era granite building sat firmly in an area that embodied California's contradictions. From a vibrant, brightly colored Chinatown, the scents from dozens of Asian restaurants mingled with those from tight markets abuzz with the quick banter of the descendants of laborers who had built California's infrastructure, as well as more recent immigrants.

A few blocks southeast, ritzy high-rise apartments surrounded Lake Merritt, where yuppie couples jogged past yoga centers and latte shops that doubled as art galleries. Rowers in paper-thin shells skimmed across the glassy water toward the Grand Lake Theatre, where, along with films like *The Truman Show* and *The Big Lebowski*, the marquee displayed leftist slogans.

A few blocks southwest, narrow Victorians with barred windows and peeling paint had the look of abandoned prisons. After dark, from gritty alleys, gunfire could be heard. Many of the Black families crammed into this neighborhood were the children of workers who had fled racism in Mississippi and Louisiana for jobs in the nearby port, building the Liberty Ships that America desperately needed. Some had become Black Panthers, fighting police abuse. Others joined church committees trying to save the lives of young men.

Alameda County also encompasses the city of Berkeley—still home to the nation's best public university, famous for the 1960s Free Speech and antiwar movements. And it extends far eastward, where rural conservatives live near UC Berkeley's Lawrence Livermore National Laboratory, which developed the first compact nuclear warheads for ballistic missiles. To the south, Fremont is home to more immigrants from Afghanistan than any other American city.

At the epicenter of all this was the eleven-story granite and concrete courthouse, dominating an entire city block, its marble mosaics, inlaid marble floors, and brass metalwork providing the backdrop for a cacophony of lawyers re-arguing the conflicts of this heterodox county. We were about to draw jurors from all these communities and ask them to reach a consensus. Our fate would be in their hands.

When Lynn, Kalani, and I pushed open the courtroom doors, Jon Lowy and Nancy Hersh were already there, shuffling through notes and conferring. Eric Gorovitz of the Trauma Foundation was discussing the case with a young, Black lawyer whom Nancy had invited to come help us with jury selection.

At Beretta's table, I saw the company's oversized, domineering lawyer, Robert Gebhardt, and his colleague, sturdy ex-cop, Craig Livingston. They huddled together, whispering with a middle-aged, balding man in a suit and tie: Larry Keane from the major gun lobby organization, the National Shooting Sports Foundation (NSSF). The sugarcoated name implied that the NSSF busies itself with recreational activities, such as hunting and skeet shooting. It hadn't been hard for me to discover that NSSF and Larry Keane were deeply involved in lobbying to defeat gun regulations and promote the purchase of guns for protection, not just sport. In fact, the National Shooting Sports Foundation was the trade association for the entire gun industry.

Soon one hundred citizens from Alameda County found their way through the door of the wood-paneled courtroom of Judge Richard Hodge. The affable court clerk, whom the judge called Nick, directed them to the rows of seats in the back of the room. There were so many that some had to stand in the aisles.

Swiveling in our chairs, we saw a cross section of Alameda County: voting adults of all races from many countries; some well-dressed, others in tattered warm-up suits; some retirees, others barely out of high school.

Judge Hodge sat high above us underneath the seal of the Great State of California, which hung slightly askew on the wall behind him. "Good morning, ladies and gentlemen," he boomed cheerily. "Welcome to Department 80 of the Alameda County Superior Court. As you can see, you have been called as a jury panel from which will be selected twelve jurors, plus three alternates."

He explained that this was a wrongful death lawsuit in which Lynn and I were suing Beretta USA, a corporation that manufactures firearms. He recounted briefly how Mark had gotten the gun from his father's bedroom, removed the loaded magazine, and, thinking he'd unloaded the gun, gone back to his bedroom. His friend Kenzo was there. As he walked in, he had inserted an empty magazine into the handle of the pistol, making an impressive click.

"Mark pulled the trigger, intending to make another clicking noise. Unknown to Mark, there was a live cartridge of ammunition that was loaded in the firing chamber. The pistol fired. Kenzo was shot in the arm, the bullet passed through his arm, into his chest, and he died shortly thereafter at Children's Hospital."

Four and a half years after Kenzo's death, every time I heard someone tell what had happened that day, my breath still caught up short and my shoulders tensed and heaved.

Hodge told the prospective jurors that we, the plaintiffs, "claim that Beretta USA Corporation was negligent; that the pistol was defectively designed; that the warnings were inadequate; and that Beretta thereby caused the death of Kenzo Dix and the damages sustained by Griffin and Lynn Dix." He said Beretta "denies that it is in any way responsible for Kenzo's death or for the damages to Griffin and Lynn Dix."

He surveyed the crowd. "So that is the case before us. As you can see, it's a case of substantial gravity, one that will engage your attention, one that will take a fair amount of your time." He said the trial could take up to five weeks, but he hoped it would be shorter.

Judge Hodge said this was not a criminal case in which all twelve jurors would have to agree on a verdict. This was a civil case, "brought by one party against another party for money damages." I cringed. We were not really bringing the suit *for* money; we were bringing it to force Beretta and the rest of the gun industry to design safer guns for their customers. But there was no way we could show that to the jurors.

Judge Hodge said that civil cases are not like criminal trials. Civil cases do not require a unanimous verdict. They require nine of the twelve jurors to answer yes to a series of questions.

He said that once the jurors had heard the facts, their duty would be to apply the law to the facts to arrive at a verdict.

"You may be surprised at the legal principles which will guide you. You will want a clear, bright line that will make your task easy. And I rather expect that you will not find that. I rather expect that you will find that the instructions are somewhat general and somewhat designed to give the jury latitude to reach a decision that rests easily with your conscience, your sense of right and wrong, and again, and most importantly, consistent with the evidence."

On hearing that, I began to wonder why the instructions to the jury would be "somewhat general" when California law was explicit. Wasn't the jury supposed to apply the law as written rather than to rely on their general sense of right and wrong? I also worried that California's product liability law would apparently not be explained to the jurors until the very end of the trial. By then, wouldn't they have formed an opinion?

Now the judge set himself the task of inspiring patriotism and charging them with upholding the great American tradition of trial by jury. He asked the prospective jurors how many had ever read *To Kill A Mockingbird*, and told the lawyers to turn around and watch how many hands went up, because it was going to surprise them. A lot of people raised their hands.

Then, he took out the novel itself and, as everyone listened, read from the final courtroom argument of Atticus Finch:

There is one human institution that makes the pauper the equal of a Rockefeller, the stupid man the equal of an Einstein, and the ignorant man the equal of any college president. That institution, ladies and gentlemen, is the court. It can be the Supreme Court of the United States, or the humblest justice of the peace court, or it can be this court upon which you are privileged to serve. Our courts have their faults as does any human institution, but in this country our courts are the great levelers, and in our courts all people are created equal.

I'm no idealist to believe firmly in the integrity of our courts and in the jury system. That is no ideal to me. It is a living, working reality. Ladies and gentlemen, a court is no better than each one of you sitting before me in this jury. A court is only as sound as its jury, and the jury is only as sound as the people who make it up.

Judge Hodge did not point out that in the novel, the jurors who heard this stirring plea entirely ignored the evidence presented to them and returned an unjust verdict.

After reading the inspiring passage, he introduced our lawyer, Nancy Hersh, who jumped up and introduced her colleague, Jon Lowy, from the Center to Prevent Handgun Violence in Washington, DC. Then Nancy asked Lynn and me to stand, so we got up awkwardly and faced the crowd behind us.

Next, at Hodge's request, Beretta's lawyer, Robert Gebhardt, stood, said he was from Bronson, Bronson & McKinnon, and introduced Craig Livingston, of the same law firm, and, "Larry Keane, from Keane and Associates."

Keane's introduction hid the fact that he was vice president and chief counsel of the National Shooting Sports Foundation. The defense was presenting him as just some lawyer—as if the gun lobby was not present in the room. His real identity would remain hidden from the jurors throughout the trial.

Our lawyers were up against one of San Francisco's largest law firms, which had far more resources than they did. The presence of the trade association of the entire US gun industry made this even more of a David-versus-Goliath encounter.

Judge Hodge said that normally for jury selection he and the lawyers would question each prospective juror, but given that people might have strong feelings about the issue of firearms, the lawyers had agreed that jurors would all fill out questionnaires. There was no space on it for people to plead hardship, so Hodge told them that the blank space at the bottom was their "opportunity to unload," to try to get out of jury duty, but that this would be very hard to do. If they tried, he said with a malicious twinkle in his eye, they just might end up on the jury of the double homicide case down the hall.

Some folks behind me chuckled.

Finally, Hodge said for the rest of the day the lawyers had a great number of issues to discuss with him, but that Thursday we would select a jury, and that the following Monday, the jurors who were selected were to come in "ready to go through this trial like Sherman through Georgia."

### What to Hide from the Jurors

The lawyers and Lynn and I were invited into Judge Hodge's chambers to debate each side's *motions in limine*, its list of the items it hoped the judge would forbid opposing lawyers from discussing in front of the jury. Both teams of lawyers had done an enormous amount of preparation for this crucial meeting, sending briefs and point-by-point counterarguments back and forth to each other, and to Judge Hodge.

Why?

Because the judge's decisions about what topics would be off limits could make the difference between winning and losing the case.

We followed Judge Hodge through the mysterious door from which he would enter the courtroom each morning. His office was a long and narrow but comfortable room wrapped in bookcases, displaying brown and black legal tomes, which were now—in the age of computers—mostly for decoration. A picture on a bookcase of a smiling young man about Kalani's age caught my eye—Judge Hodge's son, who I later learned was an avid shooter and gun enthusiast.

Judge Hodge was friendly, relaxed, and eager to enjoy this display of the craft of lawyering. The two teams of lawyers, wary and on edge, having barely spoken, arranged themselves into rows of chairs opposite each other like linemen on a football field. Just three of Beretta's lawyers sat opposite us, because their lead trial lawyer, Bob Gebhardt, was unable to attend that day.

I had been watching all the lawyers with great curiosity.

Larry Keane, VP and general counsel of the National Shooting Sports Foundation (NSSF), had quickly established his pattern of frequently whispering into the ears of the others but seldom speaking directly to Judge Hodge. For a man with such power in the gun industry, and for such a vocal national lobbyist, Keane had been virtually invisible.

At first this puzzled me. Later, I realized that Keane was attending as the gun manufacturers' representative, to observe our case and learn what he could to help other gun manufacturers defeat future lawsuits, and even to devise legislation against lawsuits like ours.

Next to Keane was Craig Livingston, the solid, square-jawed former cop and junior lawyer—eager, and fully committed to the cause. Next to him sat Jeffrey Reh, Beretta's VP and general counsel.

In his dark business suit, and with his usual opaque expression, he appeared ready for battle.

Judge Hodge settled into the high-backed leather chair behind his desk. He smiled wryly, as if to let us all know he had seen all the tricks a lawyer might come up with. Sunlight blazed in through large windows behind the judge, giving him a certain celestial advantage over the lawyers squinting his way.

Eager to begin, Hodge said we would start with the plaintiffs' motions.

We had two major ones, and each was full of legal technicalities, making it hard for a layperson like me to understand. Our first motion was to exclude discussion of "industry custom and practice." He looked at Jon and said, "Basically, what you want to keep out is that none of the safety features that you are espousing here have been adopted anywhere in the industry. Is that the basic idea?" Jon said it was.

I had read in our briefs that "industry custom and practice" means what other companies in the industry do, such as what safety features they incorporate into their firearms. We did not want Beretta to be able to imply to the jury that, *since other gun makers* did not build locks and prominent chamber-loaded indicators into their guns, that this must prove *it could not be done.*

For the next hour the lawyers argued the point, with Jon Lowy taking the lead for our side. Early in the hour, Hodge told everyone he agreed with us—that in strict liability cases like ours, it was irrelevant whether or not an *entire industry* was building unsafe and defectively designed products.[7] Eventually he granted our motion and excluded evidence of what other manufacturers may have incorporated into their designs. He went so far as to invite the lawyers on both sides to prepare an instruction to the jury telling them not to speculate about what other manufacturers may or may not have done.

With this point decided in our favor, we all took a break.

But when we came back, I was shocked to hear Judge Hodge raise a new problem.

"Now, the question, of course, is, 'What is the difference between industry custom and practice and state of the art?' " He seemed to have suddenly reconsidered and tilted against us.

Everyone on our side shifted uncomfortably. He now said that if the real reason that the industry is not incorporating these devices is because they *can't*—because there is no technological capability to do so, and not because of industry collusion—then that is another matter. How, he asked, could these issues get fully discussed by an expert in court without talking about what other manufacturers do?

As Jon listened, he inched forward in his chair, making impatient little noises—"buts" and "uhs," all ignored by the judge.

Finally, Hodge nodded Jon's way, looking peeved.

Jon swallowed and said he didn't believe that "state of the art" would be a problem in this case, because Beretta and the rest of the industry had simply refused to even *try* any of these safety devices. Their expert wasn't going to say, for example, that Colt's had tried this device, and it hadn't worked, and that other people had tried it and it hadn't worked, and had caused problems. Nobody had ever tried it at all. Jon argued that bringing out in court that nobody in the industry had tried these safety devices would be prejudicial.

Larry Keane, who'd been sitting there, cool and impassive, suddenly insisted loudly that if our experts testified that Beretta was capable of implementing these safety features, Beretta's lawyers would want to ask, "Was it done? Did anybody else do it?"

At that, Jon's voice rose in irritation. "What was *feasible* and what was *being done* have no necessary relationship whatsoever."

Judge Hodge agreed, and said, "Various industries are rife with examples of technology being available but not being employed, and product defects being found."

After more argument, Judge Hodge said, "The motion, as articulated, was to preclude evidence of industry custom and practice. That motion is granted." But then he added that evidence about engineering "state of the art" was admissible, though he admitted that the distinction was not clear, and he warned the lawyers: "I am going to be watching to see the extent to which we bring out what other manufacturers actually do."

That seemed to leave things in a muddle. I didn't know if Judge Hodge would be able to hold the line on this difficult distinction.

But at least we had won a partial victory. Beretta was not supposed to claim that since no guns had internal locks, and virtually none had prominent chamber-loaded indicators, this must prove that it could not be done.

I was relieved, since I could see that Beretta's lawyers would love to manipulate the jury by saying "Nobody's done it; that proves it can't be done."

### Comparative Fault

After another break, Judge Hodge brought up something I had never heard of: our second, and most important, motion—that the trial should *not* be argued under the rule of "comparative fault." If the judge allowed the trial to be argued under comparative fault, and if we won, the jury would then be asked to divide up the total amount of fault. They would assign a percentage of fault to Clifford, a percentage to his son Mark, and a percentage to Beretta. If the jury assigned only a small percentage of the fault to Beretta, the damages the company would have to pay might not be large enough to get the attention of the gun industry and compel it to build safer guns. This would undermine our central goal.

But more importantly, if Hodge ruled *for* comparative fault, that would affect the evidence the lawyers could present during the trial, and how the jurors would be interpreting that evidence. If the case were to be tried under comparative fault, Beretta's lawyers would be allowed to make Clifford's negligence and Mark's irresponsibility a main subject of the trial—perhaps *the* main subject. Much of the focus during the trial would be on the mistakes of Mark and his father, as opposed to focusing more strictly on whether flaws in the design of the Beretta handgun had led to Kenzo's death.

Jon argued that comparative fault should not be used because a major purpose of strict liability cases is to give manufacturers an incentive to make their products safer. Comparative fault would take away that incentive. His voice rising in intensity, he told Judge Hodge, "What's particularly extraordinary about this case is that the alleged misuse of the Beretta by Clifford and Mark was extremely foreseeable." Since Beretta knew loaded guns get into kids' hands, he argued, the company should have designed their handgun with safety devices to help prevent the injuries that are so foreseeable.

Jon Lowy cited a case in which the court had said comparative fault would only be used in strict liability cases where the plaintiff's recovery is reduced by the degree of the *plaintiff's own* lack of reasonable care. Judge Hodge replied that California law had changed dramatically since that case. More recent precedents gave corporations more protection.

But later, I came to believe that California's comparative fault precedents didn't require it to be applied to our case because we, the plaintiffs, were not responsible for Kenzo's death.

Jon Lowy looked at Hodge and asserted that under comparative fault, Beretta could just tuck a hidden warning deep in its manual and when a foreseeable injury occurred, they'd be able to point to it to shift the blame onto their customers. They wouldn't have to meet California's design criteria.

Jon said "that Beretta included in one line on page fourteen of its manual a statement, something to the effect of, 'Keep guns away from

75

children.' Beretta *knew* that this warning would not be followed. In fact, even their experts concede that!" He argued that if Beretta was to be allowed to invoke comparative fault, then they would have a ready-made defense in every single case like this when there is misuse, and they would have absolutely no incentive to improve their product.

Judge Hodge said that recent precedents gave corporations more protection than before. He brought up *Yamaha v. Paseman*, a case about defective mopeds. He said it was the best precedent in favor of comparative fault, even though the defense lawyers had never mentioned it.

That annoyed me. Judge Hodge liked showing these young whippersnapper lawyers that he knew California law better than they did. Now he was doing the work of Beretta's lawyers for them, I felt.

To my relief, Jon was familiar with the Yamaha case. He pointed out—and Hodge immediately agreed—that in the Yamaha case, the parents, who were the plaintiffs, had failed to maintain a Yamaha moped, and had failed to warn their son of the danger. So that was a case in which the plaintiffs actually *did* bear some of the fault. Jon insisted that was different, because in our case, no one was arguing that Lynn and I were at fault for Kenzo's death.

Ultimately, Judge Hodge told Jon that he knew this was significant to our case, but comparative fault came up often, and in almost all new situations the appellate courts were applying comparative fault, so he had to apply it. He said that personally, he thought the judicial trend toward comparative fault was not justified.[8] But knowing how appellate courts would rule when the case was appealed, the defendants were entitled to a comparative fault jury instruction.

At a break, Lynn and I went to a nearby Korean restaurant with Jon Lowy. He was uncharacteristically despondent, feeling that Judge Hodge's comparative fault ruling was a severe loss for us. We were disappointed to see firsthand that in California, as elsewhere, the precedents set by conservative, pro-business judges had made it more difficult for plaintiffs to win significant victories in product liability cases.[9]

I had not fully understood the significance of comparative fault. But seeing Jon's anguish, I tried to make sense of this loss. Judge Hodge's ruling meant that in this trial the opposition in the minds of the jurors was not going to be the usual one of *plaintiffs* versus defendants. Instead, it would be *Mark and his father* versus *Beretta* in regard to who was responsible for Kenzo's death. The jurors would be told to think about apportioning fault among those parties. And the court had told them that the degree of fault assigned to one of the parties could be subtracted from the others. That made Jon's job much more difficult.

### Items Beretta USA Did Not Want Jurors to Hear

When we resumed, Judge Hodge brought up Beretta's motion to prevent us from showing the jury the company's gun ads. One ad featured a Beretta handgun lying on a nightstand with a bullet next to it, and, next to that, a photo of a mother with her arms around two smiling young kids. The clock on the nightstand said 11:25 p.m. A caption under the photo said, "Tip the odds in your favor." Hidden deep in the Beretta gun manual was this sentence: "Store firearms and ammunition separately, beyond the reach of children." But the ad seemed to encourage gun owners to violate that rule.

Craig Livingston, looking sharp, began by arguing that the ads were irrelevant because Clifford "never saw any ads." In his deposition, Clifford had said that he did "not recall" seeing Beretta ads, but hadn't said he'd *never* seen any Beretta ads. He had said that he had looked at a lot of gun magazines. Many of them had Beretta ads.

Judge Hodge turned to Jon and asked why the ad was relevant.

"Beretta says they assume that every person who buys a Beretta gun will lock up their gun and keep it away from kids," Jon answered. "The

Beretta witnesses say they assume that Beretta's instructions on page fourteen of its manual—that guns be kept away from kids—will be followed by all gun owners. That's their rationale for why they don't need the safety features."

But, Jon added, this ad shows a gun clearly being marketed to a family with young kids, with a gun on a table and bullet next to it. He said Beretta knows that people will store guns somewhere that could be accessible to kids. They welcome that market, yet they assume that there will never be a gun accident because everyone follows the instructions in the manual, to store guns out of the reach of kids.

Eventually, Hodge had heard enough. He said that with reluctance, he was going to deny the defendant's motions, but that it was a close call. He accepted that since they were marketing these guns to families, this was relevant to the adequacy of the warning.

We had won that round.

Next Judge Hodge took up Beretta's motion to exclude from the trial all references to Congress's exemption of firearms from regulation by the Consumer Product Safety Commission. In 1972, Congress had created this regulatory agency to protect American citizens "against unreasonable risks of injuries associated with consumer products."[10] At the last minute, Congressman John Dingell, an NRA board member, made sure that firearms were exempted entirely from regulation.[11]

Judge Hodge said he was inclined to grant the motion.

Jon Lowy made his case: "Your Honor, I think it is legitimate to argue to the jury that guns are the only unregulated product in America, and that as a result, the only way that guns can be made safer is through jury verdicts."

Hodge jumped all over him. "That is the last thing in the world I want the jury to even think about or to have suggested to them, that this is their opportunity to be a legislature. As a matter of fact, I will tell them they are not the legislature, and they are not to legislate.

So, that was not a compelling argument. The defendants' motion is granted."

I was deeply disappointed.

Judge Hodge was certainly right that the jury should not legislate, or make new laws, and I understood his desire to avoid "political" issues in the trial. We just wanted the jury to understand the facts and to apply California's law, that when there is foreseeable misuse of a product, it must be designed with that misuse in mind. The jury *was* charged with deciding what caused Kenzo's death. If the jury didn't learn that Congress had exempted firearms from product safety regulation, they wouldn't understand how guns—specifically, this Beretta—could *continue*, year after year, to be made without important consumer safety features, and how deaths like Kenzo's could keep happening, even though they are *foreseeable* and preventable. This special exclusion had been put in the law by the powerful gun lobby. Our trial was supposed to be about the causes of Kenzo's death, and the stipulation by Congress that the Consumer Product Safety Commission cannot regulate firearms was a cause of Kenzo's death.

Finally, Judge Hodge took up two more of Beretta's motions, both of which involved limiting testimony from our expert witness, Stephen Teret, director of the Johns Hopkins Center for Gun Policy and Research. Beretta's motion to prevent Teret from giving opinion testimony argued that because he was not an engineer, he should not be allowed to testify about gun-safety devices. Jon Lowy replied that Teret would testify about the study of firearm accidents and gun-storage practices, but he would not discuss design or engineering subjects.

But then Jon said Teret would testify that at the time Clifford bought the Beretta, safety devices that could have been incorporated into the gun were available.

"But 'available' means 'available and usable,' doesn't it?" asked Hodge. "I mean, 'available' doesn't help us much."

Beretta's lawyers said those gun designs had never been tested.

Nancy Hersh replied that they couldn't have been tested for reliability because no gun manufacturers had designed or incorporated into their guns the safety devices our expert would propose.

Judge Hodge said that we had the burden of proof on this issue, which seemed to mean we were supposed to manufacture and test the guns with the safety features that our expert witnesses proposed.

But Jon Lowy had a way out of that. "Once we prove that Beretta's design contributed to Kenzo's death," Jon replied, "the burden shifts to the defendant to prove why their design is beneficial. 'Do the benefits outweigh the risks of their design?' "

Larry Keane, leader of the gun manufacturers' association, had begun grunting loudly and almost jumping out of his chair. Up to now, he had been mainly a quiet, ominous presence, so I was surprised to see him so agitated.

Hodge could no longer ignore him. "Mr. Keane, do me a favor. Just lighten up. Sit down. Have I kept you from—"

"No, Your Honor."

"—being heard one time?"

"No, Your Honor."

Soon Hodge gave Keane his turn.

"The question is whether or not the devices their expert is offering were feasible on the Beretta 92 Compact L—that there were some other devices out there is not relevant," said Keane.

I kept thinking that the Beretta company was required by law to design and distribute a gun that is as safe as reasonably possible for consumers, even if that meant redesigning it from the ground up, not just making minor modifications to the gun they were selling.

Judge Hodge had not yet ruled on whether Stephen Teret could testify about gun-safety features when he took up Beretta's related motion to prevent Stephen Teret from testifying about gun studies and statistics.

First, he asked Jon Lowy why testimony about the statistics of gun storage was relevant.

Jon replied that the thrust of Teret's statistics and studies was that there was a foreseeable risk that some gun owners would store their guns loaded and unlocked, and that unauthorized users—including children—would gain access to those guns.

Judge Hodge thought that was obvious, and didn't need studies or experts.

Jon replied that it is a contested issue, and Hodge said that he'd noticed that. Jon said because there was this foreseeable risk, Beretta should have implemented feasible safety features.

Judge Hodge asked Jon how he would respond to Beretta's argument that other accidents had to be substantially similar to our case. Jon said all that is required is that the previous injury should be enough to attract the defendant's attention to a dangerous situation. The main reason to introduce this evidence is to show "notice" to Beretta of the danger. The law holds Beretta to the standard of an expert in the field, with a duty to know what was scientifically known at the time, said Jon. Beretta had a duty to warn of the risks that were scientifically known.

"Putting your head in the sand is not a defense," Jon concluded.

Craig Livingston replied that Teret couldn't point to any of the studies and show that the same Beretta firearm was involved, and he couldn't show that the accident happened in a similar circumstance. Jon had mentioned studies by Teret and others in the *Journal of the American Medical Association* and the *Journal of Public Health* as examples Teret would use to show that this kind of accident happens.

But Livingston said, "Not to besmirch the medical journals, but publications like that are not the kind of thing that is disseminated and is expected to be widely read by people outside of that particular area of interest. There is no evidence at all that we received any of these statistics prior to the date of distribution of this particular firearm. It's not as though Mr. Teret was sending these to every gun manufacturer in the country to put them on notice that this information is out there."

So, head in the sand *was* going to be their defense.

Jon quickly read the appropriate legal precedent. "Manufacturers are strictly liable for injuries caused by their failure to give warnings for dangers that were known to the scientific community at the time they manufactured and distributed the product." He looked up at Judge Hodge. "It is not a defense to say 'We don't subscribe to that magazine.' Or, 'When we read about gun accidents, we don't read the full article.' Additionally, all the guns in these accidents had one identical defect, which is that all of them had no design to prevent unauthorized use."

After considerable debate, Judge Hodge denied one of Beretta's motions but accepted the other. Teret could testify about unintentional firearm injuries and how gun owners store their guns. But the judge severely restricted the scope of Teret's testimony. He ruled firmly that Teret could not talk about gun-design issues, and Teret was forbidden from indicating that it was foreseeable that X, Y, or Z event in our case had happened. Our safety engineer expert would have the full burden of explaining what had happened, and linking events to the defects in the design of the Beretta.

That was it. We had worked our way through all the *motions in limine.*

The judge, still in good spirits despite his occasional outbursts, thanked us, and we all filed out, a little numb, each weighing how many of our motions had been granted and what parts of reality that we thought were so crucial would never reach jurors' ears.

Our side had won on industry custom and practice. This should prevent Beretta from implying to the jury that since no gun makers built internal locks into their guns, and hardly any gun makers sold guns with prominent chamber-loaded indicators, that must prove that it couldn't be done.

But we had lost on comparative fault. Beretta lawyers could elaborate on Clifford's and Mark's errors, and draw the jurors' attention away from the key moments when, if the handgun had had a built-in lock, a prominent chamber-loaded indicator, and came with proper warnings, Kenzo would still be alive. Jurors would be thinking of an either/or trade-off between the errors of Clifford and his son Mark *versus* the errors of Beretta USA, when our side thought that they were *all* at fault.

On the plus side, we had defeated Beretta's attempt to hide its gun ads from jurors.

But jurors would never be told that, among the thousands of products around us, Congress had given only firearms a special exemption from consumer product safety regulation. And Professor Stephen Teret could only give statistics and data. He could not give his opinion on gun-safety devices, or explain to the jury how some of the specific things that had happened to Mark and to Kenzo were really quite common.

Finally, we were ready to pick twelve jurors and three alternates and present them with contradictory explanations for the causes of Kenzo's death.

# 6

## Jury Selection

On Thursday, October 15, 1998, the one hundred members of the jury pool flowed back into the cavernous courtroom. Lynn, Kalani, and I sat down behind our lawyers. Piles of tattered jury questionnaires were stacked carefully in order on the table nearby. Lynn and I and our lawyers had spent most of Wednesday reading them, flagging problematic statements and discussing the jurors who were most likely to be called.

Shortly after 9:00 a.m., Judge Hodge breezed in and announced that we would select a jury in a process called *voir dire*, "to seek the truth." The purpose, he said, is to select a jury free from bias, prejudice, or sympathy. The court clerk called the first twelve randomly selected people and asked them to sit in the jury box on the side of the room.

Nancy Hersh stepped forward, smiling, and asked the white business owner in the first seat if there was anything in his experience that would put one or the other side at a disadvantage. He said he didn't think so, but then brought up that he had "opinions about frivolous lawsuits." Soon he was dismissed because fifty employees depended on projects he would need to be working on during the trial.

Next, a middle-aged white housewife, in the second seat, said that some people were "sue-happy," but that she did not know the facts of this case. "I will say that I have a strong feeling that I don't believe in guns," she said. She felt that guns need to be locked up, especially when there are small children around. Lynn and I couldn't agree more, of course. In fact, we wanted locks built into guns. But we soon discovered that she seemed biased against us; her focus was entirely on the father and his son, not at all on the design of the gun, about which she knew nothing. That gave us a glimpse of what we were up against.

People came with all sorts of ideas about guns. A heavyset white man in seat eight who had heard about the case on the news said he was an experienced gun user. He once owned some defective small and cheap pistols—Saturday Night Specials—that "stovepiped" on him when he shot them. He did not seem to know that there were no safety standards for guns, or to think that he was lucky not to have been badly injured. He was a friendly, talkative man who said that when he was in the military, he knew a soldier who, when standing watch, had taken out his gun and, "playing with it," had shot himself in the foot. I began to hope he would understand the need for prominent chamber-loaded indicators. But in a minute, it was clear that to him, the issue came down simply to being pro-gun or the opposite—no nuances whatsoever. He became the first person our side had to use one of our few challenges to dismiss.

The questioning went on in a nightmarish way, exposing all sorts of misconceptions about our case. A well-educated white woman who worked in research and development said that if a family is going to have a gun in the home, they have to make it safe for everyone. I thought everyone would agree. She had two small children and said she "did not like" guns, but that if there ever was a gun in her house, she was going to make sure her kids did not have access to it. Good. But when Nancy asked her if she was a little bit against the Dixes' case, she admitted that she was. She wanted to blame the father, Clifford, and his son, Mark. Well, so did I, I thought, fuming; in fact, they blame themselves as well, of course. But we hadn't gotten to Beretta's part yet. Hold on a bloody second. To my surprise, Judge Hodge interrupted and told her that she was at a disadvantage because she did not know what the law was, and he was not going to tell her, because even he did not know the facts of the case yet. He had seen that the prospective jurors were making all sorts of erroneous assumptions, and he was clearly but subtly warning them to hold off. But the dreadful phrase "You only get one chance to make a first impression" popped into my mind.

As the questioning continued, I began to see our problem more clearly: lots of attention on the shooter and the gun owner—only natural—but no attention on safe product design, even—*or especially*—for handguns, the most dangerous of all household consumer products.[12] People had no idea what safe product design would even mean for handguns. No one could conceive of the idea.

But these jurors had not yet heard our case. I remained optimistic.

A white, gray-haired Berkeley public school teacher in seat eleven said she was anti-corporate and pro–gun control; she said that money is the only language that most corporations speak, and that Beretta would have to make an incredibly strong case for her not to give punitive damages to the plaintiffs. But she taught her students to look at both sides of an issue, and said she would listen to both sides before making her decision, based on the evidence. Soon Judge Hodge thanked her and excused her himself. Apparently, he thought she was biased. Beretta's lawyers did not have to use one of their challenges to get rid of her.

A Black man in seat twelve who had received firearms training in the army and had a revolver at home for protection, but kept it locked, said that, based on the judge's description of the case, Beretta had the advantage. Nancy asked him if he felt there could be "shared responsibility." Judge Hodge interrupted and said he could not allow that question, because it would require him to go into a lengthy explanation of the rule of "comparative fault." This juror remained seated in the jury. I wondered how we could conduct *voir dire*—the process of selecting an unbiased jury—if we could not ask a juror if there could be shared responsibility.

Now we had been through all twelve who were originally called. Since three people had been dismissed, three new ones were called up. One was a Black man who, as he walked to his chair, could not resist flirting with the young Black lawyer sitting at our lawyers' table. Under questioning, he said he didn't have any real feelings about the case, and added that he did not see anything that would preclude him from serving. But he was the first person I felt decidedly uncomfortable about; he seemed too eager to be on the jury.

Based on something he'd said in his questionnaire, he was asked if lawyers worked for him. He replied that he was their minister. Nancy asked him if he would be able to consider the possibility that more than one person could be responsible for the death of another. Gebhardt objected. Judge Hodge explained that we would be examining the responsibility of all parties who had anything to do with the shooting, including "the parents, the young people themselves, and the manufacturer of the weapon." He told the jurors that Beretta was the only defendant in this case for reasons that they need not know right now.

His comment made me feel better, but only briefly. When Nancy thanked the minister and began questioning the next potential juror, it became evident that Judge Hodge's mention of "the parents" had confused the jurors even more than they were already confused. A Chinese-American secretary being questioned said that if you were going to have a gun for protection, or for whatever reason, you should have it locked up, and that there seemed to be more negligence on the part of the plaintiffs, because she did not think young children should have possession of a gun. Hodge had to explain to her that no one was alleging negligence on the part of the *plaintiffs*, and that this unintentional shooting had happened in *another person's* home.

That revelation seemed to surprise many. The overview that Judge Hodge had given them had been extremely brief, and it seemed that assumptions had been getting far ahead of the facts. In a few minutes, we discovered that on the previous day, this woman's husband had told her that he owned a Beretta handgun. We had to expend another of our challenges to excuse her from the jury.

Next a well-dressed white dentist was called. He felt strongly that the person who had possession of the gun last, as an adult, was responsible. Once again, I agreed with him, but he had not yet heard the whole story. Nancy asked if he would ever be able to get past the fact that the gun was in the home of an adult, and that a teenager had access to it. Could he find that the manufacturer was *also partly* responsible? He said yes, but it would be hard.

After more questioning and more confusion, Hodge relented even more on explaining comparative fault, and told the dentist that the jury could be asked to allocate the fault of *all* the people involved, including the parents in that home, the boy who pulled the trigger, and the defendants, who had helped design the gun.

But the dentist felt that only the parents of the kid who shot the gun were responsible. He did not understand why the father of the kid was not on trial here. (Clifford had settled our prior lawsuit against him, and his homeowners' insurance had paid damages, as mentioned. But the lawyers were not allowed to tell the jurors that.)

Judge Hodge instructed the dentist, "We are only going with respect to Beretta." Nancy told him the gun could be any consumer product. But the dentist said a gun is made for killing, and someone has to have responsibility for it. He said he had a gun and kept it away from his grandkids.

I sat in agony, in complete sympathy with the guy and his opinion; certainly, the father, Clifford, was at fault. But it was inconceivable to this juror that the gun industry—and Beretta, in particular—was *also* in part responsible for Kenzo's death. We had not begun that argument, and our reasons for thinking that were as yet unknown to the jurors. We had to expend another challenge to dismiss this thoughtful, well-meaning, and rational juror. As he walked away, Judge Hodge quipped that they'd be calling him if they needed him for that double homicide down the hall.

A husky young white student who attended community college at night was called.

When Nancy asked him if he could keep an open mind, he said he prided himself on it, explaining in a friendly way: "Upper-level English assignments—I am able to take two different sides and not come to an opinion. I can watch the ten o'clock news and not come to any opinions that they force down you."

Eventually the other jurors would select this genial young student as the jury foreman.

When Nancy finished questioning potential jurors, Gebhardt got his chance. He asked the jurors if they had biases against corporations, or if they could treat corporations like they were individuals. He wanted to know if anyone had a sort of David-versus-Goliath mentality that might lead him to favor the plaintiffs just because we had brought a lawsuit. When one juror said she thought that Beretta should say they were sorry, and "You have my deepest sympathies," Gebhardt replied, "But the plaintiffs are suing for money damages.

That's what the lawsuit is about." He had slipped into the jurors' minds the idea that we were doing this for money, rather than to save lives.

We had been having trouble keeping someone in seat number one. Person after person had been called to sit there and had soon been dismissed for inability to understand English or by a challenge from the lawyers of one side or the other.

Finally, a self-assured-looking seventy-three-year-old Black woman was called. On her questionnaire, she had written that she had been a psychologist and clinician for preadolescent boys, and that punitive damages were sometimes the only way a company can be forced to correct misdeeds. She'd also written that it was not acceptable to her for someone to own a handgun for self-protection. One of her relatives had been robbed at gunpoint. She believed that guns should be made as safe as possible. Yet for some reason, Gebhardt left her on the jury.

Nancy Hersh began questioning people to fill the seats of the three alternates. One woman who was very much "against guns" replied, "As much as I feel for the family and their loss, nothing, no matter what, can get that child back, no matter what they do, whether the company is right or wrong." That opinion led her to say, "I am against both parties." She seemed to believe that by arguing that the gun's design was at fault, we were excusing Clifford and Mark. Soon Judge Hodge dismissed her.

Another woman said she had "very, very strong opinions about guns." She thought they should have every kind of safety control imaginable on them. Judge Hodge said, "All right," and looked at Gebhardt. "Do you have a motion?" He answered, "Yes, sir," and asked the court to remove her. So, Hodge dismissed her, as he had many other women who had expressed strong opinions against guns. This jury was not going to be a representative cross section of jury-eligible Alameda County citizens.

When all twelve seats and three alternate seats were filled, Lynn and I huddled anxiously with our lawyers to decide whether to use our few remaining challenges. We considered the Black man who, when questioned directly, had said he was a minister, but who, on his questionnaire, hadn't indicated his occupation was minister; he'd written funeral counselor. Later, we learned that he sold burial plots. When asked about previous occupations, he had said tax preparer. On the questionnaire he indicated that he did not listen to NPR but did listen to Rush Limbaugh. Jon had hired an experienced jury consultant group who had rated each juror. They had given him an acceptable, even fairly high, rating.

But I was still uncomfortable about the fact that he seemed visibly eager to be a juror. He was well-spoken and well-educated; we knew he could be a leader on the jury. Someone had told us if you know that someone will be a leader on the jury, you should make sure that he or she is sympathetic to your side. We all agreed: How could a Black pastor in Oakland—where gun violence among the Black community is horrendous—*not* be sympathetic to our argument?

Jon spoke with Nancy Hersh's friend, the attractive young Black lawyer with whom this juror had been blatantly flirting. With a smile, she said not to worry; this guy was just like her uncle. So, although each of us harbored gnawing reservations that we only revealed to each other later, we decided to accept him.

The jurors who would be called next seemed just as bad as the worst of those we were thinking of dismissing, so we decided to stand firm with those we had. Beretta's lawyers made the same judgment.

Judge Hodge announced that we had our jury.

# PART III

# The Trial

# 7

## Opening Statements

On October 19, 1998, Lynn, Kalani and I walked into the courtroom and sat behind our lawyers. I felt optimistic; finally, a jury was going to hear about what happened to Kenzo, and about the design flaws of the Beretta handgun. Whatever preconceptions the jurors held, now they would get to hear our case.

The twelve jurors and the three alternates sat chatting in the jury box. The gallery was already almost full. It included about fifty of our friends and acquaintances, plus media people and other interested parties who had learned about our case in the newspaper or on TV.

The small side door to the judge's chambers opened. Nick, the court clerk, shouted "All rise," and Judge Hodge strode in. His long black robe and white hair swayed as he bounded up the stairs to the leather chair behind the massive wooden "bench." He sat himself down and surveyed the crowd, looking a little surprised at its size, and welcomed the jury enthusiastically. The lawyers would give their opening statements, he said, after he gave the jurors "a taste of the legal framework" that would form the basis for their opinion.

Judge Hodge looked down at the jurors sitting to his right and explained that we were claiming the Beretta handgun that killed our son was defective. "A product may be defective," he explained, "because of a defect in design or manufacture, or a failure to adequately warn the consumer of a hazard involved in the foreseeable use of the product." He said the essential elements of this claim of design defect were whether the defect was a substantial factor in the death of Kenzo Dix, and whether his death resulted from a use of the product that was foreseeable by the defendant.

Hodge read a list of items that a jury could consider in making its judgment: the gravity of the danger posed by the design; the mechanical feasibility of a safer alternate design; the possible adverse consequences to the product and to the consumer of the alternate design. With hardly a pause, the judge reiterated that a product is "defective" if it is used in a reasonably foreseeable way, but using it involves a substantial danger that would not be readily recognized by the ordinary user of the product. This danger would need to be known, or knowable, to the manufacturer in light of the best scientific knowledge available at the time it was manufactured and distributed.

Next, Judge Hodge thrust the jurors into a thicket of legal phrases. He read briskly, "A product is defective in design if it fails to perform as safely as an ordinary consumer would expect when used in an intended or reasonably foreseeable manner, or a product may be defective in design if there is a risk of danger inherent in the design which outweighs the benefits of the design." Looking up, he tried to interpret that for the jurors: "So, you weigh the risks inherent in the design versus the benefits of that design."

He mentioned some items that a jury could consider in making its judgment: the gravity of the danger posed by the design, the mechanical feasibility of a safer alternate design, the adverse consequences to the product and to the consumer of the alternate design.

The jurors looked a little dazed.

But with hardly a pause, the judge looked down at his papers and introduced some new concepts—among them that we, the plaintiffs, allege a defect based upon a failure to adequately warn the consumer.

After he read from a page of complex legalese, I thought: What a mouthful! How are ordinary people supposed to follow all that? As jurors hear the testimony, how can they know where to file away in memory the information that they will need so that later they can match it up with the laws that are supposed to guide their decision? But, to my surprise, until the very end of the lengthy trial, this quick run-through was all the jurors would hear of the laws that they were to apply.

During his introduction of the case, Judge Hodge also explained their responsibilities as jurors. "You are not to form or express any opinion about this case until it is finally submitted to you. You are not to discuss this case amongst yourselves nor with anyone else." He called these "the admonitions," and during the trial, at the end of most days, he would merely say to them, "Remember the admonitions."

———

Finally, given the nod, Nancy Hersh walked to the open area in front of the jury and turned toward them. She stood erect and confident in a dark business suit. Her hair hung free in tight curls cascading almost to her shoulders. But what everyone noticed was in her hand: the gun that had killed Kenzo. She held it up in front of the jury and reassured them that it was not loaded and had a cable locking device on it.

Taking a step toward the jury box, she held the heavy black hand-ful close so they would see it. "The chamber-loaded indicator is this little red mark right there," she said, her voice calm. With her other hand, she pointed to it, then noted that it is slightly elevated when the gun is unloaded, and when the gun is loaded it is elevated just one millimeter more.

The jurors leaned forward, squinting.

She told them that according to Beretta's own witnesses, this chamber-loaded indicator was designed for the police and the mili-tary; it was not designed to alert an ordinary user such as Clifford or Mark that a bullet is in the chamber. In fact, she continued, Beretta had never made any effort to find out whether consumers who use the firearm could know from this device whether the gun was loaded or not. Nancy explained that on a revolver you can easily rotate the cylinder and look inside to see that there are no bullets and the gun cannot fire. But a semiautomatic is different; a bullet can remain in the chamber even when the magazine is removed, and it will fire that bullet even if no magazine is in it, or if an empty one is put back in.

Nancy started speaking faster, with increasing zeal. She said a small part of the manual somewhere—not highlighted—says that when a cartridge is in the chamber, the upper part of the extractor protrudes and shows red, and it can be felt by touch. The manual says it is therefore *unnecessary*—she emphasized the word—to work the slide to see whether the gun is loaded. That's the only mention of the chamber-loaded indicator in the manual, she said. And the manual—which she promised they would soon see—fails to men-tion that the chamber-loaded indicator is red even when the gun is *unloaded*. She told them that Beretta's own expert would himself say that the chamber-loaded indicator is made for "informed users."

Her words almost tripping one on top of the other, Nancy said Beretta, which marketed its gun not just to the military and police, but to ordinary citizens, could have put a more-visible chamber-loaded indicator on the gun and could have engraved a warning on it, saying that a bullet can still remain in the chamber even when the magazine is taken out or is empty.

She held the gun up and said it was defective without a more-visible and prominent chamber-loaded indicator. It was also defective, because it did not have a built-in lock, and because the manual failed to warn of the dangers, or to explain them adequately.

Even Beretta employees would tell them, she stated, that Beretta did nothing to determine whether gun owners store their guns away from kids or store them loaded, and that Beretta *is aware* that people think a gun is unloaded when they take the loaded magazine out of a semiautomatic.

"This is a case of shared responsibility," she said. Clifford and Mark were negligent, no doubt about it, and were partly responsible for Kenzo's death. But Beretta was responsible, too. The company could have manufactured a product that would have prevented this death, and they didn't. An ordinary consumer is likely to believe that if you take the magazine out, the gun is not loaded. The gun itself, and also its manual, could have alerted this population of home users of this risk much more clearly. She said our lawyers will show that adding an internal lock and an effective chamber-loaded indicator, and adding warnings, had been technologically feasible for thirty years. So, the fact that Clifford and Mark were negligent does not relieve Beretta of responsibility for making a safe product in accordance with the law.

Finally, Nancy's voice became softer. Stepping close to the jurors, she told them what a loving child Kenzo was, and what a shock it was to Mark when he pulled the trigger of a gun he thought he'd unloaded, and a bullet went into Kenzo's shoulder and heart.

Then she surprised me. Lynn, she said, had gone to Kenzo's grave on his birthday only a little more than a month ago, and had found a tattered picture of him there. She held up a wrinkled, dirt-stained little photo I had never seen before. It had been left there by one of

Kenzo's friends, with a note: "Happy 20th Birthday." I realized that Kenzo's friends were still honoring his memory, four and a half years after he died.

In closing, Nancy said she wanted to read the jurors something that would give them a feel for what Kenzo was like: his essay called "My Gift," in which he had said that when someday he passed away, he wanted to leave something that people could remember him by. He hoped to leave to his own children a lot of the knowledge he had gained—things he would slowly teach them over a long period of time. Even though this would not make him famous or known after his death, he said that knowledge—the lessons learned about the nature of the world and human beings—was the most important thing he could pass on to his children, which they could in turn pass on to future generations.

Every time I heard this homework essay that Kenzo had scrawled at his desk in his bedroom late one night, it brought me pleasure inevitably mixed with regret. Had he lived, what a delight he would have been to his children. I found again in his words the joy he had brought to my life. But side by side with that joy was an expectation of future joys: of Kenzo as a young man in love, then a husband. There would have been the joys of a daughter-in-law, of Kenzo as a father; of me, playing with his children—all never to be.

The memories of past joys seemed like double picture frames on a doting father's wall. Paired with each memory I treasured came the joys of an imagined future faded to nothing. Beside each fond memory there was only a blank where lives should have been.

—

The loud, indignant voice of Beretta's lawyer Robert Gebhardt jolted me out of my reverie. He stood before the jury in a suit and cowboy boots, in what seemed a calculated attempt to present himself as a folksy man-of-the-people rather than a wealthy, big-time corporate defense lawyer.

To begin his opening statement, Gebhardt told the jurors that although the pistol that killed Kenzo was designed and manufactured by Beretta USA's parent company in Italy, Beretta USA was proud of the gun and accepted responsibility for its design. The Italian Beretta company was five hundred years old, he said, one of the oldest corporations in the world.

Now, holding the gun that killed Kenzo in his hand, Gebhardt told the jurors that the US military had selected this model off the shelf in the mid-1980s. It had been subjected to the most rigorous durability, reliability, and ease-of-handling tests. Nancy objected that this was a violation of the judge's ruling on our *in limine* motion. He shouldn't have been allowed to say the gun had been tested by the military, when we were not allowed to say that Congress had forbidden the Consumer Product Safety Commission from testing firearms to see if they could be made safer as household consumer products. If Gebhardt got to say it had been tested, then we should be able to say, "No, it hasn't been tested for consumers." But Judge Hodge brushed aside her objection.

Gebhardt continued, "This case involves pulling the trigger of a loaded Beretta Compact L. The gun operated as it was designed and manufactured to do: a bullet was fired, and the consequences were tragic." Gebhardt's voice sounded peeved that he had to be in this courtroom defending this product at all. He began telling the jury in detail how the gun works. He seemed to enjoy manipulating it. He slammed the slide on top of the gun back, explaining how a round is forced into the chamber. Then, as he clutched the gun, he explained its various parts, pointing it around the courtroom. He described some safety features on it—the firing pin block, the trigger block, the "safety"—all of which were probably well-designed and irrelevant to Kenzo's death.

Gebhardt said you had to pull the hammer back to cock older single-action guns, and sometimes accidents happened when they were loaded and someone tried to release the hammer by letting it down. But the Beretta is a safer double-action gun.

I had learned by then that many of these safety features had been on handguns for decades. But I had been watching the jury. As Gebhardt had begun to play with this little black death machine of immense power—real as well as imagined, dangerous and much-storied—I could feel their excitement surge.

On an easel, Gebhardt placed a picture of the Beretta handgun cut down the middle, its insides exposed like a dissected cadaver. He pointed out various parts, such as the trigger bar, which he demonstrated by pulling the gun's trigger. He showed how the firing pin was held away from the bullet by "an inertial spring, which is a safety feature," but that when the hammer strikes, it pushes that firing pin into the bullet, causing an explosion that's 35,000 pounds per square inch. "Hence the need to keep the firing chamber totally closed," he said.

Gebhardt conveyed at length that the gun was an engineering marvel, and that tampering with its design in any way would be a mistake. However, he added, "This gun is inherently dangerous, and we are serious about the instructions and warnings issued with the gun, and they do tell the user about safe-storage practices."

On he went, hardly able to contain his enthusiasm. He said that because the Beretta is inherently dangerous, there are advanced, state-of-the-art safety devices to prevent inadvertent discharge. One of them is unique to this product. The ejector is a little tooth on the gun's slide that catches onto the spent cartridge casings and pulls them out. "And Beretta has designed it so that not only is it an ejector, it is also a chamber-loaded indicator. It sticks out when there is a bullet in the chamber."

He freely admitted that when there is no bullet in the chamber, "You can see a little red. No question about it; okay?" He pointed to the red spot on the gun, then put a spent casing into the chamber. "And would you look at the chamber-loaded indicator now? It's different. It does stick out. You can feel it if you want to." He demonstrated. "So, there it is without it; and there it is with it—readily apparent," he informed them, very quickly continuing. "Even if there is some confusion about the fact that it shows some red without a bullet in the chamber, that's a false positive. Somebody looks at this and can say, 'I see a little red. There might be a bullet in the chamber.' It's not a false negative; it's a false positive. It's a positive safety feature of this gun."

*But wait*, I thought, *a false positive is a type of misleading error.*

He started talking about how much experience Clifford had with all the guns he had owned over the years. When he said, "Some of you may conclude at the end of this trial he was a gun fanatic," Nancy objected and he withdrew it. "He was at least a gun enthusiast," said Gebhardt, having planted the "gun fanatic" idea in jurors' minds early on.

As Gebhardt stood there with the gun that killed Kenzo, that he'd been pointing around the room, he said that Clifford had taught Mark the basics of gun safety: to treat all guns as if they were loaded, and never to point a gun at anyone. Clifford taught Mark how to clear the gun and how to make sure it is not loaded—and that was done by opening the slide. "He forbade Mark from playing with this gun, and Mark knew all about gun safety," he said. Beretta does know that these guns are sold to people for home protection, and that children reside in homes, and "we also know that the buying of a gun affords a certain amount of protection to the owner and gives him peace of mind."

Having arrived at a major argument of the defense, he placed a large copy of four pages from the manual that came with the Beretta on an easel and pointed to the words: "An accident is always the result of basic safety neglect. Accident prevention is user responsibility." (The English in the section, which was a translation from the Italian that filled the first thirteen pages of the manual, was shaky at times.) Looking back over his shoulder at the jury, he emphasized two lines that he said were not mentioned in the plaintiffs' opening: "Store firearms and ammunition separately, beyond the reach of children. Be sure cartridge chamber is empty." He said, "That's basic safety. It's right there in the owner's manual that Clifford said he read."

Now Gebhardt itemized a list of things Clifford could have done to keep the gun from Mark: take his gun to his workplace, where he was that Sunday, moving and installing business computers; take the gun's slide with him; lock the gun or the ammunition in a lockable case. Then he listed what Mark had done: retrieve the gun when he knew he was not supposed to; play with the gun; treat it like a toy to impress his friend; fail to treat the gun as if it were loaded; fail to look into the chamber, as he'd been taught. He read from Mark's deposition, "Did you clear the weapon?—No, I didn't. I had forgotten to."

"The statement has been made that he thought it was unloaded," he said. "I believe the evidence is going to show that he didn't even consider whether it was loaded or not. The evidence will be that one hundred percent of the responsibility for this accident rests with Clifford and Mark."

Gebhardt stood before the jury in his cowboy boots and boomed that he was "headed toward the corral," but he aimed one last salvo at our gun expert, Les Roane, who would soon testify that Beretta should have made the chamber-loaded indicator stick up on top of the gun. He said Beretta's expert was going to say that if you drilled a hole and put a chamber-loaded indicator on top, and if there was a bad round, the gun would explode in the shooter's face. "And the main thing is that you'd have to redesign the entire gun," said Gebhardt.

He also told the jury that the defense would present evidence that every so-called safety idea that Beretta USA received got careful consideration by its VP and general counsel, Jeffrey Reh.

I glanced at Reh sitting at their lawyers' table and noticed that he was carefully observing the jurors. Any proposed safety inventions, said Gebhardt, would have to pass muster with Reh before he would send them on to the engineers in Italy, where the gun is designed.

Gebhardt's opening was as forceful and as clear as his bass voice. The Beretta was perfect in its design, and the manual that came with it warned owners of every danger. Everything that happened was entirely the fault of Clifford and Mark.

By the time Gebhardt had finished his opening statement, I was a wreck. I realized that the legal requirement to design a consumer product with full knowledge of the *foreseeable misuse* in mind had gotten lost in a blizzard of words.

It was hard to disagree with much of what Gebhardt had said: Clifford and Mark had made so many mistakes that it was easy to focus on them; in fact, it was difficult to get past them and see that there was more fault here than just theirs.

But I knew it was true. And that is what our lawyers would somehow have to impress upon the jury.

# 8

## What Happened and Why Did It Happen?

### *Emotional Testimony*

The next Tuesday, when Kalani and I picked up Lynn to go to the courthouse, we were nervous. They were both to be called as our first witnesses to tell the jury about Kenzo.

I asked Lynn how she felt about it during our drive to the courthouse.

"After all," she said, "we'll be telling them about Kenzo. That couldn't be so bad, could it?" She flashed a tense, bittersweet smile at me, then over her shoulder at Kalani in the backseat. I couldn't tell whether she was saying that to help Kalani through his jitters or just trying to calm her own nerves.

In court with the jurors and alternates settled in the jury box, Nancy Hersh called Lynn to the stand. Lynn looked poised and businesslike but a little shaky as she walked past the jurors and was sworn in.

Nancy began by asking her about her background growing up in Hawaii, meeting me when we were both in graduate school at the University of Hawaii, getting married, moving to the University of California, San Diego, where I went to get my PhD in cultural anthropology, and going with me to South Korea to do anthropology fieldwork.

She told the jurors that she had studied teaching English as a second language, and in Korea had commuted to Daejon city by bus, an hour and a half each way on a bumpy, treacherous dirt road, to teach English to Korean college students and help US soldiers pass their high school equivalency exams. Recalling our time in the village with a smile and a shrug, she told the jury that it was so cold, and the thatched-roof houses so poorly insulated, that during the winter we had to wear our down jackets indoors.

Nancy asked her about Kenzo's full name. She said, "Griffin—for his father—Kenzo Kalei Dix." She explained that in Japanese characters, *ken* means "health," which we'd chosen because he had looked so healthy and robust when he was born, and *zo* stands for "creativity." In Hawaiian, *Kalei* means "beloved child."

When asked if Kenzo was affectionate, Lynn's face brightened.

"Even when he was little, he was always looking for his older brother, whom he called 'Buppa.' He'd say, 'Where is Buppa?' and go find him, sit next to him, and lean on him. He would always—every day—give me a hug and a kiss, you know. I mean to the day..."

This thought stopped her. She paused to take a breath.

"Hello or good-bye was always a big hug. Even when he was in elementary school, after dinner we sat around the kitchen table, and he would sit on my lap, just kind of hanging out there, and we would talk. Then, when he got older and too big—much bigger than me—he sometimes would sit on my lap, just to tease me, actually."

She looked down into the space in front of her, as if for a moment she was back in those days. But then her eyes smiled at another thought, and she said, "Kenzo complained, 'Oh, Mom, you call me all these names!' " I could hear his voice in hers. "I called him Obi Wan Kenzobi after Obi Wan Kenobi in *Star Wars*. I called his older brother Sunshine, because we always said he brought so much sunshine into our lives, and then Kenzo was Sunbeam, because he also brought a lot of light. I remember also calling him Potato. I asked him, 'You know why I call you Potato, Kenzo?'

" 'Why?' " The way she mimicked his voice, I could just see the skeptical but curious look on his face.

"Because you can boil a potato; you can make mashed potatoes; you can make French fries; you can bake them. You can do all kinds of good things with potatoes, and that's you, Kenzo; you're good in so many ways. So you are my Potato."

She looked again into the space in front of her.

"It's so natural to give your love to someone, and especially to your child. He was deeply loved, and for me, it's a big loss in my life, because I don't have Kenzo to give..."

She had to stop for a moment to compose herself, but then went on.

"Even now, whenever I see an emergency ambulance going by, I think about when he died, and I feel like I should have been there. I wanted to be there for him and give him my love. But also...I am missing his love—the love coming from him to me—his warmth and affection. So suddenly, this whole part of my life—there is a big gap, and it's not as though you can just cleanly cut it out and put it away and it's gone."

She spoke her words with a slight lilt of Hawaii, plaintive, matter-of-fact.

After a pause, she continued. "I mean, when a child is gone, suddenly you go to his bedroom, and nobody's there. The phone doesn't ring so much anymore, which I thought I would like, because it used to ring all the time—pretty soon you don't answer it, because you know it's not for you. But now it's too quiet in the house. And the dinner table—you don't set the place for that person. You feel the absence. I don't know how I can say it. You just feel the absence."

For a moment, there was silence.

Quietly, Nancy said, "I'm going to show you a picture. Could you tell us the story that goes with it?"

From her computer, she projected a slide onto a screen across the courtroom. It was a picture I had taken on our little deck, of Lynn staggering under the weight of a beaming Kenzo, who had jumped up into her arms. He's hugging her, with his long legs around her waist, mugging a grin for the camera, and she's grinning, too, but mightily strained; she looks like she's about to topple over from the weight of this big kid—all arms and legs sticking out.

"Oh," she said, "Kenzo liked to do this...running leap. You know, I would say 'Hup,' and he would run to me and jump, and I would catch him in my arms, and then we would laugh. But then he was getting to be ten or eleven and too big to do hups, because he would *actually knock me down!* So, I said, 'Kenzo, this is it—the last hup.' And so, we memorialized that. We photographed him doing his last hup."

110

"And he would do special things, like frame pictures for you?"

Lynn nodded. "I was *terrible*. I always took pictures but never got them framed. He would ask me what I wanted for my birthday or Mother's Day, so I said, 'I don't want you to buy me anything. Far more precious to me would be something that you did. So just write me a card or sing me a song or something like that. So he framed a picture for me. He loved the picture, and I did, too."

Nancy touched the computer and a picture came into view. Lynn had bought Kalani and Kenzo thin white cotton kimonos with a blue Japanese pattern. They both put them on, and Lynn sat them down side by side and took this picture of them. Kenzo's arm is around his older brother's shoulder, and he's thrown his head back, leaning

111

all his weight on Kalani. Again, he's got a big grin for Lynn and the camera, but this time his grin is saying how much he loves his brother.

"So, for my birthday present, he got some wrapping paper and made it into a frame that he decorated. He put plastic over it and taped it up." It always looked like the Scotch tape holding the plastic wrapping might come loose any minute, but today, it probably means as much to Lynn as anything she owns.

Nancy asked Lynn about the day Kenzo died, and my elation was gone.

She told the jury about that ordinary Sunday afternoon when the phone rang and it was the woman from Oakland Children's Hospital who said, "You need to come immediately," and how, at the hospital, the doctor came in and said they'd done everything they could but they couldn't save Kenzo. He'd been shot.

"Oh, God. I could hardly speak. I mean…afterwards, you think of a hundred questions you could have asked the doctor. But, then…I remember…just…I could hardly breathe. I mean, you can't imagine your child dead, because the child is life, you know. You can't imagine he's dead."

After a break, Kalani was called. He stood up from beside us and walked hesitantly to the witness box. Wearing a brown shirt with a well-matched coat and tie that Lynn had gotten him, he looked unusually dapper.

After he was sworn in, Nancy asked him his age.

"Twenty-two."

"How would you describe your relationship with Kenzo?"

Self-assured, speaking in a soft voice, he said, "It was a good relationship; I think we treated each other very well as brothers. He was always there for me. He was always on my side whenever there was any dispute with other people, or even with, you know, my parents, he would usually be on my side."

I couldn't hold back a smile.

112

"And he was really loving. He would do things like give me presents when it wasn't even my birthday or anything. He enjoyed surprising me with presents sometimes—things I really wanted."

He continued on with no prompt from Nancy.

"We were really good friends. Recently I started thinking about how much we played together. From early on, all the way up through high school, he was my best friend, and I played with him every day of my whole life."

He spoke of the fun they had together in an understated way, as if it was just ordinary. It was so true. And it was breaking my heart.

"We didn't have too many friends come over to the house when we were younger, so it was just me and him playing together all the time, and we had a blast. We would go biking. We rode scooters a lot around the neighborhood. I went to a carpentry class and built a scooter—two actually, one for him. We played basketball, football—all kinds of sports. On family trips in the car, I would be the Dungeon Master when we'd play Dungeons and Dragons. I'd set up all sorts of adventures for him and lead him through them. We went backpacking a lot; we went hiking, camping, and to the East Coast and to Hawaii to visit relatives, and he was always my companion through all of that. When we would do family things that sometimes weren't so fun, I'd always know it wouldn't be too bad because Kenzo was there, and I wouldn't be bored."

Asked about when he first heard from us that Kenzo had died, Kalani said he came into the living room and knew immediately that something was wrong. Lynn and I were both crying. He said that after we told him, at first he was in such shock that he did not feel anything. But then, as it grew dark and we were all sitting there together, suddenly the phone rang. It was one of Kalani's friends asking him to come over. He had to tell the friend. That was when he broke down in tears and realized fully that his life had changed forever.

He glanced down and said, "My life has definitely been a lot harder since Kenzo left." I noted the euphemism, and was curious about what he would say next. "For a while, right after he died, I was really shaken, and I withdrew from other people. And when I went off to college—it was really hard times."

When I'd learned that Kalani was having trouble concentrating at college, I went up to Humboldt State and saw that Kalani and his friends were not taking advantage of the opportunities that college offered. In their second year, they rented a house off campus, which they never seemed to clean, and where, as a curiosity, they kept in an aquarium a large, vicious snapping turtle they had picked up somewhere. It seemed to be as much the focus of their interest as schoolwork. Mostly, I suspected, they sat around, talking and drinking beer.

After Kalani's sophomore year, he dropped out of Humboldt State. I drove up, bought a carload of cleaning supplies, and helped them clean layer upon layer of accumulated grime so they could get back most of their security deposit. By then their poor turtle had died of neglect.

From the stand, Kalani said Kenzo's loss was the spark that led Lynn and me to divorce.

114

"They got divorced soon after, because I was going away to college, and I'm sure if he was still around, living at the house, they wouldn't have gotten a divorce."

After his testimony, Judge Hodge followed his usual practice of asking the witness questions from jurors, which they wrote down and gave to him so he could review them before he asked them to the witness.

Now, turning toward Kalani, he read what one juror had written on a card: "Is Kenzo's death something you remember often?"

"Every day—and this is true—every day I think about him and miss him. When I'm in sad moods, I feel like I think about him too much. You know, it's better for me to think about him in happy times."

Finally, after dropping out of several colleges, he had decided on his own to take a Microsoft computer technology course. He studied hard, passed a series of difficult certification tests, and got a good job in information technology for the Berkeley school district. He had finished his BA by attending night school while working full-time. None of that was easy after losing his brother. Now, poised and articulate, he quietly but fully explained his emotional travails without apologies to a group of total strangers. I was proud of him.

In the days that followed, I thought about the testimony I had heard Kalani give. I realized how little we had said to each other about what we were feeling after the loss of Kenzo; that was something that I deeply regretted. I thought of the irony of listening to him tell a jury of strangers things that he and I had not discussed with each other, except in the most general way. Each of us in our family struggled separately at a time when we could have been more help to each other.

For Kalani, losing his brother was like losing a part of himself. Kenzo and he were so close, they were almost like a part of each other—and then Kenzo was suddenly gone. He had lost something central to who he was, and a large part of who he would have become.

My loss was not the same as Kalani's loss. Brothers who grow up together bond and fuse in ways obscure to parents, no matter how close the parents are to their children. So, disentangling his new self from that bond—finding the good memories to revisit, learning to face and eventually bury the demons of such a tragedy and loss—were different experiences for Kalani than they were for me, or for Lynn. But rebuilding himself was certainly no easier.

### *The Boy Who Shot Kenzo*

Jon Lowy had decided we needed to call Mark to testify because if we didn't, the Beretta lawyers would. But for us, his testimony was a minefield. If they could pin everything on Mark, the role in Kenzo's death played by Beretta USA in the design and marketing of the handgun could remain hidden. Somehow, we had to get through Mark's testimony with as little damage as possible.

I had not seen Mark for a while and did not know what to expect. Shortly after Kenzo died, I had met him occasionally when he and Kenzo's other friends had come over to our house. I had always made a point—awkwardly, I fear—of saying hello to him. I thought it good that after the initial shock, their group had remained his friend and had supported him. Although they recognized that he had made a dreadful mistake, everyone knew it was unintentional.

A few years before the trial, I had run into him when he was waiting tables at Fat Apple's, just below the Sunset Mortuary, where Kenzo was buried. Mark had told me he had taken a year off from college, and that working so near Kenzo's grave was just a coincidence. He said he didn't go to the grave often because going there "doesn't do a lot for me," and that he tried to forget what had happened that day.

I understood completely, and thought to myself, God only knows what that boy has been through.

When Mark was called to the witness stand, in came a man wearing a dark shirt and a coat and tie with mismatched pants. Mark was eighteen, going on nineteen. He didn't look like the fourteen-year-old boy I had known four and a half years ago—Kenzo's friend, so full of life and joy. He trudged past the jury box, stoop-shouldered and wary, focusing only on the floor in front of him. He looked sullen and resistant, as if he did not want to be here at all.

A wave of sorrow welled up in me.

After being sworn in, he told the jury of his friendship with Kenzo, which had begun in the fifth grade. When the questions turned to the day he shot Kenzo, he became visibly shaken, staring down at the empty space in front of him, speaking in a monotone. Whenever Jon asked him a question, Mark looked at him, then put his head down as if to hide. Several times Judge Hodge had to ask Mark to speak up. Occasionally Mark had to ask Jon to repeat a question because his mind seemed to have wandered, or was still on the last question. At times, Mark just sat silently after Jon spoke to him and Jon had to rephrase his question and try again. To the jury, Mark may have looked unresponsive or even rebellious, but I knew he was having enormous trouble taking his mind back to that day—the day he had tried so hard to forget.

Softly, almost inaudibly, he said that day when they were in his room he suddenly thought it would be "kind of cool" to show Kenzo his father's Beretta. So, without telling Kenzo, he had gone to his father's bedroom to get the gun, kept in a camera bag next to his father's bed—the gun his father had told him not to touch. In answer to Jon Lowy's questions, he said, "I released the magazine and pulled the magazine out to see if the gun was loaded." He had looked at the magazine in his hand, seen it had bullets in it, put it in the camera bag, and taken an empty one back upstairs. When he entered his bedroom, he put the empty magazine into the gun.

"Did you think the gun was unloaded at that point?"

"Yes," he said, raising his head to look at Jon.

When the magazine clicked into the handgun, he said, Kenzo turned around, saw it, and said something like, "Wow." Mark released the safety so he could pull the trigger.

"And why did you want to pull the trigger?"

"To—it was like a toy. It was like having a toy gun to shoot."

"Were you aiming at anything in particular?"

"No, nothing in particular."

"What was the sound like when the gun went off?"

"Just kind of a deep, deafening boom."

He said he'd shot that Beretta once, several months before, at the shooting range with his father, who had told him not to pull the trigger unless he wanted to shoot something. His father had also told him other things about handling a gun, but he had not done them that day.

"Why?" Jon asked, keeping his voice neutral.

"I don't know. I was just—like most teenagers—defiant of their parents at one point or another."

"Did your father ever explain to you how a semiautomatic pistol is loaded? How the bullet actually gets into the chamber?"

No, he hadn't, Mark said.

"And was there anything on the Beretta gun that you knew of that indicated to you that the gun that you thought was unloaded was actually loaded?"

"On May twenty-ninth? No."

He said that after he heard the blast, he saw Kenzo slumped over and initially thought he was joking.

"When did you realize he wasn't joking?"

"When I went to go—go shake on him, and I realized—I saw blood, and realized I had shot him."

He described how he had tried desperately to resuscitate Kenzo as well as he could.

"Did you say anything to Kenzo?" Jon asked.

118

"Yeah. I told him I was sorry, and that I loved him. I just repeated that over and over."

His father's fiancée came into the room, and he shouted at her to call 911.

Jon asked him if he'd put the gun back in his father's bedroom, and Mark said he had taken it back and put it in the bag.

"Why did you do that?"

"I thought if—it sounds pretty stupid—but I thought if I could put the gun back, my dad would never know—kind of erasing everything."

The paramedics came and told him to get out, and he went to his sister's room, where she comforted him while the police tried to talk to him.

"Mark, between the time when you picked up your father's Beretta and the gun went off, did you look down at the gun?"

Yes, he said.

"If you had seen a warning written on the gun itself—"

Jumping up quickly, Gebhardt said, "Excuse me."

Judge Hodge sustained the objection; the question was speculative.

"Your father had told you to clear the chamber of the gun at some point, is that right?" Jon asked.

"Yes."

"Why didn't you do that on May twenty-ninth?"

"It had been some time since I'd last cleared the Beretta, or even practiced unloading it, and I had forgotten."

"Mark, did you have any intent at all to shoot your friend Kenzo?"

"No."

"Did you have any idea whatsoever the gun was loaded?"

"No."

"And do you take full responsibility for what you did to your friend Kenzo on May twenty-ninth, 1994?"

"Yes," he said softly.

"That's all I have." Jon turned him over to Gebhardt.

119

Before Gebhardt could start, the juror who was a burial plot salesman and minister tried to hand in a question for Mark. Hodge told him to wait until after the cross-examination.

Gebhardt began, "Your dad—is it safe to say he liked guns?"

"Yes." Mark said his father had a couple of pistols, a Colt .45, and a rifle at home.

"And he had .22s in the house for as long as you can remember, right?"

"No," Mark said. Gebhardt took out the deposition Mark had given under oath and showed him where he had agreed that his father had had the .22s for as long as Mark could remember.

Gebhardt asked if, at the shooting range when Mark had fired the Beretta, his dad was putting one bullet at a time in the chamber, or whether he was putting one bullet in the magazine for Mark to shoot. Mark didn't remember.

"Or were you shooting a whole clip?"

"I don't remember."

I saw that Mark had completely shut down. He was blocking everything from his memory. Gebhardt kept pointing out places in his deposition—taken more than two years before—where he had been able to answer the questions that now he could no longer answer. I worried that Mark's desperate effort to avoid the trauma of that day looked to the jury like dishonesty or unwillingness to cooperate. I knew him; he was not being dishonest. He really could not go there. It was too painful for him.

Gebhardt turned again to the time when Mark had gotten the Beretta from his father's bedroom. He asked Mark if he did that to be defiant.

"No. I did it to show Kenzo the gun."

When Mark was asked if he'd talked with Kenzo about his father's guns before, Mark didn't remember. Asked if his father had shown him how to clear the gun, Mark replied, "A few months previous."

"Basically, he told you to take the clip out. Then you pull the slide back. If there is a bullet in the chamber, it's supposed to pop out, and then you look inside to see if there is a bullet. Make sure that it's empty, right?"

"Yes," Mark said.

"You thought the gun was empty, didn't you?"

"Yes."

"And the fact is, you forgot to check the gun to make sure it was empty, right?"

"I forgot to clear it."

Gebhardt had Mark admit that his father had told him the only time you switch the safety off is if you are going to pull the trigger. "And he told you that you were to consider all guns loaded. You were supposed to consider all guns as if they had a bullet in the chamber, right?"

"No. In the sense that I didn't know there was a bullet in the chamber. But I treated the Beretta like it was loaded, and I emptied the clip, or removed the clip, to see if it was loaded." He said these words with more intensity.

After Mark's suddenly defensive response, Gebhardt quickly said, "I will move on. Did your dad tell you there was no such thing as an unloaded gun?"

"I don't remember."

Gebhardt showed Mark where he had said yes to that question in his deposition.

Mark admitted he had been instructed on clearing semiautomatic handguns when he had shot the .22s. Asked if his father had ever told him he was buying the Beretta for home protection purposes, Mark said he had. But he didn't remember his father ever telling him that he kept a round in the chamber.

He was asked if he remembered Clifford ever telling him that he wanted him to have access to the gun in case an intruder came into the house.

Mark said he didn't remember.

Gebhardt was very clever. By now Mark's litany of "I don't remembers" made it sound as if anything Gebhardt asked, and Mark couldn't answer, must be true.

Gebhardt kept hammering him. Had his dad ever told him, here's the gun if he needed it, but there's a bullet in the chamber? Mark didn't remember. Gebhardt was asking him questions like this because they exposed either Mark's fault or Clifford's. Either way the spotlight was not focused on the failure of the design of the Beretta handgun.

When Mark did not remember about showing the Beretta to friends, Gebhardt read Mark's deposition in which he had said he had shown it to two of his friends one time and to another friend on another occasion.

"You cleared the weapon when you showed the other friends, didn't you?"

"I don't remember."

"Do you remember when you gave a statement to the police, Mark?"

When Gebhardt pulled out a copy of Mark's deposition testimony, he said, "Your Honor, may I please stand over the witness and read it?"

Hodge said, "Sure," then paused. "Although, why don't you *just read it?*"

Gebhardt had been intimidating the witness enough already.

Now, keeping his distance, he read from the statement that Mark had made to the police that night, in which he had said he had shown the Beretta to friends before, and had checked the slide. So, he had known how to check it then but had later forgotten.

Asked if he knew about the red dot on the extractor that Beretta calls its chamber-loaded indicator, Mark said, "No. I didn't know there was even a load indicator on the Beretta."

"Is it your testimony that you did not see a red dot on the right side of the gun, or that you don't *remember* seeing a red dot on the right side of the gun?"

"It's my testimony that I had no idea there was a load indicator on the right side of the gun."

Finally, Gebhardt was done. I felt relief, having had some idea what Mark had been through. But then Hodge collected questions from the jury. I had noticed that the burial plot salesman / minister / former tax preparer had been writing questions throughout Mark's testimony.

Previously, when the jury was not present, Gebhardt had objected to Judge Hodge's practice of allowing jurors to send him questions, which he would then ask the witnesses, on behalf of the jurors. Gebhardt said he had never been in a trial in which the judge allowed that. He did not like Hodge to receive questions from jurors and then ask them without giving him a chance to object to them. And he did not want to object to a juror's question in front of the jurors for fear of alienating them.

But Hodge was adamant, saying he was at the forefront of a movement. He said that many other judges had begun to allow juror questions, and they often asked good ones. "What astonishes me," he said, "is how often counsel misses the boat as to what's up." He reiterated that he was a devout believer in the wisdom of juries, and wanted "to bring the jury into the process, more than simply making them sit there like automatons."

Judge Hodge looked at a card in his hand. A juror—I suspected it was the burial plot guy—had written, "Why is it that you've forgotten so many of the answers to the questions that were asked of you at the deposition?"

"It's been five years," Mark replied. "Honestly, I try not to think about what happened, and think more of Kenzo as a person. When you think about somebody that you cared about that passed away, you don't want to think about how they died. You want to think about the good times."

Hodge asked, "So, you have just blocked out a lot of this information?"

"It's been five years, and I have forgotten a lot of things."

On redirect, Jon returned to why Mark had forgotten so much. He established that the deposition had been taken more than two years before, and that the shooting had happened four and a half years before. Mark also told him they have not had any guns in the house since that day, four and a half years before.

On re-cross, Gebhardt asked if Mark had met with our lawyers before he testified. Yes, he had. "Didn't they tell you to read that deposition because you were going to be asked questions concerning it?"

"Yes, but—"

"But what?" Gebhardt asked.

Mark gave no answer, but it seemed clear—at least to me—that he had not been able to revisit what had happened that day. He just couldn't.

When Gebhardt finished, Hodge asked the jurors if they had more questions. The burial plot salesman passed him one, which Hodge summarized: "The basic question is whether or not you feel that any of the lawyers coached you in how you were supposed to respond to these questions."

"No. I am under oath. Everything is honest," Mark stated.

Hodge released the jury until nine o'clock the next morning. "Remember your admonitions," he said as everyone gathered up their things and scurried out.

### The Adolescent Psychiatrist

The next day, Nancy Hersh called Dr. Hans Steiner to testify. He was a child and adolescent psychiatry professor at Stanford University with impressive credentials: director of the teaching of child psychiatry at the Stanford medical school, and of graduate students and post-docs studying normal adolescent psychiatry. He also saw patients and was a consultant to schools and to the California Youth Authority, where he directed numerous clinical research programs.

Speaking assertively in a German accent, Dr. Steiner said that to be a full professor at Stanford, you must be recognized as number one, two, or three in your specialty, and that he would soon go to Australia to give the keynote address at the annual convention of the psychiatry association. He was a scholar at the top of his field, not a professional expert witness. I wondered if his academic way of speaking—occasionally using professional jargon—would be off-putting to jurors.

Because Nancy Hersh knew Beretta's lawyers would bring it up, she asked him if he was being compensated for his time on this case. Yes, at $350 an hour.

I looked over at the jury and saw the burial plot guy shake his head in anger. He seemed to have the impression that Steiner was being paid so much that he'd say anything we wanted.

Steiner said he had reviewed Mark's and Clifford's depositions as well as the deposition of the police officer in the case. He had been asked to form an opinion about whether Mark's behavior was within the range of normal adolescent development. This was relevant to the issue of foreseeable misuse: whether Mark's behavior was predictable.

First, Steiner said, adolescence—from about age eleven to age nineteen or so—is a very turbulent and confusing time of development. Normal adolescents are attracted to objects of power, like cars and guns, and are predisposed toward impulsive actions.

For an adolescent of Mark's age, what he did was quite foreseeable, Steiner said. Boys in this age range are in the midst of an incredible mosaic of conflicting states, rapidly expanding abilities, and physiological changes. He said their muscle mass doubles, and the testosterone level in males goes up three-hundred-fold, and that's a big problem. Their cognitive capacity expands, as well, and all these new competencies are like new toys that they don't know what to do with. So, they tend to practice, sometimes where their parents won't know, and they try to form a new identity, integrating all of these factors. So, he added, in forming their identity, adolescents try out different roles and competencies, and some of them are obviously somewhat risky.

"When they do something dangerous, people usually say, 'Well, where are the parents?' But here is a scary fact: From age eleven forward, children rely progressively less on input from their parents to guide their actions." But the parents' judgment is still much better than that of the adolescent, Steiner said. When children are eight or nine, the parents know 80 percent of what they are up to; by the time they are eighteen, the parents know 20 percent. Adolescents conceal a lot. While that may seem bad, it's a necessary developmental step for them to form their own judgment, their own peer group, and to become self-reliant. "They go into this long orbit, and then they come back, usually in their mid-twenties, and then, once again, treat you like a friend."

Steiner said that he only got a short glimpse of Mark's father, Clifford, from his deposition. From what he could tell, Clifford tried to do his best, "but he didn't meet whatever standards I'm sure are out there." He said Mark wasn't being defiant or crazed; he was just testing the limits, testing himself, "doing what most kids his age do." Steiner continued: "In this case, it went horribly awry."

He repeated that what had happened was quite foreseeable. Since powerful, fascinating objects, such as fast cars and guns, are a problematic mixture for this age range, "you have to work at it from many different angles to keep things safe and under control."

He said this message about adolescent behavior has led most schools to educate their students about sex practices and AIDS. It would probably be useful to have similar education programs in schools regarding the dangers of guns, and about gun safety, but we don't generally do that.[13] With cars, we insist they get training before they get a license, and we put passive restraints in cars, and you *have to* wear them, too.

Primary care doctors have an important role to play, too, he said, glancing at the jury. Just as doctors now ask patients about alcohol consumption and domestic violence, they should also ask about guns. But in his clinical practice, he said he had learned that few doctors ask about guns, gun storage, or gun safety.

Steiner said that, just like with cars, where we've learned that passive and active restraints reduce injuries, we have to think of all kinds of creative ways of reducing gunshot injuries.

Craig Livingston, Beretta USA's other lawyer, jumped up, shouting, "Objection, Your Honor, lack of foundation." But Judge Hodge overruled him.

Steiner was able to finish his thought. "We have to think of creative ways of making guns, rifles, and other firearms as safe as possible."

Livingston did not want the jury to hear this from any witness.

Nancy was through, and Livingston approached to cross-examine Steiner.

"Would you agree, Doctor, that those who are in the best position to observe this risk-taking activity and to do something about it are the parents?"

"It depends on the age of the child," Steiner said. "Once a child begins to go to school, their activities become somewhat obscure from parental eyes."

"Well, Doctor, if an adolescent has demonstrated that he doesn't have the maturity to handle driving a car, for example—they've demonstrated they drive the car erratically and have gotten some tickets—you can take away the keys, can't you?"

"That's correct."

"And if you have a gun that you don't want them to have access to, you lock it up, right?"

"That's correct."

Exactly, I thought. If only Clifford's guns had had built-in locks, as cars do on the door and in the ignition. But instead, on the Beretta there was no built-in way for Clifford to keep it inaccessible to Mark while still quickly accessible to himself.

Livingston had no more questions.

"Okay. Questions from the jury?" Hodge smiled with evident eagerness. "This may be the hardest part, Doctor." In a moment he examined the cards from jurors.

In response to Steiner's remarks about adolescent attraction to objects of power, and his mention that when an elementary school forbade gun-like toys, the boys had made other objects into guns, a juror asked, "In general, do you think it is better to expose adolescents to those images of power or to deny them access to them?"

"The best mixture is you expose them *and* you stick around for the explanation and the interaction afterwards. That's what seems to work best. So, it's a very careful balancing act. And it's not just a parent; it's all of us. It's the neighbors; it's the friends; it's the teachers; it's the pediatricians. It's the works."

Judge Hodge nodded, and after shuffling through a few cards from jurors, he picked one and squinted at the handwriting. "Would you have wanted to talk with Mark prior to giving your testimony in this matter?"

Steiner looked at the jury and said he did want to talk with him, but for a very different reason: He was concerned about Mark. He said he couldn't imagine that this had left him untouched. He'd talked with many young men and women who'd been in this situation. Most had been traumatized by it for a long time, and most of them need to see a psychiatrist. He said, "There is some indication in his testimony that he had some early signs of PTSD. But since I haven't interviewed him, I can't really say that."

When someone asked what PTSD was, Steiner said, "Oh, I'm sorry, post-traumatic stress disorder, which is usually induced by sudden, unexpected episodes, traumatic episodes—the Vietnam vet syndrome."

Hodge asked for follow-up from counsel, and Nancy stood up. "Does post-traumatic stress disorder have consequences for memory of events?"

Steiner had not seen Mark testify, but he said, "It could very well. Yes. I work with kids in the California Youth Authority who have actually been traumatized either by their own committing of an offense—in other words, their shooting someone—or witnessing violence in the community. Their memory for what has happened is sometimes very spotty and needs to be carefully reconstructed in the course of their treatment. You very often get a lot of accounts at one time that you don't get at another time, and the two don't necessarily hang together. This is, in fact, how you work with them. You keep track of these and then say, 'Well, let's see, last time we met you told me this, and then this time you told me this. How does it fit together?' Because it doesn't quite fit, and that gets them going."

Given that Steiner had no way of knowing that the jury had just seen that Mark had not been able to remember a lot of the details from his previous deposition and the events of the day he shot Kenzo, I thought that Steiner's characterization was remarkably on target. I, too, was worried about Kenzo's friend.

Then Craig Livingston stood up for his re-cross. "Doctor, you haven't examined Mark, so you don't really have any idea whether or not he's suffering from post-traumatic stress disorder, do you?"

"No, not at all."

### *The Injury Prevention Expert*

Dressed in a loose tie and worn sports jacket, Stephen Teret looked exactly like someone central casting would choose to play a professor and academic researcher. After he was sworn in, Jon Lowy's first questions established that Teret was director of the Johns Hopkins Center for Gun Policy and Research in the university's school of public health. Teret said he studied and taught courses in the epidemiology of firearm injuries: the circumstances under which they occur, to whom, and how they can be prevented.

"Are there some basic tenets of injury prevention?" Jon asked.

Teret replied that based on a large number of studies over the course of decades, we know that some things will work better than others in preventing injuries. "What we know—which is in some ways counterintuitive to new students, so we have to convince them of this—is that the most effective way is not to try to educate everybody to always be careful, but rather to change the products we live with." He said that, for example, many children used to be poisoned by bottles of aspirin. Studies showed that you could say to parents, "Always be careful—make sure that your kids don't get into the aspirin bottle," and that might prevent some injuries. But a more effective way was to do two things: put child-resistant caps on aspirin bottles, and put fewer pills than would be lethal in aspirin bottles. These two interventions—made at the level of the manufacturers—brought down the rate of children who got aspirin poisoning, he said.

Still introducing Teret to the jury, Jon asked him if he was being compensated for his time. He replied that sometimes he charged a fee for testifying in court, but would not be asking for compensation in this case. When Jon asked why, he said, "Some cases present an opportunity for a social value in making social policy, and if they do, I'm happy to offer my services at no charge."

Looking unhappy, Hodge turned to the jurors. "And let me say to the jury at this juncture, the jury does not sit here in this case to make social policy. The jury sits here to decide on the facts of this case, whether the defendant is or is not responsible under the product defects theory that is being advanced, and to assess the relative comparative fault of the other players. But you sit as a jury in this case, not as a legislature."

I considered what they both had said. It seemed to me from what I was learning that a major reason for product liability cases had always been to uphold existing law that could save lives. We weren't asking the jury to make new law.

Jon began on the topic of unintentional gun deaths and gun storage by asking Teret about a study he had done of all the fatal unintentional shootings in California committed by children age fourteen and under. Teret responded that in about half of those that occurred in residences, the gun was stored loaded and unlocked. In three-quarters, the children had been playing with the gun, and in almost one-quarter, the child who pulled the trigger stated that he or she did not know the gun was loaded. He said, based on surveys, that *handguns* bought for self-protection were especially likely to be stored loaded and within easy reach.

Teret was asked about the brands of the guns used in accidental gun deaths. He said that most studies did not collect data about the make and model of the gun.

That fact rattled around in my brain. We wanted to be able to tell the jury how many Beretta handguns had been involved in unintentional shootings. The gun lobby was one reason that this information was not available. I had recently learned that in 1995—influenced by the gun lobby—Congress had cut the budget of the Centers for Disease Control and Prevention (CDC) by $2.6 million—the exact amount it had requested for research on gun injuries.[14] If the budget had not been cut, probably more information about brands of guns used in unintentional deaths and nonfatal injuries[15] would have been collected, and more lives—especially those of gun owners and their family members—would have been saved.

Thereafter, the CDC funded very little research on firearms injuries, even though firearms were, and still are, a leading cause of death of young Americans.[16] And that is partly why parents—like Clifford and me—did not fully understand the risks of firearms to our children.

The jurors did not know about this political interference into the CDC's research—but the absence of this information was influencing our trial.

Jon began asking about unintentional shootings and safety features, specifically magazine-disconnect safety devices. Teret testified that a significant percentage of people believe that a gun is unloaded if the magazine is either empty or removed from the gun. He read a question from a National Opinion Research Council survey among a nationally representative sample of adults: "Some handguns, called pistols, hold ammunition in a clip or magazine that fits into the handle of the gun. If the person holding any of these pistols removes the clip or magazine from the gun, can the gun still possibly be shot?" According to the survey, 35 percent had either said—incorrectly—that the gun cannot be shot, or they did not know if it could be shot.

Another survey found that 41 percent of gun owners said they personally knew of someone who had been shot in a gun accident. Nonetheless, more than 75 percent of gun owners said they never worry that someone in their home will be injured by a gun they keep there, and an even larger percentage of gun owners who have children in their household never worry.

Jon had Teret read from a sheet enumerating the number of unintentional gun deaths year by year. As the numbers mounted, I found it hard to imagine the pain and suffering involved in all of those unintentional gun deaths. In 1981, there were 1,871 such deaths; in 1982: 1,756; in 1983: 1,695. He went on to 1993. That year, when

Beretta had sold Clifford the Beretta, there were 1,521 unintentional gun deaths. In just the fourteen years from 1980 through 1993, there had been 22,263 unintentional gun deaths.

For every fatal unintentional shooting, there are about 12.5 non-fatal ones serious enough to receive medical attention, such as at a hospital, said Teret. Thus, from 1980 through 1993, there were *over one-quarter of a million* unintentional *nonfatal* shootings serious enough to require medical care. To me, that seemed "notice" enough to the gun industry that there was a problem in the design of their guns.

Teret said males of "about age thirteen to up toward nineteen" are most at risk of being involved in unintentional shootings. The rate of unintentional gun deaths for males of that age group, compared to other groups, is off the charts, and there are patterns, he said. "We know what the high-risk groups are."

I glanced over at the jurors. They looked sleepy.

In conclusion, Teret verified that the documents he had consulted about unintentional shootings by children were published before August 31, 1993, the day that Clifford bought the Beretta. (August 31 was also—uncannily—Kenzo's birthday.)

Finally, he affirmed that all the information he had presented—how people store their guns, what people know about whether pistols can fire with a magazine removed, the number of unintentional gun deaths, etc.—was scientifically known and published at the time that Clifford had bought the Beretta handgun, which meant that Beretta could have known it.

Jon Lowy said he had no further questions, turned, and sat down.

It was getting late. Hodge looked fondly at the weary jurors. "We will be in recess until nine in the morning. Remember the admonitions," he said.

———

When everyone was settled the next morning, Gebhardt's cowboy boots echoed across the courtroom as he approached Stephen Teret and they began their duel.

Gebhardt, a corpulent man, stood close to Teret's face, looked down on him, and boomed. Wasn't it true, he asked, that no national study looked at gun injuries to children to determine whether the guns are locked or unlocked? Teret admitted it was.

He also agreed that no studies counted the number of times an accident had been avoided because the owner carried out safety procedures, and no studies counted the number of accidental shootings *averted* because a child or adult had observed a chamber-loaded indicator. Teret patiently explained that you could not study a negative—something that didn't happen.

"So, what you do is you look at [gun] accidents," said Gebhardt, "but it's virtually impossible for you to look at the benefits?"

"No, I would not agree with that," Teret quickly protested. But before he could discuss the studies that compare the risks of gun ownership versus the benefits and mention how seldom guns are used for legitimate self-defense,[17] Gebhardt moved on to his next series of questions. He led Teret back to his study of 131 California unintentional gun deaths among children aged fourteen and under. Since no Beretta guns were mentioned in the study, Gebhardt tried to imply that this showed Beretta guns were safer.

Teret countered that researchers lack a baseline to show that a particular type of gun is especially likely to be used in unintentional shootings. In the United States, he said, those data are kept by the gun manufacturers and not reported to the public or the government, so we lack that information.

Next Gebhardt attacked Teret's statement that many gun own-ers—even those with children—disobey gun-safety instructions and store their firearms unsafely. Gebhardt brought up the random national telephone survey of 605 gun owners called "Loaded Guns in the Home," by Doug Weil and David Hemenway, published in the *Journal of the American Medical Association* (*JAMA*).[18] He said, "Looking at the results, it says that, 'People who live in households without children were *all* more likely to keep a gun loaded than other individuals.'"

Teret noticed immediately that this made no sense, and that Geb-hardt was trying to deceive the jury. He said, "I would strike the word 'all.' I'm looking for the sentence. Did you read the sentence right?"

He hadn't, of course. But Gebhardt, who was not under oath, answered, "Yes," read his partial sentence again, and replied, "That's what it says."

Later, when I looked up the sentence in the study, I had to almost admire Gebhardt's cunning. He had read only part of the sentence in a way that completely changed the meaning of the word "all." The original sentence (with the part that Gebhardt read italicized) is: "Handgun owners, individuals who own a firearm principally for protection, and *people who live(d) in households without children were all more likely to keep a gun loaded than other individuals.*"

The partial sentence Gebhardt read made it sound as if *all* people who live in households *with* children store their guns *unloaded*. That would contradict Teret and make it sound like gun accidents involving children are not as foreseeable as Teret had said they were.

Before Teret had a chance to locate the full sentence, Gebhardt had deftly asked him another question. A moment later, Gebhardt asked Teret if, in another of his articles, he had criticized the avail-able data about the characteristics of the firearms that are involved in unintentional shootings.

"Yes, I do criticize that," he said, adding that there was no uniform database with this information, so researchers had to go to specific studies like those he had talked about in his article in order to accomplish their research goal.

Gebhardt tried to cast doubt on the studies Teret had summarized by using Teret's own call for better data against him. However, Teret's data did demonstrate the foreseeable misuse of firearms, and it clearly showed that gun owners regularly disregard safety procedures, frequently causing harm.

I was to see this over and over: the gun lobby causing a problem, then complaining about the very problem it had created. Researchers had to rely mostly on small-scale studies because the gun lobby and Congress had essentially stopped the CDC from funding research on gun injuries, and had prevented the creation of a national database of firearm injuries that could help us all—including the gun industry and gun owners—understand how to prevent gun injuries.

Gebhardt picked up the pace. In answer to a quick series of questions, Teret admitted that he had no information to indicate the number of Berettas involved in accidental shootings, and no information on the number of guns with chamber-loaded indicators that are involved in accidental shootings, as well as no information that measures the types of safety devices on guns that were involved in accidental shootings.

"We lacked those kinds of information, which is why in my article I call for a national system," Teret said. Finally, he had to admit that he knew of no studies that differentiate between the accident rate of guns with chamber-loaded indicators and those without them.

On redirect, Jon Lowy asked Teret more about a federal government study that had chamber-loaded indicator information. Teret pulled the U.S. General Accounting Office study from the pile in front of him. He read that 23 percent of the deaths that occurred when people accidentally shot and killed themselves or others with firearms which they thought were unloaded, could have been prevented by a chamber-loaded indicator.

### The Beretta USA Executive

After the jury left for the day, Judge Hodge wanted to discuss a memorandum by the Beretta lawyers arguing that they should be able to bring into evidence the lack of other claims like ours against Beretta USA. Beretta hoped to assert—or at least, to imply—to the jury that Kenzo's unintentional gun death was the only one ever committed with a Beretta handgun. They based their argument on a precedent which had allowed Honda Motor Company to claim that a type of accident was the first of its kind.

Jon Lowy argued passionately that Honda had a complex system to monitor all accidents in which Honda cars were involved, but Beretta had no such system that was remotely comparable, and was thus unlikely to know if there had been accidents like Kenzo's. The information about gun accidents, if collected at all, sits in police departments all over the country, Jon said. Beretta never collected it. Letting Beretta assert that Kenzo's death was the only one of its kind with a Beretta would mislead the jury.

Nancy Hersh pointed out that lots of regulations governed cars like Honda. But gun manufacturers are exempt from such statutes and laws. Beretta had no incentive to collect the information, because they had never been sued in a case like this before. She said the only incentive manufacturers have to put safety concepts into their products is if they are sued and somebody wins. That's why product liability doctrine was created.

Seeing an opening, Jon argued that if the court allowed Beretta to talk about the lack of claims like ours against it, then we should be able to bring into evidence that the Consumer Product Safety Commission is not allowed to regulate firearms. If they are allowed to compare their products to those that have federal oversight, and have monitoring of defects, he said, then we've got to be able to tell the jury that guns are very different and have no such monitoring. Beretta shouldn't be able to have it both ways, he argued. They shouldn't be able to maintain the assumption that guns were regulated like other consumer products, but also use the lack of information about accidents with Beretta guns as "proof" that there were no such accidents.

Judge Hodge decided that the only way to resolve the issue was to put Beretta's VP and general counsel, Jeffrey Reh, on the stand, and ask him whether he had a system in place for collecting information about other accidental shootings with Beretta guns.

I watched closely, because I was very interested in Jeffrey Reh, the man who led the company that sold the gun that killed Kenzo. He had said almost nothing so far. Reh, who was middle-aged and well-dressed in a conservative suit and tie, testified without the jury present. He said he had instructed the company's manufacturers' representatives to let him know of any incidents or complaints they heard about. At the time Kenzo died, he said, they knew of no unintentional shootings "where someone thought a Model 92 was loaded, but it wasn't."

I noticed how carefully specific his language was, using "Model 92"—and then I discovered why. When Nancy Hersh cross-examined Reh, he admitted that, including our case, there had been four cases filed against Beretta about unintentional shootings with Beretta handguns.

Under questioning, he admitted that he had never undertaken a review of police data about unintentional shootings to see if Berettas were involved. "So, unless someone comes to you to file a complaint, or they contact Beretta and say, 'My child was killed by another child and a Beretta was involved,' or some sales rep reports it to you, you have no way of knowing that a Beretta was involved in an unintentional shooting, do you?" Nancy asked.

Reh replied straight-faced that if a sales rep saw a newspaper or TV report, he was supposed to relate that to him. Nancy interrupted him sharply and said that this would require the brand of the gun to be named in the article or TV program. He tried to argue that if the gun was *shown* on TV, his salespeople would usually recognize it as a Beretta. He contended that most newspaper articles about unintentional shootings identify the brand of the gun. But he admitted that he had not heard about Kenzo's shooting from a newspaper and did not investigate the 1,000 to 1,500 or so unintentional gun deaths per year to see if a Beretta was involved. Nor did he investigate the 20,000 or so unintentional gun injuries to see if a Beretta was involved.

Finally, Judge Hodge ruled that Beretta USA's "random collection method" was insufficient. Allowing them to pretend they had a good system for discovering other incidents with their guns could be quite prejudicial and misleading.

But now both sides had a problem. With Hodge's ruling, Beretta could present no evidence about the absence of other similar unintentional shootings. However, unfortunately, because the jurors had not been allowed to hear Reh's sworn testimony, they wouldn't know how *inadequate* Beretta's system of data collection was. That harmed us. Beretta could plead ignorance of similar shootings with the specific model of Beretta used to kill Kenzo because—head-in-the-sand—the company did not look for that information.

In addition, the jurors would still not hear about those other unintentional shootings with Beretta guns. No research showed that Beretta handguns had been used in unintentional shootings. So the jurors might assume—incorrectly—that no Berettas had been involved in them before Kenzo was killed.

That night as I lay in bed, I thought again about when Kenzo turned fifteen. Like many parents, I didn't know that a gun was the most likely cause of death of kids his age in my state, and others. Even experts like Teret lacked crucial information, such as the brands of guns involved, because of the gun lobby's influence in Congress.

Judge Hodge was adamant that anything "political" must be excluded from the trial. Yet the prior political activities of Beretta, the National Shooting Sports Foundation, and the rest of the gun lobby were impacting the trial in important ways. They saturated everything.

It seemed to me that it was prejudicial to ignore the gun lobby's political influences, such as the law forbidding consumer-product-safety regulation of firearms; the restriction on federal funding of research on gun deaths and injuries, and the consequent missing data; and the various state laws restricting civil litigation against the gun industry, leading to the paucity of information obtained through discovery. This was all extremely political, I thought.

Late into the night, alone, I kept thinking about what Teret had said. I had a new respect for public health researchers like Teret, who made injury prevention—specifically, the scientific study of gun deaths and injuries and their prevention—their life's work. Their goal was gun safety. But what did it take to prove foreseeable misuse?

I realized that our trial over the causes of Kenzo's death was but one skirmish in a much larger struggle, about which the jury would hear nothing.

As I lay there sleepless in the dark, I thought of the many children all across America whose fate would be decided by this ongoing struggle.

# 9

## The Gun's Design, The Gun's Owner

### *The Systems Safety Engineer*

Promptly at nine the following Monday morning, Judge Hodge strode out of his little side door and up the steps to his throne. He looked to see if all the jurors were there, lamented Saturday's loss by the Cal football team, then reminded the jurors that they shouldn't listen when the lawyers argued their side of the case in the media.

Given the nod, Nancy Hersh called Dr. Vaughn Adams. A solid, square-jawed man who looked about sixty walked past the jury, took the oath, and told the jury he had a PhD in engineering, with a specialization in systems safety engineering and human factors design.

He had taught for eighteen years, including at Stanford and Rice universities, and then started his own consulting company.

Our previous witness, Stephen Teret, had testified that unintentional shootings, like Mark's, were foreseeable. Dr. Adams was called to focus on what was wrong with the design of the gun that had killed Kenzo—why that gun was dangerous for people who had less training than the police or military, and how Beretta could have helped buyers like Clifford better understand how to use the Beretta safely.

Adams would fault Beretta U.S.A. on three counts: 1) The gun the company sold did not have an internal locking device to prevent children or other unauthorized users from firing it; 2) The warnings in the Beretta manual were too inconspicuous to have an impact on behavior; and 3) The Beretta's tiny chamber-loaded indicator should have been much more prominent, not only on the gun itself, but in the section of the manual that explained where it was located on the gun and what it was for.

In answer to Nancy's prompt, Adams began with a critique of the manual. As if he were lecturing a class, he said the product literature that came with the gun presumed that the owner had as much knowledge as someone in the military or law enforcement. Also, mention of the fact that some consumers kept the firearm for personal protection was "virtually nonexistent" in the manual, which said almost nothing about the potential danger that other members of the household, such as children, might gain access to the gun. Adams said there should have been a section in the manual dedicated to that problem.

I glanced over my shoulder at Larry Keane and Jeffrey Reh. They had turned their chairs slightly toward the jury and, taking care not to be too obvious, were examining the reactions of each juror to Adams's testimony. Clearly, they had some experience with this.

Nancy Hersh reiterated that Clifford kept the gun loaded and unlocked by his bed for protection, and asked Adams how he took that into consideration in forming his opinions. "We know that it happens," he said, glancing at the jurors. "Beretta is clearly aware that it occurs. I don't support it; I don't condone it, but it occurs."

Getting back to the manual, he stated emphatically that the manual was vitally important because "that's the information that goes to the consumer. It can either influence or not influence him." If the manual is strong, it will change behavior. Some hazards are controlled by the gun itself, such as not firing when it is dropped. But the hazard of a bullet being in the chamber of a gun, of which the person who is handling the firearm is unaware, is a hazard that is *not* controlled by this product. So it needs special emphasis in the manual, he said.

"In this case, there is nothing either in the manual or on the Beretta that effectively warns somebody that a bullet might be chambered?" Nancy asked, with incredulity in her voice.

"Correct."

Adams looked over at the jurors and pointed out that the first thirteen pages of the manual were in Italian.[19] He said there should be a separate manual in English for English-speaking consumers, and that all the warnings should appear together in the front of the manual in English. "That's an opportunity to use the strength of the terms '*danger, warning, caution*!' Each hazard notice should also be repeated wherever that hazard reappears, such as where there are instructions about cleaning the firearm," he emphasized.

Nancy put an image of two pages of the manual on an easel. Page 14 was the first place "Basic Safety" appeared in English. Adams read: "Always treat a firearm as if it's loaded. Never point a firearm at anything you don't want to shoot." He shook his head. "They are good general tenets, *but we can't comply with them.* When we are cleaning our firearm, that gun is going to be pointed in many directions where we don't want to shoot." If firearms are brought into this courtroom, he added, that muzzle is going to be pointed "where we don't want to shoot."

143

He had that right. Already, in Bob Gebhardt's opening statement, while waving the gun around the courtroom, he had said repeatedly that a crucial rule was never to point a gun at anything you didn't want to shoot. "These rules are just difficult to comply with under all circumstances," Adams explained, "and that takes away from the strength of the warnings about the hazards that we want to control."

Adams turned to the warning in the Beretta manual: "Store firearms and ammunition separately beyond the reach of children. Be sure cartridge chamber is empty." This is well and good, he said, except for one problem: "This warning presupposes that the firearm is a *recreational* firearm." A person who purchased the firearm for *protection* will presumably want a gun to be readily available in case of an emergency, such as a home intrusion. For guns expressly marketed to people who want them for protection, Adams advocated a statement pulled out and emphasized separately in the manual: "If you want to use the firearm for protection, and need to have fairly immediate access, this is what you need to do to be safe..."

I thought to myself how simple this would have been: a large font, the word "Caution," and a few warnings and instructions specifically for people who want their gun for protection. It would have cost nothing.

Adams said none of Beretta's safety instructions were actual warnings. Warnings, he said, are pulled out for emphasis. They should have a statement of the hazard, what its *consequences* could be, and a statement of *what you should do* to prevent those consequences.

Nancy put on the easel a blowup of a sample warning Adams had prepared. The jurors saw a tag with a bright yellow "Caution" triangle and a red exclamation point in the center. The triangle had warnings, such as the risks of unauthorized users having access to guns, and the risk of a bullet remaining in the chamber unknown to users. Warnings like this, Adams said, should have been on the manual's cover and attached to the trigger guard so every customer would see them before he could use the gun.

He showed a blowup of the side of the gun that killed Kenzo. On it he had superimposed a warning that he said should be etched on the barrel: "Bullet can remain in chamber when magazine removed or empty." Mark would have seen that warning every time he held the gun, I thought. It could have saved Kenzo's life.

Nancy thanked Adams and said she was done.

I had sat listening, astounded at how obvious these things were, and how easy to carry out. I couldn't understand why Beretta had not done them.

Rising with a slightly annoyed look, Gebhardt began his cross-examination not by defending the gun or the manual but by attacking Adams's integrity and expertise. He brought up case after case that Adams had previously worked on, quickly switching from one to another. One case involved the Boy Scouts. Gebhardt said Adams had been an expert witness for the plaintiffs, testifying that a flagpole was an attractive nuisance, liable to cause harm to children, and was negligently designed. His tone implied how utterly ridiculous such a claim was.

Adams began to get visibly angry, insisting that this was a complete mischaracterization of the case.

"I got the essence of it, though, didn't I?" needled Gebhardt.

"No, not really, you didn't," sputtered Adams, on the verge of losing his composure.

Quickly moving on, Gebhardt attacked Adams's expertise in gun design, arguing that he had never sat down with a firearm engineer to design a component part of a firearm.

Quick volleys of questions followed, with Gebhardt continuing to switch rapidly from subject to subject. It was a masterwork of obfuscation. Gebhardt's condescending tone alone might convince some that Adams had altered his opinion depending on which side he was testifying for.

Finally, Gebhardt challenged Adams's criticism of Beretta's owner's manual. "You know that there is no evidence that Mark ever *read* the owner's manual?"

"Not that I have seen."

"And do you know that Clifford forbade Mark to touch or play with the gun?"

"That's my understanding. Yes."

It was a warm afternoon, and it felt like the oxygen had been sucked out of the courtroom. But Gebhardt wasn't slowing down. He pointed to the statements in the manual under "Basic Safety" and forced Adams to agree that the "accident" would never have happened if Clifford or Mark had followed them.

Like a gunslinger in a Western bellying up to the bar, Gebhardt walked up to Adams and peered down at him. "Okay. Basically what you did is, you studied this case and you went through and figured everything Clifford and Mark did wrong, and you say *we* should have had a warning about it. Is that basically what you did?"

"No..."

But before Adams could say what he *had* done or anything about product safety engineering, Gebhardt had asked his next question.

"Don't you take Beretta to task because it didn't make a specific statement about how the owner should store the gun, and, therefore, it left it up to everybody to make his own choice?"

"I agree with that, yes, but—"

Gebhardt boomed: "You don't want—"

Nancy's shrill objection cut through to complain that Gebhardt was consistently not allowing Adams to complete his answers.

Hodge peered down at Gebhardt from his bench. "You do jump the gun often. You make my job—"

"You should be married to me, Your Honor."

146

"The mind boggles, Mr. Gebhardt. You do interrupt in an untimely fashion, regularly. So, maybe you would just stop that."

Gebhardt put a contrite look on his face. It was a play; he was a good actor. Everyone laughed. His stage role—a bully, but a lovable, joking bully—had distracted the jury from whatever point Adams had been about to make.

Gebhardt kept hammering away about personal responsibility and freedom of choice. "You want to take responsibility away from the owner and give it to the manufacturer."

But he had overreached.

Adams responded: "Precisely. Yes. This is what Beretta itself did in regard to the drop-fire safety device." This was a Beretta safety device that Gebhardt had touted as its innovation to prevent the gun from firing when dropped. Score one for the beleaguered Dr. Adams.

Now it was Nancy's turn for redirect, her chance to reply to Geb-hardt's cross-examination. She questioned Adams again about the inadequacy of the section in Beretta's manual on the chamber-loaded indicator. Adams was vehement: "I don't think if I tried to integrate that chamber-loaded indicator into a manual, I could do it with greater *secrecy*. It's hidden; it's not clear; there is no prominence given to it. It's very difficult to see and understand."

"Is there anything in the 'Basic Safety' section of the manual that says to lock the gun up?" Nancy asked.

"No, there is not," he stressed.

"How would the warning that you have suggested in this case have prevented a death like Kenzo Dix's?"

"Had there been a strong, compelling warning," said Adams, "it would have told Mark that a round was chambered. He would not have pulled the trigger."

She asked Adams about Clifford. Would warnings have been sufficient?

Adams said, "I believe that it's more than likely that he would have taken greater precautions. I think Clifford testified that had he known of a means of safeguarding [his gun], he would have purchased a gun with those devices in it."

Adams was referring to a sworn statement Clifford had made in one of his earliest—and therefore, probably most accurate—depositions. Nancy Hersh had asked Clifford about a conversation they'd had previously. She'd asked him if there had been a safer gun available, would he have purchased it, rather than the purchase he made. He recalled saying yes. He had been asked what his understanding of "safer gun" was, and he'd said one that came with a ring on your finger that would activate the gun. Later, Clifford did not mention this.

Adams continued, saying that if the manufacturer provided a lock and warnings that were strong and motivational, the user would be more likely to use the lock. But that doesn't let the consumer off the hook, he said. The consumer will still have to consider safety.

After Nancy finished, Hodge read Adams a question on a card from a juror: "Although Mark did not read the owner's manual, he indicated that he knew how to clear the chamber, and that it needed to be done. 'I just forgot.' How would a change in the warnings have prevented him from this forgetting?"

The burial plot salesman had been busy, but it was a good question.

A change in the warning *on the firearm* would have alerted him, replied Adams. "Mark would have seen an engraved explanation of the chamber-loaded indicator on the gun, saying that a bullet could remain in the chamber." Adams also said that if the warning and information in the manual had been more prominent, Mark probably would have heard about it and recognized at the time that a round was in the chamber. "But there was no way of knowing because Beretta did none of this."

Judge Hodge pulled up another card that I think also came from the burial plot salesman: "What is the lack of clarity that you perceive in the following warning: 'Store firearms and ammunition separately beyond the reach of children. Be sure the cartridge chamber is empty'?"

Adams didn't hesitate. "I think that's probably stated fairly straight for a user who is not going to be using a firearm for personal protection. But the user who is going to use it for personal protection and wants it ready at hand will generally disregard it and think, 'That doesn't apply to me, because I am using it for a different purpose.' I think that's an essential issue in this matter," he said. There is a difference between a general admonition to *always* store firearms and ammunition apart and having a gun in a state of readiness so you can gain quick access for personal protection.[20]

### *The Gun Owner*

On a foggy Tuesday, Mark's father Clifford, a stocky, well-built man with a thin mustache, walked slowly to the witness stand and took the oath. Reluctantly, we had called him to testify, knowing that if we didn't, Beretta would. We wanted the jury to see as little of him as possible. We knew that the Beretta lawyers had spent a lot of time with him, and that recently his memory had been shifting in a perilous direction. Beretta wanted the jurors to see a lot of him.

This was partially due to Judge Hodge's comparative fault ruling. The jurors had been told they might be asked to assign a percentage of fault for Kenzo's death to Clifford, to Mark, and to Beretta USA. That ruling influenced what evidence could be presented to jurors, and also established a framework for their thinking about the evidence. In many jurors' minds, the more Clifford was at fault, the less Beretta was.

But we felt that the fault was not a zero-sum trade-off between Clifford and Mark versus Beretta. Instead, we knew that they could *all* be greatly at fault. In fact, to some extent, the *more* Clifford and his son were at fault, the *more* Beretta could be at fault for not having emphasized warnings for *this common type of customer*, and for not providing the safety features on the pistol that would help people like him and his son not commit the types of *foreseeable misuses* to which they were prone.

When Nancy Hersh began questioning Clifford, at first, he spoke reluctantly in a diffident manner, his sentences terse and guarded. Nancy's questioning established that he was a forty-three-year-old divorced man, born and raised in Berkeley, who now lived in the city's flatlands with his "significant other" and his father, as well as Mark. He had first become interested in guns as a teenager when his brother gave him a BB gun. He had started target-shooting at about age eighteen. In addition to the Colt and Beretta semiautomatic pistols, which he had acquired shortly before the tragedy, he owned two .22 caliber pistols for target practice, as well as a Ruger 10/22 carbine. But from the late 1970s until 1993, he had had no interest in shooting at all.

Nancy asked him why he had bought the Beretta.

"Home protection."

"What happened that made you feel you needed a gun for home protection?"

"The neighborhood had taken a real downturn. There was a lot of drug dealing—a lot of shooting. You'd hear gunshots nearly every night coming from two blocks away."

He had started looking for a reliable gun for $500 to $600 with a high capacity of rounds. He shopped at Bay Area gun shops and gun shows, and occasionally bought magazines with articles and ads about guns. The gun dealers never gave him any safety literature, he said. In the stores, lock boxes and trigger locks were in a different section from the guns. He didn't remember seeing any of them.

After he got the Beretta, he went to the Richmond Rod and Gun Club to learn how to use it, but never took a training or gun-safety course. At the shooting range he kept hearing the sound of rapid fire from one area, so one day he walked over and saw men competing in the sport of "practical shooting." They were running rapidly through a course, firing at targets and trying to get the best score. He met competitors in this sport and started practicing for it.

When Nancy asked him how he had planned to store the new gun, he answered, "Because it was for home protection, I wanted it available for me to get to." So he kept it loaded next to his bed with a bullet in the chamber. He said his understanding of the purpose of the gun's manual was "to inform me how to use it," and that he had read it.

She asked when he had first learned there was a chamber-loaded indicator on the Beretta.

"I recalled reading about it," he said, "but actually I had forgotten about it until the first time we spoke in your office." After Kenzo was killed, he testified, the defense counsel showed him pictures of the gun, but he did not recognize the chamber-loaded indicator. He never noticed it was on the gun during the time he was using it.

Had he seen any Beretta ads before he bought the gun, she asked.

Possibly, he said, but he couldn't remember any specific ones.

At first, he had appeared to view Nancy as his opponent. Now he was loosening up a bit. He was still taciturn, but was not uncooperative.

She asked why he had picked this particular Beretta gun.

"One, because it fit into my hand; two, a friend of mine had told me that it had passed a lot of tests for the military and police departments, and so I felt it was reliable."

Clifford told the jury that he'd taken Mark to the shooting range, "to take the mystique of a gun away." He recalled that Mark had fired the Beretta with him at the shooting range a few months before the accident.

Nancy asked if he was putting one round at a time into the magazine and then letting Mark fire it, and then putting another one in and letting him fire it.

Clifford said yes.

"And did you show him how to load a round into the magazine?"

"I think I tried to, but the spring was too heavy for him to push the round in at the time."

"Did you show him how to clear the gun?"

"I don't remember that day having him do that," he replied.

He explained that when Mark had fired the Beretta, there had been only one bullet in it, so there was no need to clear an unfired round from its chamber. He did not pull back the slide and look into the chamber to see if it was empty. So Mark had not learned about clearing the chamber by doing it repeatedly.

The training Clifford gave his son seems to have emphasized firing the gun rather than practicing safety procedures. But Clifford said that he had told Mark gun-safety rules, such as: Don't load the gun until you're standing at the firing line. Always keep the gun pointed downrange. Don't take it off safety and put your finger on the trigger until you are ready to fire.

Nancy asked him if he had demonstrated anything about the Beretta to Mark at another time, aside from that time at the range.

"I remember once when I was cleaning the gun at home that I was trying to get his attention, but I think I was competing with the television."

"Did you want Mark to have access to the Beretta for home protection in May of 1994?"

"If there were an emergency," he said.

But in his deposition, taken nearer the time Kenzo was killed, he'd given a different answer, so Nancy read part of that deposition: Did he want Mark to have access to the Beretta 9mm, our lawyers had asked. He'd answered, "No." When asked why not, he'd said, "He didn't have the experience in handling the weapon."

152

On hearing what he'd said in that deposition, Clifford agreed with it in court, and repeated that Mark did not have enough experience to handle the guns, and that he had told him not to touch them.

He confirmed that on the day Mark shot Kenzo, Mark had taken out the loaded magazine and put in an empty one. "[Mark] thought it was empty. He thought he had cleared it."

"And before that day, did you ever consider that an event like that could take place in your house?"

"No."

We all paused to take that in.

Judge Hodge began reading questions from the many note cards he had received.

A juror asked if there was any reason Clifford didn't lock his guns up during the day, and then make them accessible to himself at night, when he thought he might use them.

Clifford looked up at Hodge and said, "Eventually I wanted Mark to be able to have the knowledge to use them. I wanted them available for him to use."

That word "eventually" was important. It seems that exactly *when* the training would end, and *when* Mark would be ready to use the gun, "eventually," in case of an emergency, was unclear in Clifford's mind.

I thought this was probably common in homes with guns and adolescents.

Hodge read from another card: "If Mark didn't have experience with either weapon, why did you leave the weapon on the floor?"

"I didn't think he would disobey me," he answered. He breathed out softly. For me this was the saddest and cruelest of ironies: Clifford had reason to trust his son; Mark was generally a good, obedient kid. If this were an opera, this was where Clifford would sing his tormented aria. Clifford, too, was a victim of this tragedy.

Hodge was receiving more little cards from the jurors.

"When you field-stripped the weapon, did you notice the chamber-loaded indicator?"

"No."

"Do you know how Mark learned to clear the chamber?"

"It was probably something that I was trying to work into the drill."

I cringed; it sounded so haphazard.

Looking down at Clifford, Judge Hodge asked, "Well, had you taught him how to clear the chamber?"

"Yes."

"And when was that?"

"I believe I had started at home."

Vague. Everything he said about teaching Mark to clear the chamber was vague.

Hodge sorted through more cards.

A juror asked if he was aware that there could be a round in the chamber even after unloading the clip. He said he was, but then, in answer to a follow-up question, said he couldn't remember whether he had communicated that to Mark.

Clifford said he hadn't noticed when he was shooting the Beretta at the shooting range that it had a chamber-loaded indicator.

Hodge followed up. "Did you have any curiosity about what the red dot meant?"

Clifford looked up at him, "It's not that...it's not that visible."

When Beretta's lawyer, Craig Livingston, cross-examined Clifford, he politely but ardently grilled him about keeping his Beretta and Colt .45 in a camera bag, loaded, on the floor next to his bed. Clifford repeated that he kept the Beretta loaded with a magazine and a round in the chamber so he wouldn't have to make the sound of racking a round into the chamber if an intruder came in.

Next Livingston asked, "Your bedroom wasn't locked because there isn't a door on it; isn't that right?"

"That's correct," answered Clifford.

We never learned why his bedroom was open directly to his backyard with no door.

Next came what now seems to me is testimony with very important implications.

Clifford repeated that when he took Mark to the shooting range, because the spring on the new magazine was too stiff for Mark to handle, he had loaded one round at a time into the magazine for his son and then put it down on the waist-high bench.

Mark picked up both the empty gun and the magazine with just one round in it, inserted the magazine into the gun, and racked the one round from the magazine into the chamber. Then Mark raised his arms in front of his face to aim, fired the round, ejected the magazine, and put it down on the bench for Clifford.

Livingston was arguing that Mark would have, or should have, known that a bullet could be in the chamber even when the magazine was empty, making him—not the gun's design—responsible for Kenzo's death. But, for me, this series of questions shows that *if* this gun had had a *prominent* chamber-loaded indicator, this sequence would have made the indicator very obvious to Mark. Every time he manipulated the slide on top of the gun to "rack" the round into the empty chamber, the red indicator would have popped up. Then, when he raised the gun in front of his face, it would have been there, very conspicuous. Then, each time when he fired that single bullet, and there were no more rounds left in the magazine to be loaded into the chamber, he would have seen that the red indicator that had been in front of his eyes had disappeared.

The day when Kenzo was visiting his home, Mark would have seen the red chamber-loaded indicator sticking up again in front of his face and known that the gun was still loaded, *if* the Beretta had had a *prominent* chamber-loaded indicator. The Beretta should also have had an engraved message, such as LOADED WHEN UP.

Now Livingston tried to pin down that Clifford had shown Mark how to clear the gun. He went over to a table on which there were some exhibits and picked up the gun that had killed Kenzo. Standing solidly in front of the jury, Livingston said, "I have got a dummy round here. It's a plastic round. Deputy Buckmaster has already checked it out. It's safe." He pointed the barrel upward then tipped it back downward until it was aimed at the floor. He looked at Clifford. "Clearing the gun takes whatever round that's in the chamber and throws it out the side; right?"

With evident delight, Livingston, the powerful former cop, yanked back the slide, making a loud metal-on-metal *thunk*. The plastic round sailed through the air and landed on the floor in front of the jury box. "Just like that. Is that clearing the gun?"

"Yes."

"And you taught Mark how to do that, right?"

He answered, "Yes," but we never heard in Clifford's own words how he'd taught Mark to clear the gun. We had only heard about his competing with the television while trying to demonstrate something about the gun to Mark.

Livingston asked Clifford if he'd given Mark some of the basic safety instructions about handling the gun, such as, "Never point at anybody you don't intend to shoot." And "Never take the gun off safety unless you intend to shoot it"; and "Always treat a gun as though it's loaded. There is no such thing as an unloaded gun."

"Yes," said Clifford, to each of those. I noticed again that Livingston was pointing the gun around the crowded courtroom, violating the same safety rules he was blaming Mark for disobeying. But with each new question, I felt the jury's opinion of Mark turn more negative, which drew even more attention away from the faults of the gun's design.

Moments later Livingston asked, "Isn't it true that you kept that Beretta pistol unlocked and loaded in that camera bag in your bedroom, accessible to Mark, so that if he had to use it in an emergency—an intruder coming into the house when you were away—he could do that?"

"Yes," replied Clifford, and when asked if he had wanted Mark "to be able to get to the gun and use it if someone was coming in the window and was going to hurt him or somebody else in the house," Clifford said yes again.

On redirect Nancy asked Clifford: "Did you want [Mark] to use [the Beretta] for home protection in 1994, with his lack of experience?"

"I eventually wanted Mark and his stepmother to be able to use them; I mean, to comfortably…"

"And what does *eventually* mean? Sometime after that?"

"Well, after, you know, spending more time at the range."

"What were your plans with respect to your future training with Mark and weapons?"

"Just to give him more exposure. And I don't know if I had any really set plans…"

With that, Nancy ended her questioning.

Clifford's testimony left scars in my memory like those from a burn. He was unclear in his own mind on where the line was between the training period, when Mark was forbidden from touching the gun, and the time when "eventually" Mark would be trained and allowed access to it. His uncertainty gave Beretta's lawyers an opening to argue that Mark was allowed access in case of some ill-defined emergency. Thus, Beretta could argue that Clifford would not have used an internal lock even if the gun had been designed with one.

It seemed to me that certainly Mark had been forbidden from touching the gun, but this *was foreseeable*. Situations like this happen frequently, as the testimony by Professor Stephen Teret and the psychological testimony of Professor Hans Steiner had shown. But I feared that the jury may not have recognized that these mistakes were common and foreseeable. Clifford's unsafe gun storage, the denial of the risks, the haphazard safety training, and the aggregate statistics on how common they were, all seemed to float loose and disconnected in the air, like feathery bits of goose down, perhaps to drift away before we could collect them into a coherent closing argument supported by the law, which was not going to be explained to the jurors until the end of the trial.

And there was soon more bad news to come—in fact, a disaster.

Our trial was occasionally covered in national and international media, and often in local newspapers and television. One day an editor of a computer publication, Dan Brekke, read about it and remembered that one evening ten years before, he'd received a concerned call from his estranged wife telling him that their son, Eamon Banta, had told her that while visiting Mark's house that day, Mark had shown him a real gun. Brekke had spoken with Eamon to get the specifics, then called Clifford to inform him of his son's dangerous behavior.

Thinking this information might be relevant to our trial, Brekke had called the police and told them about it. When it got to Beretta's defense lawyers, they insisted on calling Dan Brekke to testify.

Brekke's testimony added to the long list of Clifford's alleged errors. Not only had he left his gun out, loaded and unlocked, he'd continued to do so even though he'd been warned that Mark had shown one of his father's guns to a friend before.

On the stand, Clifford testified that he did not remember the call, which he had received five years before Kenzo was shot, and about ten years before his courtroom testimony.

How I wish that that telephone conversation had been enough to change the way he stored his guns.

### Plaintiffs' Gun Design Expert

As the trial continued, so did my turmoil. I had known Clifford's son, Mark, but not Clifford himself. Both of them had made horrendous

158

mistakes, I felt. But I continued to feel good about what we were doing. Win or lose, I thought the trial had benefits. The media coverage of our case was making some people think about the risks of guns in homes and encouraging some gun owners to store their firearms safely.

Second, Jeffrey Reh and Larry Keane, two of the most influential figures in the gun lobby, were hearing our arguments in court. Perhaps by forcing them to listen to our experts talk about how unsafe their gun designs were for ordinary consumers, we could convince them to make their guns safer, and save lives.

Also, our trial was giving Jon Lowy and the Brady organization an opportunity to see how a major gun maker and importer worked internally, and to learn its arguments. Jon, a relatively young lawyer with enormous potential, was involved in a complex case against a major gun company and a top executive of the National Shooting Sports Foundation. And we were discovering which of our expert witnesses were good.

In fact, we were about to see how well one of our key witnesses would do.

Jon called Lester Roane to the stand. A tall and fit man who looked to be in his sixties ambled past the jury and took the oath. His profile brought to my mind the worn face on an old Indian-head nickel. Jon's initial questions established that Roane was chief engineer at H. P. White Laboratory in Virginia. At the time it was the top gun-testing company in the nation, and Roane was responsible for planning and conducting tests.

Roane answered Jon's questions in a gravel-voiced, self-assured way, mentioning that he'd been an NRA member since he was a teenager. I took a liking to his folksy charm, but he made me nervous. He made his living from contracts with gun manufacturers. Jon had learned that he believed guns should be made safer with internal locks and prominent chamber-loaded indicators. But we also knew he was suspicious of Californians, of the gun laws that we were passing, and of "gun control"—whatever that meant to him. I was afraid he might say something that would undermine our case.

Roane told the jury he had an engineering degree from Virginia Tech and a master's in public administration from Harvard. After his undergraduate degree, he'd worked for an aircraft company. But, as he put it, "I was invited by Uncle Sam to come and accept his greetings. I spent a couple of months in basic training, learning to do push-ups and move a rifle and pick up cigarette butts and say, 'Yes, sir.'" As a soldier, because of his training and experience, he worked on the guidance system of cruise missiles at the White Sands Missile Range in New Mexico.

"So, if you say something is not rocket science, you actually have a foundation to say that?" Jon asked.

"I suppose so," he smiled. "Yes, sir." He was thoroughly a military man.

As division chief of the US Army Small Arms Systems Agency at the Aberdeen Proving Ground in Maryland, he had managed an engineering unit "overseeing the movement of small arms: rifles, pistols, shotguns, through the prototype design phase into initial production." He led the team that modified the design of the M16, the basic infantry semiautomatic rifle. They designed a "burst control" device so M16s would fire three rounds when the trigger was pulled. That improved the hit rate and conserved ammunition.

In 1984 Roane began working at H. P. White Labs, whose clients included Beretta and many other gun manufacturers. Jon asked about the gun design work he'd done there, including a lawsuit that arose after a teenager out hunting had been injured when he dropped a shotgun that lacked a safety and it went off. Roane had designed three alternative safeties, one of which was incorporated into the gun.

He said he had testified at fourteen trials involving gun design, and in about half of those he'd testified for the defendant. His company is paid for the work he does on cases like this, he said, but he gets "not a nickel."

Finally, Jon asked him to stand in front of the jury box and to put a Beretta with a dummy round in the chamber side by side with one with an empty chamber. Roane told the jury: "You can see the difference—*maybe*—between the unloaded and loaded one." The jurors in the back row stood and leaned forward to get a closer look.

Squinting at them, a juror asked, "Which one is loaded?"

"Good question. This one is loaded," Roane said, pointing.

The burial plot salesman: "I can see it."

Judge Hodge: "Hold on. Hold on. Hold on. I can't have one juror giving answers to the other juror's questions. One has the chamber-loaded indicator showing the red dot and one doesn't, right?"

Roane: "That's correct."

Jon corrected his witness, pointing out that they both show red in either state.

Judge Hodge allowed Roane to hand the jurors the guns and they played a little "hot potato" with them, passing them along, whispering to each other, pointing and squinting, fascinated, eager, afraid, while I watched, not ten feet away. One of those two Beretta handguns had killed Kenzo.

Soon we took a break. I was ready.

Back in the witness box, Roane explained that he had made his own plastic model of a Beretta equipped with a prominent chamber-loaded indicator. He couldn't install his prototype on a Beretta because after machining they undergo heat-treating, which makes them extremely hard, and he had no access to one before this process.

Pointing to his model, he demonstrated that when there is a round in the chamber, a small red marker becomes quite evident on the top of the slide, where you look down the barrel as you point it to shoot. The marker disappears when no round is in the chamber.

Holding it up for the jurors to see, he pointed out that the marker is not big enough to interfere with the line of sight. His design involved making a longitudinal slot in the top of the slide, the device that moves back and forth on the top of semiautomatic handguns. In other words, it would be possible to manufacture the handgun with a clear, red marker.

He added that it was also feasible to engrave a warning on the side of the gun, as well as words explaining that the red marker is a chamber-loaded indicator. "You could engrave almost anything on the gun. You could engrave the Gettysburg Address, I suppose."

He showed the jurors the chamber-loaded indicator on a Jennings 9 pistol, much lower in quality, but one that, oddly, had a well-designed chamber-loaded indicator.

Jon asked why it was preferable to Beretta's.

"It visually provides a real dramatic difference," said Roane. But on the Beretta, the difference between the loaded and unloaded condition is very small and difficult to detect, he emphasized.

Judge Hodge already had a question from a juror. "Does the engraving take away from the strength of the steel at all?"

"Not in any meaningful sense, no. Obviously anytime you even scratch something at some theoretical level, you reduce its strength. But in terms of practical strength reduction, no, it does not."

"All right," said Hodge, picking another card. "Would your chamber-loaded indicator design decrease the reliability of the gun in any significant fashion?"

"No, it would not."

Jon asked if the cut in the slide for the chamber-loaded indicator would have any adverse effect on the functioning or reliability of the gun.

"Well, again, by cutting a slot in the slide, you are reducing the strength of the slide. But it's in an area where it doesn't require high strength." Roane explained that the beveled area on the bottom of

162

the slide is the feed ramp; it guides the cartridge out of the magazine and into the gun's chamber. "It's not unheard of at all for cartridge cases to blow out and release hot gas," he said, "in some cases, to blow out and blow the gun apart." He had seen that on hundreds of guns, but it always happens over the feed ramp. "Just like a tire or a balloon is going to blow out at the place where it's weakest," he said, "the cartridge case blows out at the place where it's not supported—right over the feed ramp." It never blows up, which is where the slot for the chamber-loaded indicator is cut. There would be no more problem with dirt and debris than there is with the other parts of the gun.

Jon asked Roane about the three prototypes for integral locks on Berettas, which he had built for our trial. He described each one in some detail. One was a small lock with a key. He said that although his prototype was only a demonstration model, adding this low-tech, two-piece lock to the Beretta would be child's play for Beretta engineers. You could clean the gun the same way you already clean it.

The second was a combination lock. It had a small push-button and was installed in his prototype by drilling a tiny hole in the Beretta's frame. When you push the mechanism down, the hammer could not be retracted.

His third prototype was an adaptation of a Saf-T-Lok device for the Beretta; no key was required. To unlock it, you pushed buttons in a sequence. The Saf-T-Lok company manufactured small combination locks to work on a number of other semiautomatic pistols. He explained that it had been proven reliable in two tests. In one, for example, the gun had been fired 36,000 times, with no maintenance or cleaning. Nothing broke or failed.

Next Jon addressed Clifford's concern that his gun be available quickly in case of an emergency. Roane replied that with his models, the gun could be quickly accessible, but still safe.

Now it was Beretta's turn. Gebhardt rose to cross-examine the witness. He began by establishing that H. P. White Labs, where Roane had worked for so many years, was not in the business of designing or manufacturing guns. Its bread-and-butter work was *testing* firearms.

Gebhardt asked Roane if he thought the Beretta was unreasonably dangerous as designed.

"No, I don't," said Roane, which seemed to contradict his earlier testimony. But soon he said he would, nevertheless, advocate building into the gun the safety features he had just talked about—a reliable integral lock and a prominent chamber-loaded indicator. They were good features, and the reliability of the gun would remain high.

Gebhardt continued to pick at Roane. He quickly got him to confirm that when a company comes to him with a concept such as adding some feature to a gun, he generally gives opinions on its reliability based on analysis or testing. Gebhardt asked him why this jury wasn't entitled to that.

Roane began to say that they are entitled to it, and to explain, but Gebhardt cut him off and placed into evidence a copy of the first page of an H. P. White Labs brochure, which said, "One test is worth a thousand expert opinions." He pointed to a place that said, "Assisted by computer modeling and analysis, designs can be assessed for potential performance before tests are conducted."

Roane admitted he hadn't done any of that.

"But you have given opinions to this jury that your prototypes are not going to affect the reliability of the gun, right?"

"That's correct," replied Roane.

In a minute, Gebhardt turned to Roane's design for locking the gun by blocking the trigger bar. "You haven't done a stress analysis to determine the effect of drilling holes?"

Roane said he hadn't.

"How many holes can you put in there before it starts to look like Swiss cheese, and it's going to fall apart?"

"I don't know."

"So, you don't know, as you sit here today, whether or not the addition of that hole is going to create some kind of stress problem?"

"I know that it is definitely going to weaken the frame. It is not in my opinion likely to reduce the reliability or the durability of the gun to an unacceptable level."

"And one test is worth a thousand expert opinions?"

"My preference is always to test," he replied, adding that it was economically prohibitive. He said if the clients had been willing to pay for them, he would have been delighted to do them, and then he would have had answers to Gebhardt's questions.

Next came questions about the Saf-T-Lok Roane had adapted for the Beretta.

"Is the grip size of a gun important for consumer acceptance?"

Roane admitted it could be.

"Well, I mean, this one, you need almost two hands to hold it. You need a tripod or something like that. You had to make it a lot bigger to incorporate your lock, didn't you?"

"You are entitled to your opinion about using a tripod. I have very small hands, and I didn't have any difficulty using it as it is."

Gebhardt kept criticizing Roane's models as if they were ready for production, even though Roane had explained they were mere prototypes.

"Based on your experience, whatever it is, in designing guns, is that a good design feature, to have all that paraphernalia hanging out the side of that gun?"

"It would be preferable not to have it."

With that, Gebhardt sat down, looking satisfied.

After a lunch break Jon stepped forward for redirect. In response to Gebhardt's slighting of Roane's gun design experience, Jon asked him if he had led a team that designed two modifications of the army's general-issue M16, and had also led a team to design from scratch a prototype of a dual-cycle army rifle.

"That's correct," answered Roane, forthright and assertive.

Finally, to answer the objection that Roane's company had not sufficiently tested his prototypes, Jon asked him how much all that testing Gebhardt had asked about would have cost. Approximately $5,000 to $20,000 *per test* for the stress, endurance, reliability, and environmental tests, so the cost could be as much as $100,000, he said.

Clearly the cost was prohibitive for us to fully test Roane's prototype designs through to production. In essence, we would have had to take a step into the gun manufacturing business. But that was unnecessary, because Roane had designed and tested enough guns to know which designs were reliable.

After Jon's re-cross-examination, Hodge unfolded a card with a question from a juror: "Do you think that the Beretta 92L, with your modification, would pass all the tests you need to do so that it could go out to consumers?"

"I think that it would, with any of those modifications," Roane answered without hesitation.

It was Thursday, and the court did not meet on Friday. Hodge said he knew Roane would love to get back to Virginia rather than have to stay in California for a three-day weekend. Roane enthusiastically agreed.

When Judge Hodge excused him, he nodded at the judge with a boyish look of delight, stepped lightly down from the stand, and almost trotted out of the courtroom.

### Beretta's Gun Design Expert Witness

Soon it was time for a pivotal moment in the trial: Beretta USA's gun design expert would attempt to prove that the company was in no way responsible for ending Kenzo's life.

Gebhardt, looking annoyed yet determined, rose and clumped toward the judge. In a John Wayne sort of way—faux reluctant yet confident, loud and slow—he called Seth Bredbury to the stand. When the court attendant opened the door in the back of the courtroom, a dapper, poised man in late middle age walked through. His black hair was neatly combed. Bredbury looked professional but friendly—your neighbor, only more trustworthy and better dressed.

He took the stand and swore to tell nothing but the truth. Gebhardt ran him through the preliminaries. He had received a bachelor of science degree in mechanical engineering from MIT, where his undergraduate courses had included design, stress analysis, and strength of materials.

He said that after college, from 1964, he had worked at the Springfield Armory in Massachusetts for two years. During the first six months, he was an engineering trainee, and then was assigned to the Test Branch, where they tested "new development-type work" on military firearms. (On inadequate testing of military guns, see this endnote.[21])

From 1968 through 1978 Bredbury worked for Colt's Manufacturing Company in Hartford, Connecticut, where he said he ran the Test and Analytical Group. It supported the designers, analyzing the stresses on parts and looking at what happens dynamically during the firing of an automatic weapon.

Following that, he worked for almost two decades as what he called a "Kelly Girl engineer," doing temporary engineering jobs here and there. Almost two decades was a long time, and I wondered why he had left Colt's.

Gebhardt asked if he had done computer modeling in his recent work.

He had.

"In the design process?"

"Yes, I have."

"Well, I guess basically your entire career has been designing, analyzing, testing, and manufacturing guns?"

167

"Yes," said Bredbury.

I noticed that the compound wording of the question allowed Bredbury to answer yes without explaining how much of his work had been in gun design as opposed to testing. Gebhardt had criticized our expert, Roane, for being a tester of firearms rather than a designer.

"Now I want you to tell this jury what distinguishes you and your background from Mr. Roane and his background," said Gebhardt.

"In my career, I've been part of a design team that works with designers, the analytical, and the test people who are working in one company as one unit, so that we work together; we are always involved in the design. And a great deal of the time that I have spent, I have been doing actual design."

He further explained that Mr. Roane works at H. P. White Labs, an independent testing house. "We send them a specific item and say, 'Please test this according to such and such,' and they test it and send me back the parts—whether they have broken or not—and the results. And so, they are kind of out of the design loop."

Bredbury said most of the court cases he had worked on involved accidental shootings, and that he had worked on about one hundred gun lawsuits, one for the plaintiff, the others for the gun manufacturer.

Wait a minute, I thought: he's worked on about one hundred lawsuits against gun makers, mostly involving accidental shootings? How dangerous are these guns? And do they consider all of these injuries and deaths just the necessary, unavoidable cost of doing business?

But Bredbury said that he'd actually testified in trials as an expert witness only about ten times. This made sense. Most lawsuits settle out of court, often with secret payouts to plaintiffs willing to sign nondisclosure agreements that keep them quiet.

Bredbury said the Beretta 92 is a well-designed gun. It's designed to be easy to operate safely by the user, and very reliable.

Gebhardt handed Bredbury a Beretta 92 pistol—though not the one that killed Kenzo—and asked why the gun was well designed.

Putting the gun down on the railing in front of him, Bredbury replied, "It's a gun that doesn't have a lot of extraneous controls. It's simple to operate. It doesn't fool you. It doesn't make you think about how to use it. It does what you think it's going to do all the time."

*It doesn't fool you.*

Immediately, visions of Mark taking out the loaded magazine and thinking the gun was unloaded ran through my head.

Now Bredbury's bona fides as a designer were polished with questions and answers to describe a series of design steps that sounded like they came from an Engineering 101 textbook: get design specifications, create some design concepts, make a preliminary design, make a prototype, etc.

As Bredbury brought up each step, Gebhardt—loudly, and with second-grade classroom techniques—repeated its name with heightened emphasis, almost winking at the jury like a vaudeville comic. To make sure he captured the jury's attention, he wrote each step down on butcher paper he had put on an easel in front of the jury box.

"Okay. Preliminary Design." (He scrawled *Prelim. Design*.) "And what does that entail?"

Bredbury emphasized that you have to consider the risks and benefits throughout the entire process, and that when you make any change in the gun's design, you have to consider how it affects all the other parts.

Finally, they took up the design of the Jennings 9 chamber-loaded indicator, which Roane had said could be incorporated into the Beretta.

Bredbury emphasized many poor qualities of the Jennings, and on this he was correct. The Jennings 9 was one of many cheap, poorly made, junk guns. We were only saying that its chamber-loaded indicator's design could be incorporated into the Beretta, with appropriate changes.

As I listened, I grew angry. The problems with the junk guns, or Saturday Night Specials, he was complaining about had been created, in part, by the gun industry and its lobby, when they got Congress to exempt firearms from federal consumer product safety regulation, and later, to exempt US-made handguns from the law prohibiting importation of unsafe handguns. This was the pattern I had seen before: the gun industry creating problems, then complaining about the problems that they had created.

Next Bredbury demonstrated how the chamber-loaded indicator on the Jennings gun works. He stood next to a drawing of the Jennings and explained that when you pull the trigger, the round goes off, then the slide comes whizzing back; it throws out an empty cartridge case, and pushes a new one up out of the magazine. On the Jennings, when the new cartridge slides into the chamber, it lifts the chamber-loaded indicator up so you can know the gun is loaded.

The jurors were leaning forward, having no problem understanding his drawings.

Gebhardt then pointed to a drawing of the Beretta and asked, "Do you see any problem in setting the Jennings design into the Beretta design? How does it look?"

"It looks not so good." He said that the distance from the top of the cartridge to the top of the slide was a lot smaller on the Beretta than on the Jennings.

"What's wrong with that?" asked Gebhardt.

"Well, I have got this spring and this washer and something to hold it in, and I have about this much space for it." Demonstrating a tiny gap with his hands, he said there was not enough space for the sloping pin and other parts. Also, the holes you'd drill on top of the Beretta's slide would weaken it. Eventually it would crack.

Roane had said the cut wouldn't weaken it enough to reduce its practical life.

Gebhardt brought up "case head ruptures" in which the back part of a cartridge case can explode from too much pressure when a bullet is fired.

Bredbury said that when case head ruptures occur in a gun with the Jennings-type chamber-loaded indicator, the gas doesn't just blow down. Instead, it goes everywhere, because there is so much of it under high pressure. He added that the little parts in there have a very good chance of being blown out by the gas, "so they will be coming out toward the shooter."

Bredbury said he had once tested a bolt-action rifle that had a chamber-loaded indicator somewhat similar to that of the Jennings. When a case head ruptured, the bullet still went down the barrel, but a piece of hardened steel became a secondary bullet and came out the side of the gun.

This was visceral; the jury was all ears.

Bredbury briefly considered a few modifications you would need to make on the Beretta in order to incorporate the Jennings design. None would work.

For example, the slide could be made thicker so that the chamber-loaded indicator did not get in the way of the sights. (Roane had said it didn't have to.) But if the slide were thicker, when it came whizzing back, the barrel (which is part of the slide) would bump into the chamber-loaded indicator. Trying to fix one problem would lead to another. Some of the potential fixes would result in cartridge case head separations every time, he said, with dire consequences for the shooter. The gun could blow up in his face.

Bredbury explained things patiently and clearly, but the various terms and conditions were sometimes complex. A little juror confusion seemed not necessarily a bad thing for Bredbury, so long as he was seen as the expert. He concluded that it was not possible to put a Jennings-type chamber-loaded indicator onto the Beretta.

When Bredbury got to Roane's three integral lock designs for the Beretta, he contradicted Roane's testimony at every point. The locks would break here or fail there. If they were installed on the Beretta, one of them would make the grip too fat, and people with small hands would not be able to use the gun. Pieces of the lock would protrude, and if you needed to take the gun out of your pocket quickly, it would snag. He said Roane had not done adequate environmental tests on his models, like tests done on the Beretta in Italy, such as the dust test, where you put the gun in what amounts to a dust storm, or the water immersion test, or the hot or cold temperatures tests. Dirt would build up and Roane's designs could not be cleaned adequately. After much use, they would explode, sending a rush of dangerous gas and parts into the face of the user.

In closing, Gebhardt asked, "Now, you have said that this Beretta is safe and reliable, right? Is it possible to make it more safe and more reliable?"

"I don't believe that with the current state of technology, you could make it safer or more reliable."

Jon Lowy had been fidgeting in his chair in front of me, growing more agitated as he listened, furiously scribbling notes and occasionally thumbing through stacks of papers. He was visibly eager to cross-examine Bredbury.

Finally, Jon began. "What percent of your current income—working income—do you get from serving as a hired expert for gun companies?"

"A hundred percent," answered Bredbury, showing no affect whatsoever.

"Many of these cases, in fact, *all of them*, they are unintentional shootings, is that right?"

"Yes." But Bredbury added that he is hired by the gun company to look at the circumstances and the gun. If he agrees with the gun company's position—that there is nothing wrong with the gun—then he works for them.

"Of course, if you don't work for them, you don't work."

Bredbury agreed. He said he was paid $130 per hour and had spent two weeks on this case. I did the math. Eighty hours times

$130 is $10,400. A tidy sum for saying, as he apparently had over and over, that there was nothing wrong with the gun, and that each new accidental shooting was entirely the fault of the person who used it.

Jon asked him about some cases he'd worked on. Didn't he know that many people handle a gun and forget to check the chamber? Didn't he know that people often store guns loaded and unlocked, accessible to children?

Bredbury said some people do that, but they are acting irresponsibly. "Some people drink and drive, too," he added.

Jon got Bredbury to agree that in all the cases he had worked on, a user had forgotten to check the chamber and then had pulled the trigger and unintentionally killed or injured someone.

I was amazed. Apparently, the gun industry, including the lawyer sitting at Beretta's table, Larry Keane, and his National Shooting Sports Foundation, had a professional "expert witness" who made a living from lawsuits in which someone was killed or injured because someone had forgotten to check the chamber and did not know a round was in it.

How could anyone claim that current gun designs were safe, I wondered?

In answer to Jon's questioning, his face expressionless, Bredbury admitted he had worked on cases where even highly trained police officers had forgotten to check the chamber, then pulled the trigger, and unintentionally shot themselves or others.

Jon asked about a case that sounded somewhat similar to ours. Bredbury admitted to testifying in a case in which a boy shot someone after he'd removed the magazine, and had assumed that the gun was unloaded.

"Like the police officer, like the other kid, he forgot to check the chamber?"

"Right."

Jon Lowy asked him if the friend died in that case, but Bredbury said he didn't remember whether he died or was badly injured.

That struck me too. He could not remember if the boy had died. It seemed like these were not real people to him.

Bredbury agreed that Mark had intended to unload the gun when he removed the loaded magazine, but then added: "He did know how to check the chamber to see whether or not there was a round in the chamber."

Jon agreed. "Right. He forgot to check the chamber, just as that police officer forgot to check the chamber in the case that you worked on?"

"Right," said Bredbury.

Next, Jon questioned Bredbury's qualifications. "Your only work on a safety modification of a gun was over twenty years ago, when you worked on a project regarding installing a manual safety in which you were not even the designer?"

Bredbury's answer was evasive, so Jon read from Bredbury's deposition, in which he'd said his Test and Analytical Group had given support to engineers, but he wasn't the designer.

Bredbury admitted that he had never attempted to design an internal lock for a gun, and had never considered whether an internal lock could be incorporated into a gun. Nor had he ever thought about how to alert a user that a round is in the chamber.

Jon began to build a rhythm of questions to which Bredbury had to assent. Who was actually responsible for designing a safe gun? Wasn't it true that neither the Dixes nor the Center to Prevent Handgun Violence is a gun manufacturer with a large staff of firearms design engineers, but Beretta has ample resources to build a prototype?

Jon pursued him. "Mr. Gebhardt called Mr. Roane's prototypes various names—breadboards and gizmos...I forgot all the names. But you have never even done what Mr. Roane did in building a prototype of a gun with an internal lock?"

"No," Bredbury said. "You could look at those things on a piece of paper, and probably you wouldn't even have to go as far as a piece of paper if you think about it, and realize there is no point in building one of those." Yet he was forced to admit that Roane had gone farther toward building a lockable gun than he or Beretta had.

"You don't fault Mr. Roane for trying to come up with design alternatives that might save the lives of some kids, do you?"

"No, that's what he was hired to do by you folks. Why not? He should."

I wondered if the jury remembered that Roane had said he thought prominent chamber-loaded indicators and integral locks are needed and would save lives?

To my surprise, Bredbury agreed fully that you had to take into account how consumers would use the product, and that some gun owners—especially those with a gun for home protection—often want ready access to their gun. He agreed that when they hear the bump in the night, they want to have the gun in hand, round in the chamber, ready to fire.

"And some of them do, in fact, have kids in the home?" Jon asked.

"Yes," Bredbury agreed. But he added that if they had children, storing their guns loaded and unlocked was a serious mistake. "They have to weigh the risks of exposing their children to this hazard....If you've got little kids around who might get at the gun, you have got to tip the scales a little bit and increase your access time. It's your personal responsibility."

Jon said Bredbury wouldn't get any argument from him about that, but these were the risks that *Beretta*, too, should have weighed, since *Beretta* knows that kids get ahold of their fathers' guns.

Finally, Jon turned to the options for storing a gun if you want quick access.

Bredbury favored cable locks. A cable lock for a gun looks like a small cable-type bicycle lock. It is fitted through the disassembled semiautomatic handgun and locked.

Jon began by mentioning that if you want to lock your gun with a cable lock, first you have to realize you need one; then, you have to go and buy one and bring it home. It doesn't come with the gun. Then, every time you want to lock your gun, you have to disassemble it, thread the cable through the gun, and lock it.

At a table, in front of the jury, Jon demonstrated how long it takes to *unlock* a cable lock. He pointed out that the process took much longer than, say, having a built-in lock on your gun.

Jon demonstrated that the instructions in Beretta's manual, such as "Keep your guns locked up," were unrealistic if you want quick access to the gun, leaving the gun owner to make whatever choices he would—often bad ones—without adequate safety instructions from Beretta. The company told its customers to store ammunition in a different place from the gun—a good idea, but bound to be violated by people who thought they needed quick access.

Jon was wrapping up his cross-examination.

"Do you agree that if the gun could be designed to warn users like Mark that a round is in the chamber, and that the life of a child could be saved as a result, that would be a benefit?"

Bredbury ignored the question, arguing instead that Jon should be asking if a chamber-loaded indictor could be designed so that it would not compromise the gun, adding, "I haven't seen such a device."

Jon was clearly miffed. "You are not aware of Beretta ever attempting to make a more prominent chamber-loaded indicator or to make a lockable gun?"

"That's correct."

"That's all I have," said Jon. He wheeled and marched back to his chair.

176

Judge Hodge sorted through the cards he'd received from jurors, and read, "How do you weigh the loss of life against a mere increase or decrease in efficiency? How do you, in your mind, make this risk/benefit analysis?"

"I know that some people will be killed because of decisions that I have made," Bredbury answered. He said if you are dealing with items like this, you better face it.

It was Gebhardt's turn for redirect: "Do you as a designer account for the users' personal responsibility in storing their guns and following instructions?"

"It is the personal responsibility of the user—anyone who has a gun," Bredbury replied. "They have a right to have a gun, but with that right comes a responsibility to control its use, and, as a designer, I have to consider that they will do that."

I tried to process that sentence. It was said as if he judiciously "had to consider" (tried to figure out) whether gun users act responsibly, but then he assumed "they will do that"—this from a man who had admitted he had worked on about one hundred cases in which a gun had fired when its user did not want it to, and it had killed or injured someone.

Would Bredbury's well-rehearsed criticisms of so many "irresponsible" gun users, wrapped in his sensible-sounding expertise, conceal the defects of this gun design for consumers? Would the jury excuse the corporation's failures to *help* many gun owners safely control their guns?

I couldn't tell.

# 10

## Personal Testimony: Kenzo's Ten-Year Plan

The last thing to do in presenting our case was to show the jury the nature of our loss. Over Gebhardt's objection, Judge Hodge had ruled that to consider whether Lynn and I were entitled to compensation for the loss of someone we loved, there had to be evidence exploring the nature of that love. Lynn had already given her testimony.

As my time to testify approached, I began to dread it. I feared that anything I said in court about my loss of Kenzo might appear flat and listless, when, in fact, I would be holding my turbulent feelings in, protecting myself from them. Kenzo's disappearance had been so traumatic, so sudden, that it was incomprehensible. How could I explain it to someone else when I couldn't begin to understand it myself? It was a fearful black hole.

But as the day drew near, and Jon Lowy told me what I would be asked to speak about, I felt relieved. Most of my testimony could be about Kenzo's boyhood and our life with him. I could do that.

In the courtroom, when Jon called me, I left my seat next to Lynn and Kalani, walked to the stand, and swore to tell the truth. I spoke mostly of moments from our everyday life with Kenzo. Perhaps to others what I recalled about Kenzo's life seemed no more than ordinary. But, to me, they were what had made our lives with Kenzo so special. My task was somehow to make Kenzo's daily affection apparent to others as I tried to give the whole truth about his fifteen-year life—in fifteen minutes.

We started slowly, with me telling the jury about my background: volunteering for the Peace Corps in Korea after graduating from Rice University, then helping set up a Hawaii State public school English as a second language program, and teaching in Honolulu's version of an inner-city high school. Lynn and I had met and married when I was a graduate student studying cultural anthropology at the University of Hawaii. We had moved to UC San Diego where I received my PhD. Then I had taught anthropology at Santa Clara University. Eventually my interest in current events led me to the newspaper business, and then to the nascent personal computer industry. I became research director at *MacWEEK*. Later I started my own computer industry research and consulting business.

"What are your memories of Kenzo as a young boy?" asked Jon.

"As a toddler, he was cute and cuddly and always had a good attitude. He was very, very huggable and just fun. I used to play 'ring around the rosy' with him, drop him between my legs, but at the last second keep him from hitting the ground. He loved that. Both Lynn and I enjoyed watching him traipse around after his older brother.

"For a while," I continued, "he went to a babysitter a few houses down—a retired couple who took good care of him and read to him a lot. Their home had a warm, affectionate atmosphere. They baked soft, fragrant loaves of bread. Kenzo would walk with us back to our house, snuggling a warm loaf in his arms like a newborn child."

I told them of evenings when our family would all slip out the side door to hunt for snails invading our little strawberry patch. When Kenzo found one he'd pluck it, carefully pick his way over to the bucket, and drop it in. Hearing it plop on the bottom, we'd look up and see Kenzo smiling proudly at Kalani with a bit of a gloat.

"What sports did he play?" Jon asked.

"He played soccer and then basketball and baseball. I was coach of the soccer team, and later, the Little League baseball team."

Our Little League team. Kenzo is far right, front row.
I'm in the dark shirt, back row.

I recalled that in elementary school Kenzo joined the Berkeley
Bears co-ed baseball team. One day from the mound he took his
biggest windup and threw a wild pitch right into the head of a gentle friend, the daughter of a couple that we liked. She fell immobile
at the plate. As parents and kids circled around, she slowly came to,
and was fine. But Kenzo was so shocked that for a while, he refused
to pitch again. Later, I would take him to a park a block from our
house, crouch down, and set a target. He'd take a full windup with
good balance and blast the ball into my mitt. I called practice balls
and strikes tight as any umpire. By the time he was old enough to
play on the Little League team, he liked pitching again.

"What were his interests?

I told the jury that, like his brother, he loved music. In Berkeley
Arts Magnet Middle School, Kenzo joined the raucous Latin Percussion Band. One day we borrowed a friend's video camera and took
some family movies. In the courtroom we showed a few clips.

One was of Kenzo, Mark, and another friend on the small stage
in the school gym during a Percussion Band concert. In makeshift,

oversized silver band uniforms, the boys beat drums and gongs and swayed gaily to wild beats as parents rocked with delight, amazed at the skill, but unable to conceal their laughter at the occasional unrehearsed and offbeat solo.

When I see Mark next to Kenzo in that blurry video, I just see two enchanted boys rapt in good fun with their friends.

Another video was of Kenzo hamming it up for the camera, jumping into Lynn's lap for one of her big hugs. Kenzo's grandmother, sitting next to her, had to jump out of the way and shield her face. She feigned shock but couldn't stop grinning.

I told the jury that when Kenzo was about thirteen, he needed a chair for his room. One day, I was driving home from work when out of the corner of my eye I saw a menacing creature. On second look it was only a giant stuffed bear, hunched and forlorn amid some other junk in a yard sale, waiting for buyers. I pulled over, examined the slightly tattered, almost life-size teddy bear, and paid a minimal sum for it.

On the way to our house I wondered if Kenzo might dismiss it coldly: Was he getting too old and cynical for such a cuddly object? His friends might mock him mercilessly. But when he came home and saw it slouched in the corner of his room, he rushed to it, tested it, turned, sat on the floor, and fell back against it tentatively; when he leaned into its soft belly, it hugged him. Beaming, he rested his arms comfortably on its big furry legs. When his friends visited, they took their cue from Kenzo, accepted it, and spent many hours sitting with it, joking and having fun.

Maybe this would mean nothing to others, I said, but to me it was one of those unexpected little delights that suddenly poked its head up as my children grew and defined themselves. It showed me that Kenzo remained unashamed to show affection even though he had entered the sometimes-cruel, peer-driven teen years. He retained that quality to the end of his life.

I told the jury that Kenzo made gifts for us—he was a marvel at gift giving.

"He would just make things for people. He made me little yellow clay tennis balls along with a clay tennis racket." I still have them.

When I started my own company, he made me a name tag to wear at the computer conferences I was going to. It was an oblong bulge of hardened clay painted white with my name carefully printed in black. There was a pin sticking out the back so I could fix it onto my shirt.

I had not yet rented an office, so he made me a door sign for the room I was using at home: "Grif's Office." Curling seaweed floated up from a sandy bottom where pastel shells lay. Multicolored fish swam past my name. It was more apt than he knew: I had just started my company, and sometimes felt underwater.

As I spoke to the jury, I realized how unsatisfactory my words were. It wasn't these little objects that meant so much to me. What really mattered was fleeting and indescribable: the little expressions of joy I saw on Kenzo's face as he gave me these creative gifts.

The scene was surreal. Here I was, speaking to sleepy strangers in a jury box about odd trinkets that Kenzo had given me. They meant so much to me, but in truth they were merely token reminders—only placeholders for memories that were already fading.

"Did you ever play sports against Kenzo?" Jon asked.

"Yes, he played in a Japanese-American basketball league, and I played against him in the father–son game." I explained that every Friday night during basketball season I'd take Kenzo to his team practice and help coach or just shoot baskets. Every year the kids got taller and more skillful—dribbling the ball between their legs, getting to the rebounds faster, passing the ball quickly in complex plays. And every year the dads got older and slower.

At the end of the season the father–son game came around, and it was always fun to see what would happen. The last year we played, when I was sent in, Kenzo came over to guard me, and he covered me like a blanket. He was doggedly persistent, sticking close to my chest. I could hardly get a shot off.

After the game, with everyone exhausted and cheerfully milling around, I congratulated him on how well he had played. He looked a little embarrassed in front of his friends, but I knew what I said stayed with him. That year he made the Berkeley High School freshman basketball team. During the team's games, he didn't get so many minutes of playing time, but he was good, and steadily getting better.

"Did you know Mark?"

"I got to know Mark pretty well," I said. "I drove the two of them for a day of skiing a few months before Kenzo was killed. And once before that, with a couple of other parents, I took a bunch of boys, including Mark, on an overnight camping trip."

Wondering whether the judge would allow me to say this, I went on.

"Mark was a very nice kid. He was always responsible, and, you know, I agreed as a parent with Kenzo's choice of Mark as a friend. He was not a kid that was always getting into trouble or taking risks. Although he made a mistake with the gun, it was a child's mistake. But it ended in tragedy."

I wanted to say that it's really up to parents and the community of adults to make sure that when a child makes a predictable childish mistake it does not end in death. But I held my tongue.

"Did you ever think about whether there would be a gun at Mark's house?"

"No, I just—you know, I never thought..."

It was hard to admit, but I had never thought to ask the parents of the boys that Kenzo played with if there were guns in their homes. Lynn and I never kept a gun in our home in Berkeley, but when I was a kid, our father had a shotgun and an old World War II pistol. I went hunting with my dad a few times. He had grown up in Virginia and, following the Southern male tradition, he bought me a single-shot bolt-action rifle when I grew into my teen years.

"Did Kenzo indicate what he wanted to do in his life?"

"Yeah, we had talked that over with him some. When he was a freshman in high school, he was asked to write an essay, a ten-year plan of what he expected to do. At fifteen, he was a kid, just into high school, sort of looking over his future at all the different things he might do."

It was a class assignment given by an energetic young English teacher. I had never seen Kenzo's ten-year plan when he wrote it. We'd found it among his things after he died. A mix of emotions came to us when we saw what he'd written. It felt like we suddenly had a new unexpected link to him, a view into his future never-to-be.

I still had a copy and read parts of it to the jury. Kenzo had said he wanted to take Spanish throughout high school, "because you can speak to different people from different cultures, and it's also great for college." Photography and drawing would be his other electives. After completing driver's training, he'd get his license and borrow his dad's car, "because it holds more people, it's safer, and has better speakers."

"News to me!" I said. Everyone laughed.

186

I read on, my head down in his ten-year plan. In his sophomore year, after summer basketball camp, he hoped to make the JV basketball team and take ceramics as his elective, because his older brother had liked it and had "made some great things." Chemistry was harder than biology, so he'd take that in winter. In his junior year, he wanted to be a photographer for the school newspaper; but he didn't want his photography to pull him away from his writing, which he said he liked to do with equal enthusiasm. He'd get a job to save some money for something big, like a trip.

"Eleventh Grade: This is where I have to really bear down and concentrate on my studies, because colleges really look at your progress in junior year," he wrote. He'd take radio journalism as an elective. "I like music of all kinds. There's talk of an actual Berkeley High radio station, and I'm excited about that." He liked the idea of being a DJ, and would take Advanced Placement Biology, "which is much harder, but colleges love to see you pass such a hard class."

As a senior, he'd apply to UC Berkeley, UC Santa Cruz, University of Oregon, and others, most of them in California, because tuition is cheaper for residents. Good Food Café, a cooking class, would be his elective, because knowing how to cook would be good for his life as a college student. "I might even earn some money catering." He'd choose Theoretical Psychology and Asian Cultures, "because I'm interested in the beliefs of different kinds of people." (He'd adopted some of my own interests.) Finally, he'd take a popular English class called "Voices of the Wilderness" to explore his interest in nature and literature.

And on, out of our house he'd go, but hardly out of our lives: "I plan for my parents to pay for as much of college as possible," he wrote.

"After college I'll probably go to graduate school to learn for myself, but mostly for employability. By that time, who knows how hard it will be to get a job?" At fifteen he was pragmatic, independent, and responsible for his own future: "I could go for being some kind of doctor that works with kids, not to treat illnesses, but to do something else with them. I like kids and work very well with them, especially from ages four and up."

He had often played with our neighbors' young kids, to the great delight of all. It sounded like he might become a pediatrician—if he ever got over his apparent dislike of actually treating illnesses.

Jon asked me about the end of Kenzo's ten-year plan.

He had written that he'd wait until after college to find someone very special and marry her. "I want to mature more before I have my two children. Two for the companionship, and two years apart, I hope, so the younger can learn from the older and the older can have someone to look down on." Whenever I read his plan, I noticed that Kenzo hoped to create a replica of our own family, and that made me feel good.

"He would have made a wonderful father," I said. "He would have brought us grandkids. He would have continued to support us and Kalani in so many ways. He was just right on track. You can't imagine a more loving, wonderful kid."

I had been looking straight at Jon the whole time, but now ventured a glance at the jury, and added, "So that was his ten-year plan. You can see a kid who just had so many interests and was kind of looking out at the world and his future...thinking of becoming an adult...all the things that he was looking forward to..."

"Do you recall the last time you saw Kenzo?"

"Yes, that was a Sunday, and I was cooking 'Delicious Nutritious Pancakes' from my *A World of Breads* cookbook that a Peace Corps friend had given us."

In my mind I recalled the savory, heavy, near-burnt smell that drifted into each bedroom, rousing the sleepers. Barefoot, in rumpled pajamas, yawning and scratching, they had staggered into the kitchen where I put plates of fat, healthy pancakes topped with cut strawberries and warm maple syrup in front of them.

In just a few minutes, Kenzo's eyes darted up at the clock. He said he had to hurry, and rushed out to get dressed, asking us to give him a ride.

"Lynn took him off to the school grounds where his art class was meeting to paint a mural at an unused outdoor handball court. You know, it was just a regular Sunday morning."

I told the jury that later Kenzo telephoned us to ask if he could go over to Mark's house.

# 11

## Closing Arguments

### *Plaintiffs: Corporate Responsibility*

On Monday, November 9, 1998, people filled the seats in the gallery and stood in the back of the courtroom. Many of our friends were there to hear the closing arguments—neighbors who had brought us meals in those first dreadful days, victims of the 101 California Street massacre and their lawyer friends, and others. I had seen how persuasive Beretta's lawyers and professional expert witnesses were, yet I was hopeful. I felt the law was on our side, if only the jury could be made to understand and apply it.

Judge Hodge began by mentioning that there had been lots of media coverage, and warning the jurors that they should not read or see any of it because it was not evidence, and could not be trusted.

The judge then gave what he called a thumbnail sketch of the legal framework of the case. He said that in a product defects case, the word *defect* has a strict legal meaning that is not the ordinary meaning. It does not mean that the gun was sold broken or with a missing screw. This is the gun that Beretta intended to sell. In this trial the word *defect* has three meanings, all of which are different from the usual meaning. It was up to the jury to determine if any of them applied to this case.

First, he said, stretching an arm toward the jury, a product is defective if 1) it fails to perform as safely as an ordinary consumer would expect when used in an intended or foreseeable manner; 2) if there is a safety risk in it, which outweighs the benefits of the design; or 3) if the manufacturer or distributor of the product fails to provide an adequate warning of a substantial danger that would not be readily recognized by a user when the product is being used in a reasonably foreseeable way.

With a look of eager anticipation—like a football fan finally sitting down to watch two good teams compete in a playoff—Judge Hodge called Jon Lowy to give his closing statement.

I knew how much this meant to Jon and how hard he had worked on our case, even though his infant twins were so far away. When I had visited the Brady Center to Prevent Handgun Violence headquarters in DC, I had been surprised and proud that Jon had put up on the wall of his small office a picture of Lynn, me, Kenzo, and Kalani. And in the many lunches of Korean food that we had shared near the courthouse in Oakland, I had heard how important Jon thought this case was, and how much he had been learning about the gun industry from it. Our goals for the case matched perfectly, and we had remained impressed with his dedication.

Jon knew how to summon a striking courtroom presence, and he did so now. He stood erect, stepped forward with papers in hand, and began by softly and genuinely thanking the jurors for their time and sacrifice. He told them that they had a great—in fact, an awesome—opportunity. Stepping directly in front of the jury box, he continued: "There are decisions made in corporate boardrooms that cost lives, decisions that if made the other way, would *save* lives. We are generally powerless to do anything about those decisions. But not today, because here you sit as jurors, and you have the power and the responsibility to weigh in on those decisions."

Jon reminded them that Bredbury himself had explained how he and Beretta weigh the risks and benefits, and had admitted that doing so was in part a matter of values. "These decisions, where lives are lost, are a question of values," said Jon. He read the question a juror had asked Bredbury about how he weighs the loss of life against the mere increase or decrease in efficiency. And he read Bredbury's answer: "I know that some people will be killed because of the decisions that I've made." Jon paused a moment to let that sink in.

Soon he focused on the law. He said that everyone agrees that Clifford and Mark were irresponsible and should have done a lot of things differently. If they had, Kenzo would not have died.

"Is this a case of parental responsibility? Of course. Did Clifford fail in some ways as a parent? No question about it. But it's not an issue in *this* case, because, as the judge told you, this is a product liability case. The defendant is Beretta, and the question is, did *Beretta* do what it could have done to prevent deaths like Kenzo's?

"The law makes an awful lot of sense," Jon said. "It says if you are selling a product that goes to households, you are obligated to do what is *feasibly possible* to prevent foreseeable injuries. The question is: 'Is it foreseeable that these injuries will occur?' Is it expectable?"

Jon's voice rose. "*A company is supposed to...in fact, has to deal with reality—with the real world. It is no excuse—and it is no defense under* the law—that the consumer did wrong if that wrong was foreseeable, if it was expected."

He paused for the jury to consider what he had just said. There was quiet in the courtroom.

This point seemed to me the key contrast between our argument and Beretta's. They wanted jurors to believe in an ideal world where every person who touches a gun knows what he "should" know, and also does what he "should" do. We wanted jurors to recognize the real—and in truth, the dangerous—world in which people make predictable mistakes, and to see that under the law, the gun manufacturer must help the ordinary gun buyer, so that their mistakes do not injure or kill someone.

Jon said that if a car is poorly made, and a drunk driver veers off the road and crashes, and the car falls apart, not only the drunk driver *but also the maker of the car* would be in the wrong. "Not that you defend what the drunken driver did, but the fact is—if you know that people are going to crash in cars, you've got to make them as crashworthy as possible. You can't just sit back and say, 'You know what? If someone misuses my product—and I know it's going to happen—then I have a ready-made excuse. If I ever get sued, I'm going to say: *They shouldn't have crashed the car.*' Of course, someone is always responsible for a car crash. You always have that excuse. But the law doesn't allow that excuse *if the misuse of the product is foreseeable*. And you will see that in the jury instruction. The company is the one that can act first; the company is in the best position to prevent these deaths before they happen. And that's not just common sense; it's the law.

"Do Clifford and Mark have some personal responsibility?" Jon continued. "*Absolutely*. But in this case, the question is: What about the responsibility of Beretta? They sell this gun to families with children. Of course, it is a potentially lethal product, but they sell it suggesting it is a safety device, and that it's going to protect your family."

194

He placed on an easel a blowup of Beretta's ad, of one of their guns on a nightstand next to a clock that showed 11:25 and a picture of a mother with two kids.

"Beretta calls it 'Homeowners Insurance,'" he said, "and this ad says, 'Tip the Odds in Your Favor.' They know a big part of their market is people who want their guns for protection, and they want access to it quickly—like Clifford. They are going to hear the bump in the night downstairs, they don't know what it is; and they want to reach for it and get it. Many of them want a round in the chamber. This is un-rebutted testimony."

Jon reminded the jurors that Beretta's experts had testified that people shouldn't store their guns unlocked with a round in the chamber, but Jon said it's irrelevant whether they *think* that's right or not. The question is: Do people *do* it?

"If people *do it*, and you're Beretta, then you've got to take that into account. You have to *try*! You hope for the best, but assume the worst. And we have lots of evidence, which Professor Teret from the Johns Hopkins Center for Gun Policy and Research talked about, showing that a substantial percentage of gun owners store their guns loaded and unlocked. It's common knowledge. And Professor Teret's testimony was un-rebutted. He testified that there are about fifty-five unintentional shootings *a day*! That includes all kinds. Some result in death; some are bullets in the brain where the person survived; some of them are not serious. This is information that Beretta knew or should have known. 'Knew or should have known,' is the same thing under the law."

Jon said Beretta knew that in the real world, many people make the mistake Mark made, forgetting to check the chamber. "Mr. Bredbury testified about cases he's worked on where highly trained policemen who carry their gun every day, who've been through training, who've been reminded of the importance of checking the chamber—*they* forgot. They have unintentionally shot themselves and others. It's a common problem. And here, with Mark, we are talking about a kid who went to the range once with his father with the Beretta."

Now he was buzzing along, speaking quickly and passionately, without referring to his notes. "Mark did not want to harm his friend Kenzo. It's the central tragedy of this case. Was it possible to prevent it? Well, here are some things that Beretta should have done to prevent this.

"First of all, develop an obvious indicator to alert any user that a round is in the chamber. *Isn't that common sense, to at least try to do that?* Beretta never *tried.* You heard that this thing they call their chamber-loaded indicator was intended for police and military, so that they could check in the dark whether their gun was loaded. But even their own witnesses backed away from the idea that you should rely on this thing."

He pushed on.

Beretta could have engraved a warning on the gun that a bullet may remain in the chamber when the magazine has been removed. Again, just common sense. Jon—a soft-spoken guy—was getting visibly worked up.

Taking a few steps back and forth in front of the jury, he continued: Beretta claims they *do* warn their customers. In their manual, it says, "Store firearms and ammunition separately beyond the reach of children. Be sure cartridge chamber is empty." But, Jon said, where is that instruction? On page 14, on about line 15. "Does anyone think that Beretta actually believed that all of its customers who bought the gun for home protection would, when they heard the bump, go to the night table for the unloaded gun, go across the room to the locked cabinet for the magazine, put them together, load the gun, and then approach the threat?"

Beretta knew a lot of people weren't going to do that, Jon said, but the company never developed a gun with an internal lock. The jury, he said, had heard what Beretta did in response to these tragedies;

they simply poked fun at Mr. Roane's prototypes. "But *Beretta* is the gun company. The Dixes are not the gun makers." He said that when the jury got their instructions, they would see that the law does not require us to go into the gun business and make a gun.

And they also heard Beretta's expert say that Roane's prototypes would fail all their tests, he said. "They could have done the tests. *But they didn't do any tests.*"

He glanced quickly at his notes and said that the law makes a lot of sense. One of the jury instructions they would see says: "If weaker and less satisfactory evidence is offered by a party when it was within such party's power to produce stronger and more satisfactory evidence, the evidence offered should be viewed with *distrust*." Beretta could have tested these prototypes to see if any of those designs would work, but Beretta chose not to, and instead simply relied on Mr. Bredbury's "opinions," which were *not* based on tests. They *should* view that testimony with *distrust*.

The jurors sitting in the box to my left were paying close attention. Some were clearly sympathetic; others had blank expressions. But they all seemed to be thinking.

After a break, Jon was back in front of the jury box to discuss the instructions that the jurors would get. He explained two tests that the jury would apply to determine if the gun was defective: the *consumer expectations test*, and the *risk/benefit test*. If either one of them was true in our case, we could win.

He said, "Under the *consumer expectations test*, the gun is defective if it fails to perform as safely as an ordinary consumer would expect when used in a reasonably foreseeable manner....The testimony is un-rebutted that many ordinary consumers believe—incorrectly—that when you remove the magazine, the gun is unloaded."

They are wrong, Jon said. They forget to check the chamber. When the gun fires, the round that is still hidden in the chamber, it is acting in a way these consumers do *not* expect.

197

Jon wasn't excusing their error; it was just an unfortunate but a *foreseeable* fact.

He then went on to argue that the *benefits* of this product do not outweigh the *risks* inherent in its design. "The risk/benefit test," he said, "is basically weighing the pluses and minuses of the gun's design." The risk of Beretta's design was that people like Mark would not know that the gun was loaded when they forgot to check the chamber. "That is a huge risk. It is the lives of children."

He asked what were the benefits, the pluses and minuses, of the so-called chamber-loaded indicator on the Beretta. Even someone as experienced with guns as Mr. Roane, our expert in gun design, said he could barely tell the difference between the loaded and unloaded condition, Jon reminded the jury.

He walked to his table, took a sip of water, headed back in front of the jury box, and said, "Basically, you are left with the question: Is Beretta doing the *best that they can* to alert users that a round is in the chamber? They never tried. *We* produced a better, more obvious indicator." Jon said that if you had an *engraved* warning on the side of the gun which explained that when the indicator is popped up, there is a round in the chamber, then that would be a better way to alert users that a round is in there.

"It was, then, Beretta's burden to prove that the pop-up, or some other indicator, could *not* work, was *not* feasible. And what did they do to prove that? *Not a single test*; not a single prototype. All they had was Mr. Bredbury's '*judgment.*'

"Mr. Bredbury's testimony is basically that if he had tried to make a prototype of another sort of chamber-loaded indicator, it would have various problems. Well, he would be in a better position to tell you what those problems are if he had actually done the testing. He didn't.

"The same thing with the feasibility of designing a gun with an integral lock: *no tests, no prototypes*, no attempt to do anything—just what he calls his 'engineering judgment.' "

Moving on, Jon brought up the third way a gun could be found defective: failure to warn.

"As Dr. Adams said: If you've got a serious risk—kids and others dying—get serious about it. Don't bury it on page fourteen, line fifteen."

The failure to warn, Jon said, is particularly important given all the statistics they'd heard—how common it is that people die because someone doesn't know that a bullet is in the chamber, and given that so many gun owners don't think it could happen to them.

He reiterated that Bredbury had worked on about one hundred cases for gun manufacturers—similar tragedies. "So many tragedies, and *still* a failure to warn."

After a pause, Jon's voice was soft.

"Beretta did not do what the law required. And by not doing that, they never gave Mark—never gave Kenzo's parents—the chance to know with absolute certainty what would have happened."

Now, he brought up the issue of compensation, how much money we were suing Beretta for, to supposedly compensate us for our loss. "It's important to know that if Kenzo's parents had their choice, they would have gone back in time, and they would have had you, as a jury, tell Beretta Corporation before Clifford ever bought his gun, 'Make your warnings emphatic; talk to your brilliant engineers; see if there is a way you can alert people that there is a round in the chamber.' The Dixes would rather have you go back in time, and also tell Beretta, 'These people who insist on storing their guns loaded with a round in the chamber, give them the option at least, of an internal lock, so there's a way they can keep it safe but have it ready in seconds.' *That* would have been their first choice.

"But it was Beretta's decision to do none of that....So now, the only remedy that you can give, and that the law allows, is money. You will have instructions on that, entitled 'Measure of Damages: Death of a Child.' There are a number of elements of loss: love, companionship, comfort, affection, society, solace, moral support of the child. All of those elements of the loss were suffered by each plaintiff separately.

"As I have said, this is not a case about engineering; it is a case about *values*. We have heard how Beretta values life. There are other ways. When a pilot calls from a multimillion-dollar fighter plane and says he's in trouble—should he eject, or try to save the plane? The tower tells him, of course, eject; your life is worth more than that plane."

Jon said that after Kenzo's death, my life expectancy would be twenty-two years and Lynn's would be twenty-eight years, so the total for the two would be fifty years. We did not just lose a fifteen-year-old boy. We lost a sixteen-year-old, and a seventeen-year-old, etc., year after year, and for each of those years the loss would be $150,000, which is a total of seven and a half million dollars, he said. "I would never ask the plaintiffs to put a number on the life of their child." It was true. He had never said anything to me about the amount he would ask from the jury. We wanted to influence Beretta and the rest of the gun industry to sell safer guns. A significant victory could do that by making it too expensive for them not to.

Jon closed his argument: "Underlying Beretta's value judgments is a belief that the loss of life—of children's lives—is not enough to warrant taking some action. When you make that sort of decision— that value judgment—you are saying that life is cheap. I suggest that there is something horribly wrong with that value judgment, and it is your responsibility—and your obligation—to make a clear statement with a verdict that you will deliver in this case: The life of a child is not cheap; it is precious."

Jon Lowy turned, paced back past the jury, and sat down.

How could we not win this trial?

## *Defendant: Personal Responsibility*

After the morning break, Gebhardt pushed himself up, strode forward, stood foursquare in front of the jury, and said: "The core of this case is personal responsibility. Clifford and Mark made a number of decisions, and they have to take personal responsibility for those decisions. I believe this lawsuit is an effort to erase that responsibility, to erode that responsibility. And the law and the evidence don't permit it. One hundred percent of the cause of this accident rests with Clifford and Mark."

But in a second, he said, "In addressing you, it may be that I misstate what the facts are, or distort what the facts are; it may be that my recollection is different than you as to what the evidence was. If I do that, please don't hold it against Beretta."

Glancing in our direction, he went on. "I believe I heard Mr. Lowy say that what Clifford and Mark did is really not an issue in this case, and I dispute that totally. Let's look at the law. Basically, Clifford and Mark had a duty to act responsibly under the circumstances; and to fail to act reasonably, that's called negligence...I maintain that in this trial I have proven to you that one hundred percent of the cause of the accident was the *negligence* of Mark and Clifford."

He launched into a recap of his argument, focusing first on the ways Clifford was negligent. "There should have been a big red flag the day Clifford got a call from a parent, four years before the accident, complaining that Mark had shown a gun to his son," he boomed. "Clifford should have taken steps to make sure that would never happen again. Clearly he didn't."

Warming to his challenge, Gebhardt quoted from a deposition in which Clifford had said that he wanted Mark to be able to use his gun in the event of an emergency, such as an intruder coming into the house. After saying that Clifford was a sophisticated gun user who engaged in practical shooting and had lots of accessories, he went on: "Clifford decided to assume the role of teacher—the safety instructor for his son. I think his true negligence relates to his obligation as a teacher to instill in his son the safety rules relating to gun handling and the need never to play with a gun. Clifford was in the best position to teach Mark rules like 'Always consider a gun loaded' and 'Don't point it at anyone.' Clifford must assume the blame for the tragic consequences of his failure to make certain that his son had the maturity to be involved with a gun and to follow the safety rules."

Gebhardt continued to stress that Mark's father was to blame. "Clifford made the decision to store the gun contrary to the instructions in the Beretta manual, which clearly state: 'Store firearms and ammunition separately beyond the reach of children. Be sure the cartridge chamber is empty.' "

Gebhardt then quoted from a deposition in which Clifford had said that he deliberately kept the gun loaded and unlocked so it would be ready for him or Mark to be used in an emergency. Picking up a Beretta 92, he held it up before the jury.

"He didn't want to take the time to do *this*," he said, slamming the magazine into the grip, "in the event of an intruder in the house." He said that leaving the gun loaded was an incredibly bad decision, and for that, Clifford must take personal responsibility for the tragedy that followed.

Moving on to the subject of Mark's negligence, Gebhardt reminded the jury that Mark had been trained by his father with the Beretta and had been told how to check to see if it was loaded: You pull back the slide and look in the chamber.

"Mark knew it was dangerous if you didn't do this," he added, "yet on the day of the accident, he didn't check; he treated the gun like a toy. I disagree with the plaintiff's proposition that when Mark removed the full ammunition clip from the gun and put in an empty clip, that he thought there was no bullet in the chamber, because it

202

suggests that he gave some conscious consideration to what he was doing. It's more probable that he wasn't thinking about anything."

Gebhardt then hammered home the point he had been making throughout the trial: "Mark disobeyed his dad. Clifford forbade Mark to show the guns or play with them, and Mark made the decision to disobey his father. It is no excuse that teenagers are risk takers and that sometimes teenagers do things that they shouldn't. We must all bear responsibility for what we do, whether we are teenagers or old people. Question number thirteen in the questionnaire that each juror will fill out asks: What percent of the fault lies with Beretta USA, and what percent with Clifford and/or Mark? You should fill that out so that one hundred percent is Clifford or Mark."

Gebhardt went on to claim that the design of the Beretta had in no way contributed to the tragic accident. He pointed out to the jury that Teret, our expert from Johns Hopkins on unintentional shooting accidents, could cite no evidence that a Beretta 92 had ever been involved in an accidental shooting.

Then he quickly changed the subject to another type of accident—the dropfire—in which the gun goes off accidentally when dropped. He explained how Beretta, "the same company that allegedly doesn't do anything to prevent accidental shootings," had incorporated into their gun a safety feature to prevent such accidents.

"And our gun *has* a chamber-loaded indicator," he boasted, ". . . and most semiautomatics don't have one." A chamber-loaded indicator, he explained, is a secondary way of telling the operator that there is a bullet in the chamber, the first being to check the slide.

"This gun," he said, pointing to the Beretta, "is state of the art as far as safety goes." Its design, he insisted, was not a substantial factor in bringing about the death. The predominant factor was Clifford's decision to leave his gun loaded, to make the gun available to his son, and not to tell him there was a bullet hidden in the chamber.

Gebhardt cited his expert engineer's testimony that a more-prominent chamber-loaded indicator would be impossible to install without critically weakening the safety and reliability of the gun, causing case heads to rupture and blow back in the user's face. And he argued that we had failed to prove that even if a more prominent chamber-loaded indicator were present, this accident would not have happened.

"A better chamber-loaded indicator design," he conceded, "might benefit people with a passing knowledge of the gun and who are looking for information: What's this thing? But," he proclaimed, "it would not benefit the Marks of the world, who are not looking at the gun for information but are playing with it."

He also dismissed our argument that an internal lock on the gun could have helped prevent this tragedy. Clifford, he said, knew all about gun locks, and had made a conscious decision not to use them because he wanted his gun available for immediate use by his son. "It's the height of speculation to assume that even if the Beretta were designed with a lock that Clifford would have ever locked it."

Pointing to us, Gebhardt continued: "The plaintiffs claim that the Beretta was defective in design because it failed to perform as safely as an ordinary consumer would expect," but he then asked: "Just who is the ordinary consumer that the law talks about but never clearly defines?" He answered: "I say the ordinary consumer is the person who knows that, if you're going to pull the trigger on a gun, something bad can happen. The ordinary consumer knows that if you fire a gun without checking the chamber, something bad can happen. Pointing a gun at somebody and pulling the trigger is a danger that any ordinary consumer knows about. The ordinary consumer is not children. Not Mark. It's more the Cliffords of the world. And this gun performed as safely as an ordinary consumer would expect."

Next, he took up the questions the jurors would have to answer. He read: " 'Was the Beretta pistol defective when it failed to perform as an ordinary consumer would expect when using it in an intended or in a reasonably foreseeable manner?' The answer should be, 'No.'

" 'Was the Beretta defective because the risk of danger inherent in its design outweighs the benefits of that design?' Answer, 'No.'

" 'Was there negligence on the part of Clifford?' Obviously, there was.

" 'Was his negligence a substantial factor in bringing about the death of Kenzo Dix?' You should answer that, 'Yes.' The same with the negligence of Mark.

"Then you get to question thirteen: 'What percent of the total fault is due to Beretta USA Corporation, Clifford and/or Mark?' One hundred percent to Clifford and Mark."

Gebhardt concluded that if the jury didn't do its duty to uphold moral and ethical values, then in some way, "the personal responsibility that flows from that duty is diluted." He continued: "I say to you, for every percentage of fault that the plaintiffs would apply to Beretta, they are saying, 'Clifford, it's not really your fault.' In order to apply any percentage of responsibility to Beretta, you must find that this gun was defective, or that the instructions were inadequate. Don't do it. The law and the evidence say there is no defect in this well-made gun. This accident was a result of a series of negligent, poor decisions. And a verdict for the defense, which is what I am suggesting the evidence and law calls for, will mean that the ethic of personal responsibility for one's acts is still a healthy concept in our society."

Looking satisfied, Gebhardt marched back to his chair and lowered his body down into it.

### Rebuttal

It was late in the day. Judge Hodge turned to Jon Lowy and asked him if he could finish his reply quickly. He said he could.

Jon stood, not looking the least bit deterred by what Gebhardt had said, and began by paraphrasing one of Gebhardt's statements still ringing in jurors' ears: "We all must bear responsibility for what we do."

"I agree with that statement," Jon said. "Mark, when he was fourteen, killed one of his best friends. You saw him face these people who lost their son, and *he* took responsibility for his actions."

He said that Clifford also accepted responsibility. If there was actually a body of evidence that *contradicted* what Professor Teret said—which was that Clifford's behavior was very common, and Mark's was very common—Beretta would have produced it on the witness stand, Jon said. But they didn't do that, and you can infer from that, that they *couldn't* do it, because Clifford's behavior *was* very common and Mark's *was* very common.

There is no question, he said, that what Clifford did was negligent and irresponsible, but, it was foreseeable to Beretta. And what Mark did—negligent, irresponsible—was foreseeable to Beretta. Jon's voice rose as he emphasized every word, *"And under the jury instructions, therefore, Beretta had to do something about it.* So, yes, this is a case about responsibility. Very much so. We don't take anything away from Clifford's responsibility, from Mark's responsibility."

But Jon said this was *also* about *corporate* responsibility, *Beretta's* responsibility. "It's about the responsibility of a company that sells its gun for six hundred bucks a pop, and brings them into households across the country, and they know about the dangers, and they know about the deaths, and they should try to prevent them. *That's* about responsibility, too. It takes nothing away from Clifford's or Mark's responsibility. You think they are off the hook? Do you think Mark for one moment thinks, because of your verdict, 'I'm off the hook?' "

I sat there recalling Mark on the stand, suffering, so conflicted, trying to cooperate but still also burying his painful thoughts about the day he had shot Kenzo. I recalled watching him struggle against

Gebhardt's onslaught. I had been deeply moved when I saw Mark attempt to give his testimony, and had felt sympathy for the boy who had shot my son. Then I had heard Professor Steiner say Mark exhibited symptoms of PTSD. What a tragedy for Mark, caused—as he'd admitted—by his own childish mistakes, but also by Beretta's, which the company refused to acknowledge.

"And the point is the law," Jon continued. "It makes good sense, because in every one of these cases there is a Clifford. And there is a Mark." But just as Jon was getting going, Gebhardt suddenly interrupted him, saying, "We are talking about this case. I don't know what other cases he is talking about."

"There is a certain amount of rhetoric permitted in the final. You may continue," Judge Hodge immediately ruled.

Jon had to start again. "The law says that the *manufacturer* has got to take action to prevent *foreseeable misuse*. If you keep on having people like Clifford, who store their guns so that kids can get ahold of them, loaded, and you *keep on* having people like Mark, who get ahold of them and forget to check the chamber, and *if you allow that as an excuse* to prevent the corporation from doing something about the problem, it will happen *over and over and over*. There will be a Kenzo Dix for every Clifford and for every Mark. And that makes no sense; and that's why the law says what it says. This case is *all about* responsibility."

Jon paused. When he spoke again, his voice was softer, but with the same intensity.

"Mr. Gebhardt talked about causation. We can't, of course, prove with certainty what would have happened in a world where Beretta did what it was supposed to do. It's impossible to do that. All we need to do is prove by a preponderance of the evidence, which means more than fifty percent. The testimony that Mark took actions to unload the gun is undisputed. He took the magazine out, found an empty magazine, and put that in. He was wrong to think he'd unloaded the gun. But he took actions that he thought unloaded it. You can infer from the evidence that an effective indicator would have stopped Mark from pulling the trigger when the gun was loaded. If there was an indicator that alerted him that a round was still in the chamber, it would have prevented this tragedy.

"What they are really saying, when they say we can't prove causation, is, 'Give us the benefit of the doubt, because the plaintiffs can't prove with certainty what would have happened if the world were different.' But that would be grossly unfair. You can infer from the evidence that Clifford finally got the message—far too late—but he finally got the message. It would have been possible to get the message even to him, and to Mark, *but Beretta never tried.*"

Jon scanned the jury. "Mr. Gebhardt said Clifford testified he knew about the chamber-loaded indicator, then forgot about it. Well, that highlights how *useless* this indicator is. It doesn't really alert you." He said maybe the military and trained police get some benefit from it. "But the ordinary consumer? He needs a constant reminder."

He glanced at his notes and said the problem of people forgetting to check if there is a round in the chamber is extraordinarily serious. It causes a lot of deaths. That's why you put that warning on the side of the gun.

"Mr. Gebhardt spoke about who is an ordinary consumer, and said the ordinary consumer is not children. Well, ordinary consumers may include children, if children gain access to these guns. An ordinary consumer could also include a police officer who forgets to check the chamber.

"Mr. Gebhardt talked about the risk/benefit analysis. We have the burden of proof on causation. But they do have the burden of proof on the risk/benefit analysis." He said Beretta could have tested all the prototypes, but they never produced any actual evidence that proved those supposed risks of Mr. Roane's designs.

Jon took a step toward the jury box and asked, "What are these supposed problems?" Bredbury had said the gun might crack after firing 10,000 or 15,000 rounds. That's several *lifetimes* of a gun.

Jon said Gebhardt had mentioned that in Italy, engineers had considered internal locks, but the jury didn't hear about that. "If Beretta Italy had tested internal locks and the results helped their case, do you think they would have kept that from you?"

Jon disagreed strongly with the statement that there would be only limited benefits of a better chamber-loaded indicator. He said that if the chamber-loaded indicator was obvious, and if there was an engraved warning that worked in conjunction with it, Clifford would have been reminded about it. It would be very obvious. And Clifford wouldn't even have had to teach Mark about it. It was Beretta's burden to prove it wasn't feasible to do it better, and they did not even approach meeting that burden of proof.

"In closing, I would say to you, the reason we have the law as it is—about a product maker's duty to do what it can to prevent foreseeable injuries caused by foreseeable misuse—is because there are Cliffords all around this country. There were before Kenzo died, and there are today. And there are Marks in those households across the country. The Berettas of this world know that if every time this happens they can escape *their responsibility* by putting it off on the Cliffords and Marks, there will be no change; there will be no more safety; and there will always be more Kenzo Dixes."

Jon returned resolutely to his table and Judge Hodge excused the jurors for the day.

Once the jury had left, Jon objected strongly to Judge Hodge that, in Gebhardt's closing, he had argued there was no evidence of other accidents involving a Beretta 92. Judge Hodge had ruled that Beretta could not make that argument because there was no foundation for doing so, since the gun industry did not keep records or try to find out specifically which brands of guns were involved in accidental shootings.

Judge Hodge admitted that Gebhardt had made a "comment," but said, "I am going to give Mr. Gebhardt the benefit of inadvertence. It certainly is not prejudicial."

Inadvertent? Not prejudicial? Gebhardt had simply ignored Judge Hodge's ruling and Judge Hodge had let him get away with it. The jury was left with the false idea that no Beretta had ever been involved in any other unintentional shootings.

This was crucial, because it seemed to contradict our argument that Mark's shooting of Kenzo was foreseeable. And Gebhardt's inadmissible statement would be in the trial transcript for the jurors to see during their deliberations.

Gebhardt's closing had been devastating, in part because so much of it was true.

Everyone agreed that Clifford's and Mark's negligence caused Kenzo's death. But, contrary to the way Gebhardt had framed it, this was not an either/or—Clifford/Mark *or* Beretta—choice. The law did not force the jury to choose between Beretta *or* Clifford/Mark and let the other entirely off the hook. They could *all* be at fault.

Gebhardt was trying to use Clifford's irresponsible storage of a "protection" gun and Mark's moments of irresponsibility to *erase* Beretta's irresponsibility. Although I thought one bad deed should not erase another, Gebhardt had made a strong argument.

Worse yet, the gun industry itself was partly responsible for creating this irresponsible subculture by emphasizing in their ads the need to have a gun for protection, and to keep it instantly available.

Could Gebhardt now succeed in making Clifford and Mark out to be 100 percent responsible for Kenzo's death? Or, would the jury recognize that the actions of the father and his son were part of a larger pattern that was, or should have been, known—foreseeable—to

Beretta, a pattern about which Beretta had failed to take actions that would prevent deaths like Kenzo's?

We were finally about to see. The case was going to the jury.

# 12

## The Verdict

Judge Hodge instructed the jurors and sent them off to deliberate. Lynn and I paced the courthouse halls with our lawyers, wondering what was going on in that small jury room. Soon we got tired of speculating and just sat on the hard, cold floor, looking at the walls, wondering if we'd be able to force the gun industry to design safer guns.

It took three days of deliberations before the clerk announced that the jury was coming back. To win the trial, we needed nine of the twelve jurors to say yes to a series of questions.

Someone had told me that if, when the jury returns, they don't look at you, that's a bad sign. The jurors filed in, looking grim, but relieved to be done. They didn't look at us.

"Ladies and gentlemen of the jury, have you reached a verdict?" asked Judge Hodge.

The community college student stood up. "Yes, we have."

The clerk got the verdict form from him and Judge Hodge read, "Question number one: Was the Beretta pistol defective because it failed to perform as safely as an ordinary consumer would expect?

"Yes: Three.

"No: Nine.

"Was the Beretta pistol defective because of a risk of danger inherent in its design which outweighs the benefits of that design?

"Yes: Three.

"No: Nine.

"Was there a defect due to Beretta's failure to give an adequate warning of a substantial danger involved in the use of the pistol?"

"Yes: Seven.

"No: Five."

A majority had voted that the warnings were defective. But we needed nine for a victory. The judge said they had not reached a verdict on this question.

"Was this defect a substantial factor in bringing about the death of Kenzo Dix?"

Ten jurors said no and only two said yes. Most had thought that, although the warnings were inadequate, this defect would not have made a difference.

———

I was devastated. We had lost, badly. And I was, despite my heavy heart, very curious to know what had happened in that jury room. How had they reached such odd, seemingly contradictory conclusions—finding that the warnings were defective, but that they were not a substantial factor in Kenzo's death? And why had we lost so badly on whether the gun had failed to perform "as safely as an ordinary consumer would expect"?

The jurors were free to go. But they were finally allowed to talk about the case.

Lynn and I followed them into a small adjoining room and talked with them. Many were quite eager to speak with us. They still looked grim. There was no air of levity, just relief.

I got into a conversation with the community college student who they had chosen as foreman. For some reason, he started telling me how one day when he was a kid, growing up in Wyoming, he and a friend were fooling around with his father's gun—as I recall, a shotgun. He thought it was unloaded and pulled the trigger. It fired into the wall. He looked at me and laughed, "Wow! Isn't that funny?"

"That happens all the time," I said. "People think the gun is unloaded, but it's not. That's why we're here."

He gave me a startled look and his smile evaporated. It had never occurred to him that his funny childhood story was Mark's story. We both knew how that had ended.

I turned and bumped into a juror who said she had voted with us. When I asked her about the deliberations, she glanced quickly around to see if anyone was listening, then up at the ceiling in exasperation and said, "Oh, it was very hard. There were very adamant people on both sides. I feel like I've been beaten up. *You don't know!*" She stepped closer and whispered, "One juror was on our side all through deliberations, right through Thursday, when we quit for the weekend. But when she came back on Monday, she had suddenly changed her vote. Everyone wondered what happened. During a break, she told me she had talked with her husband about the case over the weekend, and he'd convinced her it was completely Clifford's fault. That's what she said."

We both knew that this violated the "admonitions" that Judge Hodge had often explained: that they not form or express any opinion until the entire case was argued, and that they not discuss it among themselves or with anyone else. Her husband, after all, had not heard the testimony, or the law.

In the following days, we asked around to find the best private investigator in the Bay Area—someone to work for us to poll the jury. Beretta's law firm had already hired him! It figured; they had lots of money and were experienced at lawsuits.

So, we searched for someone else. Oddly enough, my book group happened to be reading a memoir titled *Altars in the Street* by Melody Ermachild Chavis, about a woman's attempts to clean up the drug dealing in her South Berkeley / Oakland neighborhood. The book jacket said the author was a private investigator, so I gave her name to Jon.

It turned out that Melody Ermachild (her professional name) was an experienced investigator, although mostly in capital murder cases. We hired her.

Melody conducted in-depth conversations with many of the jurors, taking careful notes. Within a few weeks she had obtained declarations from five jurors, some who had voted against us and some for us. Since some jurors feared retaliation from other jurors, I will use pseudonyms.

Melody's interviews revealed that the trial had touched deeply felt beliefs and emotions on both sides. Each declaration contained explicit and sometimes graphic descriptions of the "atmosphere of hostility" that had pervaded the jury room and interfered with reasoned deliberations.

The first task when the jurors retreated into the jury room was to choose a foreman. The community college student blurted out, "I volunteer myself," even though he had been a loner who sat in a corner during breaks, sometimes watching his portable TV. Another juror nominated Arnold, the burial plot salesman. (All the jurors' names are pseudonyms.) But one juror told Melody that most of them were so antagonized by Arnold that they told the community college student, "Well, since you're volunteering, you be foreman."

Although the student tried to be fair, he was not a strong foreman, and was greatly influenced by Arnold. He called for a vote very early. The defense won slightly more votes than the plaintiffs, but not enough for a verdict. Some jurors were undecided. The foreman immediately shifted the "burden of proof" to the pro-plaintiff jurors, asking them to explain their reasons and try to convince the majority. Those in the majority did not have to explain their reasons. Another juror said, "When we tried to persuade the 'maybes' and 'nos,' that's when Arnold would interrupt and say, 'That's not the issue! That's wrong! That's ridiculous!' You'd start a sentence and then his hand would be up, waving, or he would just interrupt."

Another juror's declaration to the court said, "At times Arnold could barely be controlled. I and others tried making various rules to help jurors be allowed to speak. We tried raising our hands before speaking. We tried making a rule that each speaker would indicate when he or she was finished speaking. None of this worked. Arnold continued to constantly interrupt. He would literally jump out of his chair like a little kid, and interject his opinion." She was bothered that Arnold kept interrupting the pro-plaintiff jurors, and was excessively rude.

Another juror said deliberations became "a screaming match because of Arnold's antics." He would interrupt "in a scathing tone, accompanied by dramatic body language, throw his body back from the table and his arms up to show his outrage at their opinions. Arnold constantly interrupted, he yelled, he belittled; he was aggressive, sarcastic, and demeaning—all of it. We were shifting from what we should have been discussing, because we always had to deal with Arnold. When I wanted to refer to the judge's instructions, Arnold or the foreman would put me down.

"The instructions were never clearly read aloud, nor were most of them ever referred to during the deliberations. I would like to have gone through the whole packet of instructions, because Judge Hodge explained what the various things meant in them. I felt that we'd have been more sure about the correct interpretations if we had done so. For example, I wanted to get a clearer picture of the issue of foreseeable misuse, but some of the others did not want to take the time."

This juror said Arnold made them feel like "hostages" and may have shortened deliberations, because jurors wanted to get away from him and the hostile environment he created.

Just before the final votes, one juror was in such a quandary over how to vote that she was crying. Arnold got up, stood behind her, and began rubbing her neck and shoulders. She and others said they thought Arnold's touching and flirting with female jurors before and during the deliberations was inappropriate.

Early in the trial, Arnold had asked all of them to write their name and address for him. Several jurors said they thought he was going to make copies for everyone, but he never did. During the trial, the jurors were either called or received mail from the mortuary where Arnold worked, asking them if they wanted to buy a funeral plot or crypt. Some were intimidated that they had been contacted at their homes.

Also, according to one juror, before the jurors had heard the full testimony or the law, Arnold had declared, "It was Clifford's responsibility to have stored the gun properly and trained his son properly. The manufacturer has no responsibility, period."

Well before we had presented all of our case, Arnold had stated to another juror, "I believe in parental responsibility, and the person at fault is Clifford." He had said, "There's too much laxness in society. People are not taking responsibility for their actions, so it's Clifford's fault." The juror said, "I heard these statements at various times: early in the trial, at breaks, while we were sitting in groups around the table in the jury room, eating donuts. During testimony by plaintiffs' experts, Arnold carried on a commentary as he sat in the jury box, speaking to the juror who sat next to him. That juror would sometimes whisper replies while I tried to ignore him. At times I would miss the witness's answer because Arnold would be speaking."

Another juror said that Arnold had "openly expressed his opinion for Beretta and against the Dixes." In the jury box, he had interfered with testimony from our experts by snorting to the juror next to him, "That's ridiculous." In fact, I had also heard him say this from my seat, less than ten yards from the jury box.

When we heard the stream of evidence that clearly showed Arnold had prejudged the case and tried to influence others before deliberations, and that he'd disrupted the deliberations, we appealed to Judge Hodge, asking him to declare a mistrial. This was jury misconduct.

However, at the last minute, two of the jurors refused to sign their declarations, even though they had told Melody that everything in their declarations was true. One of them, an immigrant from an underdeveloped country, said she wouldn't sign because she was afraid of retaliation by Arnold or by a juror who she thought had brought a gun into the jury room. (Both Arnold and the woman she thought had a gun were Black, but opinions among the jurors were not divided along racial lines.)

The other juror who did not sign his declaration had already signed a handwritten copy of it, but when the typed copy was brought for his signature, he refused to sign, saying this had already taken too much time; he didn't want to be called into court again, and was having more pressing problems with his girlfriend. Jon felt his statement showed the truth, so he submitted it, unsigned, to Judge Hodge. Melody had to go back to this juror and tell him that his unsigned declaration had been submitted. He became angry and threatened to tell Judge Hodge he'd never met Melody, or that he'd sign a statement saying she'd pestered and coerced him.

Nevertheless, Jon submitted three strong signed declarations and the unsigned one with his brief.

On January 15, 1999, Lynn and I sat with the lawyers from both sides in the empty courtroom for a hearing about our request for a new trial. When Judge Hodge burst through his side door and settled himself at the bench, he was hardly his usual cheery self.

"I don't know how to proceed," he growled. "The document I received just yesterday I read with substantial disquietude. It included an unsigned declaration, which is clearly contrary to law." For a long time, he vented his anger at the lawyers from both sides, but mostly at Jon. He was particularly incensed that in his brief, Jon had pointed out that several jurors had thought a juror, Ms. Roberts, had carried a gun with her at all times, and they thought she probably had it with her in the jury room. Judge Hodge seemed to take the mention of such an idea as an attack on his courtroom. He seemed to think that during deliberations in the jury room, practically anything goes. Finally, the judge looked down at Jon, frowned, and asked, "Did Ms. Roberts have a gun?"

"I don't know, and I can't know," he replied. "And, in fact, in my brief, I made clear that I wasn't saying that she necessarily had it."

The judge lit into him. He said that her declaration "bore the ring of truth," but it sounded to him like Jon was saying she had violated the law and should be prosecuted. He said it was only a casual comment, and that he was sure there was no gun in that jury room. He offered to have her come and be subjected to cross-examination if Jon wanted.

The judge was worked up. "You know, I've been sitting here a long time, and I've seen hundreds, thousands of jury trials. There isn't a perfect one in the lot. We don't bring to this proceeding professional jurors. We don't bring jurists in robes who have been trained. We bring people off the street, regular people, a jury of your peers, your clients' peers. And we impose upon them greatly." He said, "We require them to listen to and follow the law. We require that they listen to complicated and technical facts. This process comes flawed, and it is flawed. But, Mr. Lowy, it works. I'm sorry. It works again and again. The jury reaches the result that is appropriate under the evidence. I have very little faith in certain parts of our system, but what I believe in is having the twelve people come in and be the conscience of our community."

Jon had occasionally tried to speak. Finally, he got his chance. "Well, first of all, Your Honor, about Ms. Roberts—what I said in the brief is exactly the truth, that a juror said that Ms. Roberts said she had a gun that she carried with her all the time, and that scared the juror. Another juror told our investigator the same thing. The question, Your Honor, is what effect [this had] in the jury room." Jon said that it scared the two jurors, and that this was serious.

"And, Your Honor, I believe very much in the jury system, too," Jon continued. "This process today is one of the checks in the jury system. And cases are filed and remanded back for a new trial because of misconduct much less egregious than this."

Judge Hodge, still scowling, would have none of it. "I am finding that as a matter of fact in this case, Ms. Roberts did not have a gun, and that her comments about the gun were grossly misconstrued." He read from the declaration that Beretta's investigator had obtained. Ms. Roberts had said she never carried a gun during the trial, and that in the first courtroom we'd been in, there had been metal detectors. During jury deliberations she had told a couple of jurors that she owned a gun, and had joked, "I never leave home without it." She said there was no place on her she could have concealed a gun during the course of the trial.

As Judge Hodge read, I agreed she probably didn't have a gun in the jury room. But many people in Oakland have guns, and carry them, and many people are afraid of those with guns.

221

Now the judge seemed so angry at us that I was afraid he might be reluctant to listen to the evidence we had of jury misconduct and grant us a new trial.

Finally, he asked Jon what his best point was. With relief, Jon said we had clear evidence that Arnold had prejudged the case long before the jury had heard all the testimony, or the relevant law. He had discussed the case with other jurors and tried to influence them before deliberations even began. Jon also argued that Arnold's disruptive and aggressive behavior during deliberations was evidence he had prejudged the case.

After more harangue, Judge Hodge declared that if he believed the plaintiffs' case was unlikely to win, even if they got a new trial, then he could deny the request for a new trial. He ruled that the plaintiffs were unlikely to prevail, "given the tragic but also peculiar circumstances of Clifford's extreme negligence, and that of his son."

He thought Clifford's negligence was *peculiar!* If by "peculiar" he meant uncommon or unusual, that belief struck me as wrong, and contrary to the facts we had presented. The un-rebutted testimony of Professor Teret was that such behavior was not peculiar at all; it was extremely common, even though it was highly unfortunate and unsafe.

Although Judge Hodge did not grant us another trial, he made no ruling on the issue of jury misconduct. He believed the outcome of this trial was going to be appealed no matter what, so he would let the Appeals Court deal with it.

A week later Judge Hodge denied our motion to strike court costs. Unless his denial of our appeal for a new trial was overturned by the Appeals Court, Lynn and I would have to pay $24,246 of Beretta USA's court costs. Those costs would include, for example, the expenses incurred for Larry Keane, representative of the gun industry's trade association, to participate in the trial—it seemed to me, so that he could help other gun manufacturers defend themselves against similar lawsuits when children die due to unsafe gun designs.

Our appeal provided the evidence of jury misconduct. It also stated that un-rebutted evidence had shown that it was clearly foreseeable to Beretta that many people are killed when guns are stored loaded and unlocked. As a result of the missing but feasible internal lock, prominent chamber-loaded indicator, and emphatic warnings, the foreseeable had occurred, but could have been prevented.

We had lost the trial. Our appeal sat in some in-box as time dragged on.

# PART IV

# The Tribulations

# 13

## Heartache

Before our loss in court, I had become involved in gun violence prevention, and had met hundreds of people who had suddenly lost a loved one to gun violence.

At a Coalition to Stop Gun Violence conference, Tina Johnstone from New York told me about the death of her husband, David. He had been on a business trip in San Francisco in 1992, when a young boy who was planning to rob him shot David in the back, perhaps unintentionally, severing his spinal cord.

Tina asked me to join her and Ellen Freudenheim to organize the 1996 Silent March, an event which would educate the public about the toll of American gun violence in a uniquely moving way. We identified potential activists in almost every state, and asked them to get people to donate pairs of shoes equal in number to those killed with guns in one year in their state. They held rallies at their state capitols, displaying the shoes, then shipped the total—almost 40,000 pairs of shoes—to Washington, DC, where we laid them out at the Capitol reflecting pool on September 30, 1996. It was the nation's largest gun violence prevention rally to date, covered by every major TV network, with news stories written or broadcast in over eight hundred newspapers and TV stations.

Then, at our trial in 1998, I came face-to-face with the VP of the company that had sold the gun that killed my son, and with the VP of the trade association of the entire US gun industry, whose job was to help the industry sell as many guns as possible. Few people affected by gun violence have the opportunity to observe so closely the men who they thought were, in part, responsible for their son's death, and to hear them try to justify themselves.

What I saw in court made me even more curious about the gun industry.

While I waited impatiently to hear the results of our appeal, I got intensely involved in work on passing California and federal gun laws. I met even more victims of gun violence who were experiencing the same turmoil I was. Some of them had lost their children because of unsafe gun designs, and, as I worked in collaboration with them, I learned more about faulty gun designs and their tragic effects.

Meanwhile, I continued my computer industry research business, doing multi-client studies, mainly of professionals in electronic publishing and digital video. Although the field was exciting and my client companies were interested in my research, after Kenzo's death, my interests shifted toward gun violence prevention.

Every day I managed to get to the small office I had rented in Berkeley, almost next door to the world-famous Chez Panisse restaurant. I did what I had to in order to keep my computer industry research projects going, but as soon as I could, I would turn to studies about gun violence, especially those that pertained to the circumstances of Kenzo's death.

I shifted more and more of my paying work to the UC Berkeley undergraduates I hired. As time went on, I felt little interest in expanding my successful business. Afternoons I would sit in my cluttered office and read, feeding the beast that gnawed inside me. My investigation was no mere academic exercise; it cut to the bone.

Late in the day, I would look up and see the sun already setting. My shoulders ached with tension, my stomach was tight, my breathing shallow. The vise-like pressure in my neck and shoulders would send me rushing out into the cool evening air. I frequently walked the block to Black Oak Books on Shattuck Avenue to order specialized books on gun policy.

One day, by chance, I got an impromptu lesson in the lasting impact of trauma.

I was browsing in Black Oak Books when I noticed a young man who looked familiar. Finally, it hit me. He was Steven (a pseudonym), one of Kenzo's best friends. During their entire freshman year, he had been away in a foreign country. I had not seen him in years.

Now sporting a stylish beard, he had grown tall and strikingly handsome. I said hello and reintroduced myself. He told me he was still deeply disturbed by Kenzo's death, even though he had not been at Berkeley High School to experience the collective grief with all of Kenzo's other friends.

Speaking softly, with compassionate, sad eyes, he told me he was now attending college far away, but that whenever he left to go there, he experienced waves of anxiety. In fact, an irrational fear came over him whenever he left home on a trip. He had difficulty shaking off the thought that someone he loved, such as his mother, might be killed while he was away, and that his leaving would itself bring on the tragedy.

I felt enormous tenderness for him, and for so many of the friends who had suffered from the sudden, incomprehensible loss of Kenzo.

Gradually I filled an eight-foot-tall bookshelf in my office with books and government reports about gun laws and loopholes. I kept buying more four-drawer file cabinets, or picking up old, battered ones. I filled them with studies by academic researchers, many of whom were in university departments of public health and were asking the same questions I was. Perhaps my training as a cultural anthropologist—my need to see the cultural and political context that had led to Kenzo's death—was not so good for me. The more I learned, the more I hurt.[22]

After Christmas 1999 and New Year's, in January 2000, I began to notice something more than tension and hot anger at what I was learning. I was feeling pain in my chest. At first, I dismissed it as stress. But day by day it worsened, becoming a persistent ache that I kept trying to ignore.

One evening at my office, after a day of reading studies and discovering new political machinations, I looked out my window at the gathering dusk and suddenly sensed how tightly wound my body was. Realizing that I had been tense for hours, I straightened the piles on my desk, escaped from the stuffy room, and drove home.

From there, seeking relief, I walked down to the cemetery where Kenzo is buried. As it grew dark, a fog spread across the bay toward the hills. I could make out a few does and their fawns grazing near his grave. They looked up at me without alarm, then continued. I thought vaguely that if Kenzo's spirit was somehow there, he'd be delighted. The deer would pass the evenings together in Kenzo's easy affection. I could feel my tension ebb.

After a bit of quiet reflection on Kenzo and the joys he had brought us, I turned and climbed back uphill. By the time I approached the cemetery gate, the pain in my chest had grown intense. I could take only a few steps before I had to stop and wait for it to subside. This was something new, as if some unfriendly hand was clenching my heart each time I advanced even a few steps.

I called my doctor, who referred me to cardiologist John "Jack" Edelen, who was around my age, and willing to explain things to me. I told him about my chest pain and the stress I felt daily from Kenzo's death, our trial against Beretta, and my obsession with loopholes in gun laws. I asked him if feeling so much stress for an extended period of time could cause chest pain, and asked if it was serious.

He said yes, stress can cause heart disease. It can raise your heart rate and increase your blood pressure and your need for oxygen, which can bring on chest pain. His description of the way extended periods of stress can cause symptoms like mine seemed to fit my experience—the hours spent in my office, studying the gun lobby, and the vise-like tension in my body. Dr. Edelen also said hormones released during stress can injure the lining of the arteries, and as they heal, they may thicken, allowing plaque to build up. He scheduled a test for me the next day.

At the testing facility, they wired me up, injected contrast dye into my blood vessels, took pictures of my heart at rest, then ran me faster and faster up an inclined treadmill. When my heart reached the target rate they quickly laid me down, hooked up the monitor again, and compared the shape of my heart working at high speed with the image of it at rest.

On the monitor, I could see the slow-pulsing heart next to the racing one, digitally slowed down so the images were in sync.

"What does it show?" I asked.

The technician pointed his finger at a lower section of the racing heart. "This section is not expanding and pumping blood the way it should."

My cardiologist made time to do an angiogram the next day. They cut a hole near my groin, wired me up, shot some radioactive slush into me, and rolled me into an impressive dark cavern of a room dominated by a hard slab bed under a monstrous, mobile scanning device. Lying under it, I could see black fluid pulsing through root-like branches of the blood vessels surrounding my heart. Enough black lines pulsed that I could make out the shape of my heart itself, contracting and expanding—the basic rhythm at the core of my life.

Dr. Edelen pointed his white-gloved finger up to a spot on the monitor where a thick descending artery suddenly narrowed to almost nothing. He had to do an angioplasty and place several stents in that spot, and others, where the blood vessels feeding my heart were blocked by gummy plaque.

He held up a stent for me to see. It looked like the tiny pieces of chicken wire I had seen my grandmother in Virginia use to patch the fence that kept her chickens from scurrying outside the coop. That made me think of the big, stained chopping block where my father had axed those chickens' necks. We kids would watch them run around headless until they collapsed, then we'd take them in for my grandmother to pluck and fry on her old wood-burning stove.

Finally, they rolled me into a bright hospital room with a big window. Wires and mysterious electronic doodads surrounded my bed. A business-like blonde nurse chatted me up as she stuck an oxygen tube into my nose, helped me with my short, revealing cotton gown, shaved hair off spots on my chest, wiped cold goop on each spot, and hooked a fistful of wires from my chest and head to an impressive pink monitor. When she was done, columns of lights were flashing up and down, sending signals out somewhere.

For a while I rested alone, thinking about what had brought me there. In only a few years my younger son had been shot and killed; my older son had gone away to college; I'd moved out of my home; my wife and I had divorced; and I had taken up living alone. I had suffered the loss in our trial, and was waiting for the decision on our appeal. I had learned about all the loopholes that had led to my son's death.

From my hospital bed, I looked down into the backyards of nearby homes and wondered what sorts of traumas the people who lived there had endured.

Suddenly my reverie was interrupted. An elderly man on a gurney was rolled in through the open door. His round stomach bulged under a light green blanket. When the nurse and a hefty male helper hoisted him onto his bed, we looked at each other through gaps in the curtain between us. He had a dark complexion and a round, lined face. He smiled patiently, looking remarkably accustomed to the whole routine. As the nurse poked and swabbed him as though she was buttering a big turkey for the grill, he amiably asked her where she was from. Did she have any family? How long had she worked here? She knew her craft, too, and kept the banter going.

When she left, we introduced ourselves.

"I'm Carlos," he said, glancing sideways at me. "This will be my third open-heart surgery. I know it's going to kill me sometime soon," he said matter-of-factly. "Maybe this time, maybe next. When it's your time, it's your time. My doctor tells me not to eat fat and to take it easy. But we eat Mexican food; it's full of fat. That's what we eat. I can't change that."

He asked me why I was there. I told him about my angioplasty and the stress I was feeling from Kenzo's death and everything that had caused it.

"Yeah, that'll do it—too much stress," he said. "I have that, too. Sometimes my heart just stops. So they planted one of those shock devices near my heart. You wouldn't believe what it's like when that thing goes off—never felt anything like it." He squirmed. "I was lying in bed and all of a sudden, blam, it threw me on the floor. Like you've been hit by a freight train."

He told me about his big close-knit, fractious Mexican-American family—wife and kids, grandchildren, nieces and nephews, with generational conflicts as the younger ones became more Americanized and stopped listening to their parents. He was funny, sad, and philosophical as he lay there looking at the ceiling—facing death. Occasionally we turned our heads to make eye contact when one of us mentioned something especially revealing.

At three in the afternoon, he clicked on the TV that hung on the wall at the foot of our beds. Oprah walked onto the set, radiant as always. After some preliminaries, she announced the subject: parents and unruly teenagers. As a few guests spoke about the problem, Carlos got quiet.

Suddenly we were watching a video of a teenage girl wearing a short, tight skirt coming into a small kitchen. Her mother snapped at her in a heavy accent, "You can't go out looking like that! Anyway, remember, you're grounded." The teenager shrieked back, "Shut up and mind your own business. I'm old enough. I can make my own decisions...you're living in the past." She yelled that all her friends dressed like this, and she was tired of her mother's rules. She was going to do what she wanted.

I heard gasps, then steamy expletives exploding from the bed next to mine. I looked over. Carlos was grimacing and straining to lift his head as if to break loose from the wires and bust the TV. His face was tense and deep red. The veins in his neck bulged as if they would burst.

I was dumbfounded. In an instant he'd been transformed from the easygoing guy I'd been chatting with to a cauldron of anger. He flipped his head my way and spit out, "Fuckin' kids. No respect. Like my goddamn granddaughters and nieces."

"Hey, man, what's up with you? You'll hurt yourself. Take it easy."

I tried to calm him down, thinking he was going to fry the wires stuck in his head. This sassy teen had pushed all his buttons. I was about to press the gizmo the nurse had strung on my guardrail, but the video of the teen and her mother ended.

Carlos eased back down onto his pillow, but kept grumbling. On the TV a few experts told Carlos and me how to handle teenagers like that.

A while later I felt I could ask, "Carlos, what's up with you? How come you got so upset?"

"I know it's going to kill me someday. But those goddamned kids make me so mad. They won't listen to nobody. They'll be the death of my daughters. I know it. One of my granddaughters already ran away."

"Well, take it easy. You'll hurt yourself. If you do that again, I'll call the nurse."

But then I thought: Wait a minute. Who am I to be giving advice like that? Carlos's anger was hurting him; it was going to kill him. But at least he knew it.

After he calmed down, we watched more TV, ate canned fruit, crackers, and green Jell-O with petrified fruit. Then we both slept.

The next morning an outdoorsy nurse burst in cheerily and started plucking wires off me. I liked her no-nonsense manner, and noticed she wasn't wearing a wedding ring. So, with a tube for oxygen sticking up my nose and my head and chest hair greasy from gunk where she'd stuck wires, I asked her, "Would you like to get a cup of coffee sometime?"

With a tender look of pity, she smiled at me, lying there helpless in my little gown.

"Sorry—I make it a rule never to date my patients." She might as well have finished her sentence with "who might soon die of a heart attack."

It wasn't one of my better moments.

That night, settling down into my own bed, I thought of Carlos, the ticking time bomb. His anger wasn't solving his problems; it wasn't any help to his daughters or their families. It wasn't changing the behavior of his grandkids. It was only hurting him. The funny thing was, he seemed to know this, and admitted he was unable to control it.

And then I thought of all the ways I was like him—maybe worse. Wasn't I allowing all the things I was learning about the gun lobby to hurt me? It didn't improve the situation—it just made things worse for me, without being any help to anyone else.

I could, of course, sidestep the emotional turmoil I was feeling by avoiding the gun issue entirely, or I could build on my nascent activism by turning my tragedy into action. But if I did, I'd have to find a way to avoid letting my anger hurt me.

Carlos's sudden explosion in the hospital had placed a mirror before me. And Dr. Edelen recommended a stress management class that was helpful. After that, I began searching for other ways to become more aware of my anger, to manage it, but also to do something constructive with it. I would not let it kill me.

We would go ahead with our lawsuit if we won our appeal. I would continue my activism. I couldn't stop. I would have to find a way to ensure that everything I was learning—which rightly made me angry—would not harm me. I knew many other activists, people I respected, who were coping with the same challenges. I could see that gradually, many of them were coming to terms with their grief, and that their activism helped them find meaning and purpose out of their tragedy.

By mid-2000, most major computer companies working in electronic publishing and digital video were buying my studies. The person I worked with at Apple told me that Steve Jobs found them useful.

But preventing gun violence had become my primary interest, so I closed my research company.[23] I would work full-time on gun violence prevention from this point on.

# 14

## New Hope

### *Reversible Error*

On June 27, 2000, more than a year and a half after we had appealed the loss of our case, the California First Appellate District Court ruled unanimously, 3–0, that Judge Hodge's ruling against a mistrial had been an incorrect "reversible error." It remanded the matter back to his court to determine whether juror misconduct had occurred.

The Appeals Court said strongly that since the votes regarding "defect" of the gun had been 9 to 3, if one juror's vote was the result of juror misconduct, the injured litigants should receive a new trial. By subtracting one juror's vote, Beretta USA had 8 votes, not the 9 they needed to win.

As to Judge Hodge's statement that we were unlikely to win our case, the Appeals Court said he had used "an incorrect standard of harmless error" and had not resolved the factual dispute, so it had no choice but to reverse his ruling denying our motion for a new trial.

When we all met again with Judge Hodge, he quoted Gilbert and Sullivan: "Whenever applying the law of the case, I understand fully my place." Ultimately, he granted us a new trial because of jury misconduct.

Beretta appealed his decision; they always appealed everything they could, adding to our costs. Their appeal paid off this time. Our "failure to warn" argument—perhaps our best, as the judge had said—was stripped away. Most of the jurors (7 to 5) had voted that there was a defect due to Beretta's failure to warn adequately, primarily in the pistol's manual. But then the jurors had voted 10 to 2 that the defect was not a substantial factor in Kenzo's death. Even with one juror subtracted, the remaining 9 votes were still enough for the Appeals Court to disallow "failure to warn" as one of our causes of action in the subsequent trial.

Perhaps those jurors thought Clifford was hopeless. But I believed that with a better manual that included very prominent warnings and an engraving visible on the gun, Kenzo could still be alive. Now, however, the manual and other "warnings" could not appear as an item on the jury verdict form in the next trial. That hurt our chances.

Jon Lowy was busy with other cases, and we all decided we should seek another trial lawyer—but not immediately. So we waited for the new trial. Years passed.

### *Organizing Against Gun Industry Legal Immunity*

On November 7, 2002, at a status conference at the Superior Court in Oakland with Judge Henry Needham, we settled on a new trial

238

date distant enough in time to accommodate Beretta USA's lawyer, Craig Livingston, who had asked for the delay.

When I e-mailed Jon Lowy about it, his reply made me feel that the ground could be yanked out from under us before we ever got to trial. "The gun industry is making a big push for a federal gun-industry-immunity bill that would probably do away with your case and every other case we're involved in. It's at the top of the NRA's agenda." He said the Republicans hoped to pass it quickly. "We're fighting it, but it's tough." I wanted to do what I could to help.

A struggle on many fronts was raging over lawsuits.[24] Thirty-two US cities were suing the gun industry for endangering the public. Individuals were suing, too.[25] In response, the gun industry was trying to get Congress to grant it this special immunity from civil lawsuits.

Meanwhile, the gun violence prevention movement was evolving. In 2000, Handgun Control, Inc., had changed its name to the Brady Campaign to Prevent Gun Violence, to honor Sarah and James Brady. Jim Brady had been President Ronald Reagan's press secretary when Brady was shot and badly injured in an attempted assassination that almost killed the president. President Bill Clinton had signed the Brady Background Check bill into law in 1993, and three years later, Jim Brady had received the Presidential Medal of Freedom, the nation's highest civilian honor.

I had founded the Oakland / Alameda County Chapter of the Bell Campaign, an organization started by Andrew McGuire, whose favorite cousin had been killed with a gun when he was twelve. Our chapter became a Million Mom March chapter, and in 2000, a Brady chapter after the Million Mom March and Brady organizations merged.

That occurred because a remarkable woman, Donna Dees-Thomases, had initiated a powerful protest that helped us organize locally and nationally, and fight the gun-industry-immunity bill. On August 10, 1999, on her TV she saw frightened children from the North Valley Jewish Community Center in Granada Hills holding hands in a chain and running across a street, away from a gunman. Cops on each end of the line were anxiously scanning the area for shooters. The attacker was Buford Furrow, a member of the Aryan Nations, a militant Neo-Nazi anti-Semitic group.[26]

Dees-Thomases, a publicist with the *Late Show with David Letterman*, whose daughters attended a nursery school like that one, said, "Those children could have been mine." Starting from scratch, she began to organize what would become a huge gun violence prevention rally: the Million Mom March.

With about two dozen other activists in our Oakland Bell Campaign Chapter, I began organizing an Oakland Million Mom March rally. I had been at a low point, but this offered me something positive to work for. When Mother's Day 2000 finally arrived, over 5,000 people came and stood in light rain in Oakland. At the last minute, I decided to go to the Million Mom March in DC, where over 750,000 of us rallied on the National Mall. I met California senators Dianne Feinstein and Barbara Boxer that day, and soon after, I joined the California Million Mom March Chapters State Council.

Mary Leigh Blek, our state president, suggested I write a newsletter, *Chapter Chat*. It went out to the members of our twenty California chapters, and activists in other states. Every issue covered federal and California gun legislation, and gave tips about how to organize, as well as suggestions for writing letters to the editor and op-ed essays.

Not long after Kenzo died, I had testified before the California Assembly Public Safety Committee for a firearm safe-storage bill, which Assembly member Richard Rainey had voted against, effectively killing it. After meeting Rainey that day, I had vowed to defeat him.

The first *Chapter Chat* issue of November 17, 2000, described how our Oakland / Alameda County Chapter had joined our new Contra Costa County Chapter to distribute over 5,000 leaflets, educating people about the voting record of Richard Rainey, now a senator in the California legislature. We had raised over $800 for ads in four newspapers to help Tom Torlakson defeat Rainey. Finally, we had beaten him.

One 2002 issue of *Chapter Chat* celebrated that the Million Moms had sent the "Gun Industry to Bed, No Dinner" by repealing California's gun-industry-immunity law, which the industry had utilized to deny justice to the victims of the 101 California Street massacre, in their suit against Navegar, the company that had advertised assault weapons with "excellent resistance to fingerprints."

By then both sides of this issue had grown stronger. We had held huge Million Mom March rallies on Mother's Day 2000. But in November 2000, the Supreme Court had stopped the vote counting in Florida, handing George W. Bush the presidency, and turning the gun-industry-immunity issue into a major cause for conservatives.

In April 2002, Larry Keane testified for the "Protection of Lawful Commerce in Arms Act" (H.R. 2037) before a House subcommittee. He portrayed the National Shooting Sports Foundation as a sports organization that manages programs for "active participation in the shooting sports." Keane said lawsuits against gun makers and dealers were an improper attempt to regulate firearms, and to circumvent state legislatures and Congress.

But we just wanted product liability laws to be enforced in court against gun makers and distributors, as they were with every other product.

It looked like Republicans would send President Bush a federal immunity bill. But then, in October of 2002, a sniper began randomly shooting people who were going about their business in public places around Washington, DC, Maryland, and Virginia. These shootings dominated the news and riveted the public day after day.

After three weeks, John Allen Muhammad, forty-one, and Lee Boyd Malvo, a minor, were found sleeping in a car at an Interstate 70 rest stop in Maryland. They were arrested on weapons charges. Officers found a Bushmaster .223 caliber XM-15 assault rifle in the car. Ballistics tests identified it as the weapon used in eleven of the shootings.

The sniper story, while tragic, played into our hands. But in the 2002 election, after the September 11, 2001, terrorist attacks, Republicans took control of both the House and the Senate. Most Republicans supported the federal gun-industry-immunity bill.

Nevertheless, in January 2003, Jon Lowy and the Brady Legal Action Project joined a Washington state law firm to sue Bull's Eye Shooter Supply of Tacoma, Washington, and Bushmaster Firearms of Windham, Maine, on behalf of the families of the snipers' victims.

Their plaintiffs' brief argued that Bull's Eye had run its gun store in a grossly negligent manner, which allowed dozens of its guns to routinely "disappear" from its store. The plaintiffs also said the gun shop kept such shoddy records that it was unable to account for the DC snipers' Bushmaster assault rifle when federal agents asked for the weapon's records of sale. At least 238 guns had disappeared from Bull's Eye in the previous three years, said the brief.

Both Muhammad and Malvo had been prohibited from purchasing firearms; Muhammad's wife had obtained a restraining order against him, and Malvo was a minor. The negligent practices of gun industry defendants had allowed the two shooters to obtain the Bushmaster assault rifle, said the complaint.

The brief also said Bushmaster had failed to adequately screen the dealers of its guns to see whether they sold and stored them responsibly. Nor had Bushmaster trained its employees, implemented proper inventory control, or instituted sound sales policies (including regular training of employees on how to spot illegal sales). The foreseeable result of the negligence was illegal access to deadly weapons by prohibited persons, and the slaughter of Americans, said the brief.

The case was settled out of court. Bull's Eye's contribution to the settlement was $2 million, and Bushmaster's, $500,000. Bushmaster agreed to educate its dealers to prevent this from happening again.

The Brady Legal Action Project had won a major victory for the victims of the DC snipers.

But the gun industry kept pushing for immunity from lawsuits for gun makers like Bushmaster and gun dealers like Bull's Eye. In opposition, activists were reaching out to local media. I published an op-ed, "No Lawsuit Immunity for Gun Industry," in the *San Francisco Chronicle*, on February 19, 2003. "[I]f the gun lobby's pending legislation becomes law," I wrote, "our family will have no right to seek justice, even though my son was the victim of a defectively designed gun used by another child (a 'criminal' use). If he were killed by any other defectively designed product, from a BB gun to an automobile, the manufacturer would be held responsible."

Partly because gun violence prevention groups across the nation made many people aware of the injustice of granting immunity to gun dealers and gun makers, the leaders of the gun industry quietly decided to shelve their immunity bill and wait until the public's attention turned elsewhere.

Finally, Lynn and I and Jon Lowy knew we would get the new trial we had been promised.

# 15

## Try, Try Again

### *Bulldog*

*Here we go again*, I fretted. I knew that the experience of a new trial would bring up powerful mixed feelings, including my anger at Beretta. I assumed the second trial would be like the first.

It turned out I was wrong.

The Brady Center to Prevent Gun Violence had found a San Francisco law firm, Keker & Van Nest, and an up-and-coming star lawyer, Elliot Peters, who might represent us, if after he met us, he and his law partners thought our case had merit.

I looked up his one-page bio online. "New York University School of Law, 1985, Yale University, 1980." Okay, I thought, he's a bulldog.

245

He had graduated *cum laude* from Yale, majoring in philosophy. Good; a smart philosopher bulldog.

"Elliot litigates all manner of complex civil and white-collar criminal cases," his bio said. In addition, as a public prosecutor, he had put bad guys in jail. In fact, in 1991 he had received the Department of Justice Director's Medal for being one of the most effective federal prosecutors in the country. He had prosecuted the famous *United States v. Paccione* racketeering case concerning New York City's giant trash-hauling industry. I remembered reading about that huge case, which involved the Mob's lucrative dominance of garbage contracts.

Elliot was an expert in trash and the Mob. He sounded to me like just the guy to take on the gun lobby.

Later, after he did decide to represent us, I mused over why a corporate lawyer like Elliot Peters would take a case like ours. Then I recalled an important sentence at the end of his bio: "Elliot Peters has three children."

Soon after we met him, Elliot would entertain us with stories about his two spirited daughters and active little son. When he spoke of his kids, he could not hide the joy they gave him. Lynn and I knew he understood our love for Kenzo and Kalani. I believe Elliot's sense of the extraordinary love a parent can have for his children was the main reason that he, despite having many lucrative cases to choose from, took on a cutting-edge but difficult case like ours. He cared about protecting children.

As I got to know Elliot, I also found that, as his bio suggested, he was a tenacious inner-game-of-tennis competitor in the courtroom. His job allowed him to observe at close range the extremes of human nature in the midst of bitter disputes that had escalated into courtroom battles. He was clever at judging how far he could push his opposition in testimony and cross-examination. Maybe it was his philosophy background combined with years of prosecuting bizarre varieties of hard-core criminals, but he had become an expert judge of human character. I noticed that he plotted every action, took the steps necessary, then carefully observed his opponent's response, to see what it suggested as a follow-up. He had a feel for what could make a carefully composed rascal squirm—or make him drop his disguise just long enough for the jury to glimpse the real person hidden behind it.

Judge Gordon Baranco, a middle-aged man, began the new trial on December 2, 2003. Rather than cracking jokes to entertain the jury, as Judge Hodge had done, Judge Baranco was strict and tight-lipped. He announced his decisions quickly without allowing much argument from the lawyers. He would make the trial run like clock-work, according to his interpretation of the law.

Elliot was aided by his law partner Daralyn Durie, a tall, athletic graduate of Stanford with undergraduate degrees in human biology and comparative lit, and Jamie Slaughter, another Yalie, who was hoping to make partner.

Throughout the agonizing process of jury selection, we wondered what biases might lie hidden in the mind of each prospective juror. This time during jury selection, Elliot and Daralyn asked each poten-tial juror, "Do you believe that something can have several different causes?" They all replied that of course it can. Once again, several potential jurors said they didn't like guns and would have trouble being unbiased, so Judge Baranco dismissed them. I worried, how-ever, that the "pro-gun" ones did not announce their biases as openly. Eventually we had an entire set of twelve jurors and two alternates.

Daralyn Durie's opening statement was succinct and clear. She began by telling the jury that this trial was about whether Beretta USA had sold a gun that was defective. The Beretta gun, she said, had two specific design defects that made it unreasonably dangerous for use in a family setting for home protection: First, the chamber-loaded indicator was defectively designed and didn't do its job of telling people whether there was a bullet in the chamber; and second, the gun didn't have a built-in lock.

"And let me tell you what this case is *not* about," she declared. "There has already been a lot of discussion [during jury selection] about the responsibility of gun owners to store their guns properly and about the responsibility of gun users to use guns responsibly. We don't disagree with any of that. This case is not about whether Clifford and Mark are responsible for the death of Kenzo Dix, because they are. That is an undisputed fact. This case—and what you'll be asked to decide—is whether Beretta is *also* responsible."

Standing erect before an attentive jury, she said there were three issues: What did Beretta know? What did Beretta do? And what *should* Beretta have done? Beretta knew or should have known that some of its customers leave their guns loaded and unlocked in homes with teenagers. Beretta knew that every year in this country, many children die because exactly this kind of accident happens. Beretta knew that many people think when you take the magazine out of a pistol, you've unloaded the gun. And Beretta knew that people often forget to pull back the slide and physically look to see whether there is a bullet in the chamber.

The evidence will show, she continued, that many people die every year because they make just these mistakes. The evidence will also show that gun designers, for a hundred years, have tried to come up with solutions to the problem that a bullet may still be hidden in the chamber. Beretta sold this gun with a promise that it had solved that problem. But it hadn't. Clifford had shot this gun thousands of times and he didn't even realize that the gun had a chamber-loaded indicator, because in all of his time handling it, he'd never seen it.

The experts will tell you, she continued, that the chamber-loaded indicator on this gun is not only hard to see; it's also ambiguous, because even when the gun is *unloaded*, it sticks out a little bit and shows some red. And the evidence will show that Beretta did nothing to determine whether its customers could use this chamber-loaded indicator, or to determine whether it would be possible to make it better.

She introduced Stephen Teret's qualifications and said he would testify that accidents like this are readily foreseeable, and the *best* way to address them is to make changes in the design of the product itself. Vaughn Adams would testify that this chamber-loaded indicator is not designed in accordance with the principles of safety engineering, and he would describe the advantages of an internal lock.

She introduced our family—Lynn, Kalani, and me—and said we would also testify.

When she said, "But there is one person you will not hear from during this trial, because he's not here, and that person is Kenzo Dix," I felt a sudden wave of emotion rise in my chest. I hadn't known she was headed there.

Daralyn Durie's opening statement had been clear, straightforward, compelling, and convincing. Hope swelled inside me.

Wearing a conservative business suit, Craig Livingston rose and stood before the jury, clean-cut and eager. Here was the former cop who had been Beretta USA's junior lawyer in the previous trial. In a firm voice, he told the jury that this case was about responsibility, but that the plaintiffs were saying the Beretta Model 92 Compact L was a bad design. So the jury would hear more than they ever wanted to know about that design—how the gun is made, what its features are, "and how it played a role in this tragedy in the hands of an untrained user and in the hands of someone who had no business storing it the way it was stored."

Livingston said many Beretta Italy employees are engineers from top engineering schools in Italy. That launched him into a long introduction to the Model 92. The durability and reliability of a firearm are critical, he said, and the Model 92 is one of the safest, most reliable, most durable pistols around, and that's why it has become the choice of a lot of police departments, and the US military. It's a simple device that works reliably every time.

He said that when the military wanted to replace the venerable old Colt Model 1911 pistol, it conducted a series of tests, and the Beretta Model 92 won. He repeated several times that Beretta had already been making the gun before they'd won the military contract.

Why was he emphasizing it was a gun for consumers? I knew Beretta had sold its handgun to the military essentially at cost to penetrate the much larger market of less-trained consumers, many of whom wanted a gun immediately available for protection—and many of whom lived in homes with kids. This fact would continue to bother me as I learned that this marketing strategy was hardly unique.[27]

Livingston mentioned, with obvious admiration, that Berettas had sailed through the sandbox test, the high- and low-temperatures test, and the mud test, in which pistols are submerged in mud and then pulled out and fired.

My anger began to rise. This gun was going into consumer homes, but there was no mention of an "after-someone-takes-out-the-loaded-magazine-does-he-think-this-gun-is-still-loaded?" test, which would have been far more relevant than a sandbox or mud test. There was no mention of a "does-this-gun's-extractor-work-for-consumers-as-a-chamber-loaded-indicator?" test.

Next, Livingston went over several safety features which were probably well-designed, such as one to prevent firing when the pistol is dropped, and one to prevent the trigger from being pulled unless the slide is fully forward.

He touted the chamber-loaded indicator for its "ingenious design." The extractor pulls out the spent cartridge casing when the gun fires, but this one does double duty as a tiny chamber-loaded indicator on the side of the gun.

Livingston was delivering his lines in an easily understandable way, and the jury seemed to like him. Yet he lacked the dismissive humor and subtly contemptuous manner that Bob Gebhardt had deployed so effectively in the first trial.

Finally, Livingston stated that this tragedy began with a profound lack of parental judgment on the part of Clifford, who, he said, knew a lot about firearms. He enumerated in excruciating detail Clifford's purchase and use of his five guns, and how Clifford kept the Beretta loaded and unlocked in a camera bag next to his bed.

Beretta's lawyer systematically recited what happened that day in Mark's room.

"Without saying anything to Kenzo, Mark decides he wants to impress his friend, so he goes downstairs." He said that when Mark was in his father's bedroom, he pulled the pistol out, took the loaded magazine out, and took an empty magazine out of the bag. He didn't put it in the Beretta until he got back to his bedroom. But then, "a few feet from Kenzo, he takes the magazine, and he wants to make this sound, which is exactly what he does."

Livingston manipulated the pistol in the crowded courtroom and jammed in an empty magazine. "That's not enough for Mark; he wants to go one step better. He wants to make the sound of the hammer falling, but he's got to do something before he can make that sound, because right now the gun is on 'safe.' So, in this fatal act of foolishness, he takes the safety off. Now when he pulls the trigger, that's the sound he wants to hear."

Violating another basic safety rule, Livingston pulled the trigger and we heard a loud click when the hammer surged forward. "That's not the only sound he heard...The one thing he did not do that he knew how to do was to pull the slide back and see for himself if there is one in the chamber. It's what he had done before. It's what Clifford had told him to do. It's what he knew how to do. And when asked after this tragedy occurred, 'Why didn't you do it?' Mark's response was 'I forgot.' "

It seemed like such a devastating series of mistakes that arguing 'If the Beretta had a prominent chamber-loaded indicator, Mark would have seen it'—*no matter how true*—felt just then like standing in the face of an onrushing wave.

Next, in order to inoculate the jury against our counterargument about the utility of a prominent chamber-loaded indicator, Livingston repeated something that Gebhardt had said in the previous trial: "Now, when Mark pulled the pistol out of the bag and took the loaded magazine out, he was no longer looking for safety information; he was intent on getting upstairs and making those sounds."

This irritated me, as it was pure conjecture. But later I realized he had emphasized this for a reason. Livingston described the specific way Mark's father had let him practice shooting the Beretta at the shooting range. Clifford had repeatedly put only one round into the magazine and let Mark pick up the gun and the magazine from a table, insert the magazine into the gun, manipulate the slide to rack the single round into the empty chamber, hold the gun up with two hands in front of his face, and then fire that last round. They did that repeatedly.

When I heard this, you'd think I would have recognized that this was the moment when Kenzo's life could have been saved—if only that gun had had a prominent chamber-loaded indicator. But, in fact, each time one of Beretta's lawyers droned on with this demonstration, I am not at all sure I noticed how inevitable it would have been for Mark to learn about the prominent chamber-loaded indicator sticking up right in front of his face, then disappearing, if there *had been* a well-designed one on the Beretta.

Looking now at Gebhardt's and Livingston's arguments to the jury in those trials, I see that they understood this hole in their defense. That is why they both took such pains to emphasize their supposition that Mark wasn't looking for information on the gun when he took it from his father's bedroom upstairs and into his room, where Kenzo was. They had to inoculate the jurors against a potential argument that at the shooting range with his father—*if the gun had had a prominent chamber-loaded indicator*—Mark would have seen the little red thing pop up every time he racked the single round into the empty chamber, and then, after he'd fired that round, he would have seen it disappear.

He would have learned what that very prominent red thing meant.

### *The Gun Handling Expert*

In both trials Michael Lane (a pseudonym) testified as Beretta USA's expert in gun handling and training. He was there to say that Beretta USA was in no way responsible for Kenzo's death, because it was Clifford and Mark who had broken the rules of gun safety. He also disparaged the efficacy of safety devices on guns, such as chamber-loaded indicators and integral locks.

But this time Elliot Peters's law firm, Keker & Van Nest, had a larger staff for research on Beretta's expert witnesses than we'd had in our first trial, so Elliot was in a position to persuasively argue that Lane was an unreliable "expert," and attack his testimony.

In response to Craig Livingston's questions, Lane said he had spent three years at UCLA, and after college, had worked for the UCLA Police Department as a detective. He was drawn to guns, so for eight years, he served as the department's primary firearms instructor and range master. Soon after leaving the UCLA PD in 1994, he had begun a firearms consulting business, which involved being an expert witness in civil and criminal cases.

Lane testified that it was reckless and irresponsible for Clifford to keep the Beretta chamber-loaded and in an unsecured location. Livingston established that Clifford knew of inexpensive ways to lock his gun, such as with a cable lock. But Lane said Clifford had not used a locking device because he did not want his gun to be locked.

By then, I had been to gun shops and gun shows, where gun sales-men generally dismissed locking devices. What they said matched the NRA's firearm safety course instructors' manual, which stated—in mixed messaging—that "firearms stored for personal protection must be ready for immediate use."[28] The need to keep a gun unlocked and ready was widely accepted in this subculture. Not many lock boxes that can be quickly opened were selling yet.

When Elliot Peters cross-examined the witness, he got Lane to admit that he had not graduated from any four-year college, and also had not completed the Los Angeles Police Academy's training for officers, and had been asked to resign. As Elliot continued to question him, Lane grew more agitated. Soon beads of sweat began forming on his upper lip. Elliot exposed to the jury that he had been misleading about his level of training and experience.

Lane said he had worked as an expert witness in about fifteen cases, all but one involving firearms, but had never testified against a gun manufacturer. In the past two years all of his earned income had come from work in litigation as an expert. Lane said he billed $200 an hour.

Soon, Elliot pointed at the Beretta table, and said, "So, as you sit here, those folks over there, or the companies they represent, owe you in excess of $12,000. Correct?"

Lane said yes.

When Livingston questioned him, Lane had repeated the testimony he'd given in the first trial: that a prominent chamber-loaded indicator would not have prevented the accident, because the *only* safe way to tell if a round remained hidden in the chamber was to pull back the slide and look inside.

Now Elliot was ready for him. He put in front of the jury a blowup of a page in the Beretta manual which read: "Make sure the pistol is not already loaded by inspecting the loaded-chamber indicator." Lane had to admit that there was nothing in the manual that said to pull back the slide and check for a bullet. Since Beretta's tiny extractor / chamber-loaded indicator was inadequate as a way to tell whether or not there was a round in the chamber, it became obvious that Beretta's manual was a safety hazard for gun users. (Both chamber-loaded, and loaded-chamber indicator are used.)

The day ended, and everyone was sent home. It was December 9, 2003, and Christmas carols were everywhere. You couldn't turn on the radio without hearing "Sleigh bells ring, are you listening?" or some other jolly jingle, mostly about children and families.

I missed Kenzo. Christmas is tough for anyone who has lost a child.

As a leader of our Oakland Brady Chapter, I was organizing our Evening of Remembrance for people who had lost loved ones. In a church in Oakland, parents of every description—many of them Black—came to share their stories and pray. Every year we met and comforted at least a dozen new parents whose children had recently been shot and killed.

The next day in court, after Livingston's brief re-cross of Lane, Elliot rose for his redirect. He showed the jury and Lane a page from Beretta's website, advertising Beretta's new B●Lok gun. Lane agreed that the company's new internal lock would be simple to use, which is how Beretta characterized it. This contradicted the thrust of the testimony he had just given about how difficult an internal lock would be to use.

In the first trial, Beretta had argued that it was impossible to build an internal lock into its handgun. Now, a few years later, the company was advertising one. The company had said (probably because of our ongoing trial) that it could not make it work right, and they were not selling it. But by advertising an internal lock, they had proven our point—that they needed to take corrective action and make a safer gun.

Now we were ready for the main event: Elliot's confrontation with Beretta USA's firearms engineering expert witness, Seth Bredbury.

### *The Gun Industry's Top Hired Gun*

I knew this would be a tough test for Elliot. Bredbury was Beretta's star witness. He had forcefully argued in the first trial that given the current state of technology, the gun that killed Kenzo could not be made any safer. When he was presented with a model of a Beretta gun that our expert engineer, Lester Roane, had fitted with a prominent chamber-loaded indicator, Bredbury had said it was likely to blow up in the user's face.

All of Roane's prototypes with integral locks were just as unfeasible, Bredbury had said. Dirt buildup would make them impossible to clean, and the addition of a lock could cause them to break here or fail there.

In the second trial, much of Bredbury's testimony was similar to what he'd said in the first, but on some points, he and Livingston had devised new approaches.

"Sir, what is a hazard analysis?" Livingston inquired.

"It's a formalized method by which you try to identify a hazard to any product—what may fail—and identify what the consequences of that failure would be." Bredbury gave the impression, but never actually said, that he'd done a hazard analysis for this case.

Bredbury repeated the visceral descriptions of how the addition of a prominent chamber-loaded indicator and internal lock could make the gun potentially fatal for the user. This time he emphasized even more graphically that with Roane's prototypes, when case head ruptures occur and release gas under high pressure, a secondary projectile—the chamber-loaded indicator itself—could "fly in the face of the shooter."

Elliot Peters rose for his cross-examination and immediately grabbed the jury's attention.

"You went to MIT, is that right?" he asked. "Did you take science courses there?"

When Bredbury answered that he had, Elliot asked, "In the course of your studies, did you become familiar with something called the scientific method?"

"Sure," said Bredbury agreeably.

"In the scientific method, the scientist starts out developing a hypothesis, right?...And then the scientist tests the hypothesis by gathering facts, right? And the scientist uses experiments to gather facts, correct?"

"Among other things, yes," answered Bredbury, beginning to look a bit uncomfortable.

"In the course of your work [at the Springfield Armory], you actually performed tests on firearms, didn't you? After doing tests, you would speak to the designers about how to incorporate the results of the testing into the firearm design, right? You do testing by firing the gun yourself or having it fired by someone else, right?...You would talk to the engineers at Colt's about how to design the gun based on the results of your testing; is that right?"

Elliot's questions were coming one right after the other.

Judge Baranco reprimanded him repeatedly for going too fast for the court reporter.

But Elliot kept on. "The finite element test you testified about is a form of stress analysis, and the computer modeling software is available to a gentleman like you? You could hire someone who knows how to use that software for you? It's not hard to do, is it, Mr. Bredbury?"

Livingston objected: Argumentative.

Sustained.

Elliot plowed on. Had Bredbury ever had any discussions with Beretta engineers about how to improve the design of the chamber-loaded indicator on that product?

No.

Ever been asked by Beretta to have discussions with its engineers to find out what work they did to design it?

No.

Ever tested the 92 L himself?

No.

Elliot asked him why he hadn't done his own tests.

Bredbury replied that there was no need. "At this level of design, you can tell whether or not there's a reason to go in that direction." Bredbury remained composed, but his voice had become a bit shaky.

"Do you believe that your conclusions and opinions in this case are based upon the scientific method that you learned when you were at MIT?"

"Yes."

"But you haven't done any testing yourself, have you?"

"Argumentative," barked Livingston.

Judge Baranco agreed.

Bredbury had testified that the chamber-loaded indicator was a tactile device, so Elliot asked, "Have you done any studies or tests to see whether users can feel this tactile indicator?"

"Only other than doing it myself."

"So, the sole scientific basis for your opinion about whether it works as a tactile indicator is that *you* can use it?"

That was ruled argumentative, so Elliot rephrased.

"Other than touching it yourself, have you gathered any information from anywhere else to inform your opinion about whether it works?"

"No."

"During the time that you were forming the opinion that it works for you, were you being paid by Beretta?"

"Yes."

Bredbury admitted that he, like Lane, derived 100 percent of his income from serving as an expert witness in gun cases. He had done this for the past five years. He said he'd been retained as an expert witness in over one hundred civil cases.

"In more than ninety of those cases, did someone get hurt or killed by a bullet shot out of a gun?" Elliot asked.

Bredbury replied: "Usually that's the case." Bredbury acknowledged that in the past five years, he had made approximately a quarter of a million dollars from work on cases for gun manufacturers or distributors.

Bredbury admitted he'd never designed a complete handgun, never designed a safety device for a handgun, and had never worked on the design of a chamber-loaded indicator or internal lock. He acknowledged having said that there are no benefits to having internal locks on firearms, but that there are detriments. In response to Elliot's questions, he said he didn't consider it a benefit that you can't lose an internal lock, and that you don't have to go out and buy one. He was trying mightily to maintain his composure, but it seemed to be slipping again. He must have realized that these answers sounded false.

Elliot had been setting a trap, and Bredbury certainly knew what he was up to.

As Elliot's questions about internal locks became more pointed, Bredbury hedged every answer. But the jury had heard the thrust of his testimony, which was against the feasibility and the benefits of putting an internal lock into a Beretta pistol.

Now Elliot put in front of the jury a blowup of a page from Beretta's website, showing the company's new B●lok pistol.

"Is it simple to use, in your opinion?" asked Elliot.

"It doesn't work," said Bredbury.

Elliot wound up by directing his attention to Roane's prototype with a chamber-loaded indicator on the top, showing red when a bullet was chambered.

"Do you believe that there's any value to the user in having a reminder right there on the top of the gun that the chamber could be loaded, even if you can't see a round in there?" Elliot asked.

"I don't think it would effectively do that," Bredbury hedged. But it seemed to me that he was unable to keep a tone of desperation out of his voice. He knew the jury recognized that Roane's prototype chamber-loaded indicator clearly showed the user when a bullet was still in the chamber. The attorney and his adversary were having at it, speaking as fast as they could, like kids in a shouting match on some dirt-covered ball field. Everyone was leaning forward in rapt attention, sometimes commenting to each other. Even the elderly court reporter was nodding as she watched the action, her fingers flying.

"Do you believe that an indicator plays a valuable safety function?"

"I think it plays a relatively minor function in the operation of the gun."

"Do you believe that it's of minor significance for a user to know whether or not there's a round in the chamber?"

"No. It's critical that he know whether or not there's a round in the chamber."

That was Elliot's point. There was no need for the "Well, then..." follow-up.

"No further questions," Elliot said. He nodded, spun around, and sat down.

There was silence in the courtroom.

I took the elevator down with Elliot. With a gleam in his eye, he leaned over and whispered in my ear: "I think the gun companies are going to have to find someone else to give their testimony for them."

### One or Two More Votes

The jury was sent off to begin deliberations on Monday, December 15, 2003. Although it was getting close to Christmas, I wasn't worried that the holidays would interfere with the trial. But the next morning, with the jurors seated, Judge Baranco announced that our favorite juror, a fifty-year-old Japanese-born woman who was an executive assistant with a large corporation, had called and told him she was very ill with the flu, and could not stay on the jury. The judge replaced her with the first alternate, an elderly Vietnamese immigrant who scowled a lot, and whose command of English was minimal. We had realized during *voir dire* that she would be against us, but the next potential jurors looked just as bad, so we had not struck her as a juror.

Now, someone who was against us had taken the place of our best juror, who would have been a leader in deliberations.

The jury was sequestered. After a day, they sent a note to the judge asking to have Mark's and Clifford's testimony from the trial read to them. Then they asked to see the Beretta manual and the bright yellow tag with a prominent warning on it that our human factors expert had testified should be attached to the trigger guard of the gun when first sold.

The jury seemed to be going about its business in a conscientious way.

But when they asked to see Les Roane's prototype of a Beretta onto which he had inserted a prominent top-mounted chamber-loaded indicator, Judge Baranco said they would have to tell him in writing beforehand specifically what they wanted to see, and then the sheriff's deputy would show it to them. They would not be allowed to touch the gun or have any discussion while it was being shown to them in a locked courtroom.

They found these rules so onerous that they canceled their request to examine the gun. I was dismayed. They would not be looking at a crucial piece of evidence: Roane's prototype of a gun with a prominent chamber-loaded indicator.

As the jurors deliberated for four days, Elliot, Daralyn, Jamie, Lynn, and I wandered the courthouse halls or sat on the hard, cold floor. When we could no longer stand it, we went home, planning to rush to the court as soon as the jury was returning. We found waiting at home just as bad as wandering the halls of the courthouse.

We were back in court early Monday morning, December 22, and noticed a juror was mysteriously missing from her chair. Looking extremely perturbed, Judge Baranco marched in and explained that she had called and told him she could no longer serve because there was simply no one to watch her children, who were out of school, on Christmas vacation.

Suddenly we saw a side of the judge we had never seen—a very angry side. He said he had called her back and asked why she didn't know this before, and why she couldn't get a babysitter. She had thought her nephews would watch her kids, but at the last minute they couldn't. He asked if she could come the next day. She wasn't sure. "What do you think?" he had asked angrily. Her answer: "Oh, my God!"

We gleaned from what he said that this juror could no longer serve for emotional reasons. It had become clear during *voir dire* and the trial that she was on our side, but she was emotionally fragile. I had watched her during the trial and written in my notes that she looked especially torn by our tragedy, and by the lawyers' arguments. She had cried more than any other juror. Later we learned that when the jury room debates had become contentious, she'd said she couldn't come back.

Judge Baranco replaced her with the last alternate, Henry Daily (pseudonyms are used for all the jurors), who had been in the jury box the entire trial. We knew from *voir dire* that he was against us. However, he seemed a reasonable guy. Perhaps he might change his opinion when they went over the evidence.

But going over the evidence was a problem. With the jury back in the jury box, Judge Baranco explained, "The alternate must be given an opportunity to deliberate." He instructed them, "Set aside and disregard your past deliberations and begin all over again."

We wondered whether the jurors could possibly do that after having debated the evidence intensely for four days. Even if they *were* able to start over, it was now December 22. Wouldn't they feel enormous pressure to just reach some sort of conclusion before Christmas?

The first question the jurors had to answer was: "Did the Beretta pistol perform as safely as an ordinary consumer would have expected?" We learned that they sent the judge repeated notes, asking him for help defining "ordinary consumer," but we knew nothing more. I was beside myself with curiosity. Questions collided in my brain.

Finally, on the afternoon of Tuesday, December 23, as I anxiously paced the floor at home, I got the call: The jury was returning. I picked up Lynn and we rushed to the courtroom. The jury announced quite firmly that they were deadlocked; it was a hung jury.

I felt my chest collapse.

The foreman said the vote was 6 to 6. However, we would learn very soon, when we got to talk with the jurors, that their first vote had been 9 to 3, in our favor. During much of their debate, the vote had been 8 to 4. We needed only one more vote for 9.

Lynn and I were allowed into the small room where the lawyers had already begun talking informally with the jurors about their deliberations. Almost the entire jury was still voluntarily there, sitting at the table or standing, leaning against the wall.

I took out my pad and began furiously writing down what they were saying. The jurors told us that if the two jurors who were on our side had not left and been replaced by the two alternates, who were against us, we would have won, 10 to 2; or, if just one of them had remained on the jury, we probably would have won.

We soon learned what the reasons for the jury's exhausted, final intransigent vote had been. Initially, when the first alternate had been placed on the jury, they had been utterly unable to put aside four days of heated debate and "start all over," as if from the beginning. They were at loggerheads, and angry at each other.

Then, after the second alternate was put on, they never got to the crucial question, of whether the Beretta pistol's design was a substantial factor in causing Kenzo's death. After being told to start all over, they had gotten stuck arguing over the meaning of "ordinary consumer," a term they re-debated for an entire day.

When the jurors had asked Judge Baranco for help in defining "ordinary consumer," he had refused. That, combined with the inability of one juror and one of the alternates, who had just joined them, to understand English well enough to follow what was said during the trial and the deliberations, is what had led to the deadlock.

We had been one inch from winning.

Daralyn Durie asked the jurors, "What was the first vote?"

The jury foreman replied that it was 9 to 3, for the plaintiffs. The three included the Southeast Asian woman alternate who spoke little English, and had been the replacement for the excellent juror, who was clearly on our side, but had called in sick. Another of the three against us was an elderly male insurance claims processor whose job was to be skeptical of insurance claims, and who had been silent throughout; we never would have gotten his vote. The third vote against us was also a loner—a quiet retired man who had napped during part of the testimony.

A consistent 9–3 vote would have given us a victory. However, we soon heard that the young immigrant juror—another Southeast Asian who spoke little English—may have misunderstood the question he was voting on. His first vote had been taken before the Southeast Asian woman alternate was put on the jury; in subsequent votes, he followed her and became a pro-Beretta vote. The jury foreman said it had been 8–4 for days before the jury began stumbling over the definition of "ordinary consumer."

Beretta's lawyer, Craig Livingston, began questioning them. This was his chance to learn what they thought of the witnesses.

Paul Dolan, who had said in *voir dire* that his high school friend had committed suicide with the family's gun, spoke up. "The plaintiffs' experts were way more credible than the defendant's. The chamber-loaded indicator was not prominent. For anyone without gun training, it didn't work." He said for him, it was not visible, but the gun was manufactured well. Looking at our lawyers he added, "Showing the Beretta advertisement was effective, and the manual did not even warn them to check the slide."

Livingston asked him *how* the plaintiffs' experts were more credible.

They had facts and studies, Dolan replied, and the last expert, Bredbury, was too combative. He said that the way Bredbury reacted to their tactics worked against him and that the plaintiffs caught him saying things that contradicted something he'd said before.

Livingston asked if Roane was credible, and Dolan told him that you could see the chamber-loaded indicator on Roane's prototype easily. He told Livingston, "Something that you can see on top is better."

A woman juror who worked as a receptionist at a health-care organization looked at Lynn and me and said, "Do you realize how close you came to winning this?"

Livingston quickly interceded and asked which experts were good.

Dolan said all three of the ones for the plaintiffs were better. Lane's career was so cloudy that it made people wonder. "Couldn't they get anyone better than that?" responded Amanda Cahill, an alert office manager for a big Bay Area company.

Most agreed that our gun design expert, Lester Roane, was a credible witness. Cahill's comment was typical: "He answered the questions right away without having to figure out how it would sound." She was impressed that "Roane has been on both sides of this issue." That gave him credibility in her eyes. He was the crusty old lifetime NRA member, engineer, and head of the top gun-testing company. His testimony in the second trial had been far stronger and more unequivocal than in the first.

Livingston asked how plausible Roane's alternative designs were.

Amanda Cahill felt that the internal lock was irrelevant, because Clifford would never have used it. We were not surprised that some jurors believed that, since by the second trial, the Beretta lawyers had persuaded Clifford to sign a declaration contradicting his earlier deposition (closer to the shooting), in which he'd said that he did not want his son to access his gun because he lacked experience. After Clifford's first deposition, a lawyer who told Clifford he was "a fellow gun owner" had shown up and offered to "help" him. But he seems to have been there at least in part to influence Clifford's memory about his willingness to let Mark access his gun "in an emergency." We suspected this lawyer was being paid by Beretta USA.[29]

Livingston then asked about the Beretta's chamber-loaded indicator.

Amanda Cahill said, "For the military, it provides information they can use, but for consumers in the home, the sophistication is just the opposite. That contributed to the tragedy. If this chamber-loaded indicator had actually functioned as the manual said, then it would have served as a reminder." She mentioned that Clifford never noticed it.

Sue Talbert, who had been lifting her hand and making little motions to speak, finally got her chance. She said the experts on both sides were good, and that the Beretta is a well-manufactured gun. The engineering diagrams shown by Beretta's employee, Gabriele de Plano, had impressed her. (I held back a grimace; those standard engineering drawings had nothing to do with the adequacy of the chamber-loaded indicator in consumer homes.) But she said that Clifford was a major contributor to the terrible accident and loss. She was sorry for Mark and the emotional stress he had suffered.

The jurors were leaning forward, engaged in the conversation. For two weeks, they had been forced to watch the lawyers, unable to speak. Now they were like a friendly group of theatergoers who'd just seen a new play and had stayed to workshop it with the actors and playwright. They were eager to express their opinions.

Something was bothering me about this conversation, and later, I realized what it was: This was not mere entertainment. The jurors didn't understand the potential effect this trial could have on the gun industry. They did not realize that each year the lives of dozens of living, breathing people would either continue or would end as a result of their votes.

Of course, I was not sure of this either at the time. But later I found out.

Livingston was getting an earful. He asked, "How was Jeffrey Reh [Beretta USA's Senior VP] as a witness?"

One juror commented that Reh seemed high-strung and had a bit of a nervous tic.

Then Dolan jumped back in. "From his years at Beretta, [Reh] could have been more involved in advising Beretta in Italy to look at the studies. Beretta didn't show they had done surveys or anything. They fell short for an ordinary consumer that purchases the firearm."

We continued around the room in a haphazard way.

Amanda Cahill finally mentioned the epidemiological and statistical testimony. She said Stephen Teret was central, but that he was a little academic and dry. No one had said anything about the scientific findings Teret had explained. No one had mentioned anything that he'd said about how common it is for gun owners—especially those with handguns for protection—to store their guns loaded and unlocked.

Statistics and research did not leave as much of an impression as the concrete example before them of Clifford and the mistakes they thought he'd made—and that wasn't Teret's fault. It was just difficult to comprehend that, however dangerous and deserving of blame Clifford's behavior was, it was also extremely common. There was virtually no discussion of "foreseeable misuse"—the concept and the law behind it. But many jurors *did* recognize that this tragedy was foreseeable to Beretta; otherwise, we would not have almost won.

Livingston asked if the jurors believed his statement—that Mark had not been looking for information on the gun when he took out the loaded magazine and carried the gun and an empty magazine up to his bedroom. "Was Mark looking for that information or not?" he asked.

"He thought he had unloaded the gun," Dolan objected, criticizing the gun's design: "If you have to pull the slide back, that is not very visible."

Carl Wang, who had voted for the plaintiffs, told Livingston, "The chamber-loaded indicator was not effective, and the manual was defective. No one believed the chamber-loaded indicator worked."

I couldn't resist asking the question that had nagged me throughout the trial.

"At the shooting range, when Mark shot the Beretta thirty times with his father—firing a single bullet each time—do you think he would have seen the chamber-loaded indicator, if there had been one like the Roane prototype?"

"Yes, he would have seen it," Carl Wang replied. There was general spoken agreement and nodding of heads.

I also asked whether hearing that guns are the only consumer product that Congress made exempt from regulation by the Consumer Product Safety Commission would have made a difference. They almost jumped out of their chairs. Several said at once, "That would have been huge," or words to that effect. One said that we assume the products around us are made more or less safe, but lack of regulation by the Consumer Product Safety Commission helps explain why a chamber-loaded indicator like Beretta's is still on the market. He put it exactly as I would have!

We had already heard that the jury had gotten deadlocked on the definition of an "ordinary consumer." Now Livingston asked them about question number one on their jury form: whether the Beretta Model 92 Compact L was defective because it failed to perform as safely as an ordinary consumer would have expected.

Juror Sue Talbert, a quiet, college-educated woman from Oakland, suddenly expressed her deep frustration about their deliberations.

"We would have made progress on question three [whether the design of the gun was a substantial factor in Kenzo's death], but when one of the jurors did not show up and was replaced, and we tried to start all over from the beginning, that led us right back to question one, which involved defining 'ordinary consumer.'" She said they hardly discussed the crucial third question.

Wang said, "Some people had difficulty seeing how the design was a substantial factor. They were not evaluating the arguments." During *voir dire* Wang had paraphrased the NRA slogan—that guns don't kill people, people do—so I'd thought he was against us. We had considered striking him. Yet he had voted with us.

But the well-educated Southeast Asian woman alternate, who had difficulty understanding English, finally spoke up. "For me, it was Clifford...and Mark was a *minor*. He was not supposed to touch the gun. Beretta is not at fault."

Several jurors complained that two people on the jury could not understand English. One juror said he had wanted to complain about the non-English-speakers to the judge, but the foreman did not let him.

Paul Dolan said, "People did not interpret the questions right; they were way off." He looked at Livingston and continued, "It would have worked against you if everyone understood English."

The Southeast Asian woman understood enough to know she was being criticized. She changed the subject and asked, "Who made the questionnaire?"

"The state legislature; they made the verdict form," Daralyn answered.

In a minute Lynn asked, "Could you see multiple causes? Could you see beyond what the human beings caused?"

This stirred up some anger. Someone said, "I kept reminding them all to be open-minded. Some looked only at the human error. One woman spent an entire day telling us, 'Mark forgot.'"

"Was there any particular fact for Beretta that should have been brought out?" asked Livingston.

Sue Talbert had a suggestion: "It was so absurd that one of your experts said the picture in the ad might be a divorced father's picture showing his two daughters and his ex-wife. My ex-husband wouldn't show a picture of me, that's for sure."

When the laughter subsided, Wang said, "Beretta did not answer any of the real questions. There were a lot of safety issues left unanswered. Also, foreseeability. What about that? They had no answer."

As an anthropologist, I was intent on scribbling down what they said. But the few times I spoke, I couldn't help but try to convince this jury a bit.

Lynn was way ahead of me, thinking about the next trial. She asked, "What should the plaintiffs' lawyers have brought out? Anything else?" But her question backfired. The jurors just mentioned more problems with Beretta's arguments.

Wang continued. "I want to see or hear from the person who designed this gun. They [Beretta] made a good case that it is a well-made weapon." He looked at Livingston. "On foreseeability, we need answers. The things the plaintiffs brought up were not answered. If the knowledge was there when they made it, then why not show it?"

Now, I thought, Beretta is probably going to bring some engineering diagrams and try to say that it has been addressing the foreseeability of this all along.

Gun-owning juror Henry Daily asked, "Why doesn't the industry put chamber-loaded indicators on guns?" This surprised me; he had originally favored Beretta.

"Did you ever hear of the NRA?" I asked him with a grin.

I was thinking of the successful boycott that the gun industry and big distributors had orchestrated against Smith & Wesson when the company had agreed to President Bill Clinton's request to build safety features for consumers into its guns, and to monitor gun dealers who sold its guns, so they would not sell to straw purchasers—people illegally buying guns for someone who can't pass a background check.

S&W gun sales plummeted; its president was removed, and it was forced to abandon the agreement.

"The fact that the military uses it, was that good for Beretta?" asked Livingston.

"Consumers are different, because they have children in their homes," answered Daily. "Beretta should have done more, because there's idiots out there."

If he had been on the jury from the beginning, I thought, we might have won his vote.

Daralyn had been leaning against the wall, taking it all in. Now she stepped forward and asked, "What else should we have done?"

Amanda Cahill said, "Clarify that the consumer and purchaser are not synonymous."

Cahill was smart, and what she said aroused juror Helen Dole's frustration. "Yes, we hammered 'ordinary consumer' *all day* and could not agree on what it meant. Everyone had his own definition." The jurors' inability to agree on the meaning of *ordinary consumer* created their frustration and eventual intransigent division.

Their dispute piqued Livingston's interest, and he asked what definitions they argued about. "To me," Daily said, " 'ordinary consumer' is lots of people. It should have been Clifford *and* Mark, and it's even bigger than them alone." Even though Daily had originally favored Beretta, when he replaced the ill pro-plaintiff juror, he had voted for the plaintiffs in the jury's original 8–4 votes. Now he cautioned, "I hope Beretta wakes up, and other gun companies wake up."

"Did anyone else think Mark was an ordinary consumer?" asked Livingston.

"Yes, said Amanda Cahill, "Clifford had shown him the gun and let him fire it at the shooting range."

But clearly, others thought Mark was no ordinary consumer.

Finally, in exasperation, Cahill said, " 'Ordinary consumer' was not clear enough." She shot a dirty look at all the lawyers: "You guys should put a definition on it. We had a whole day debating it—*all of one day*."

The California legislature had created the verdict form with its *ordinary consumer* term, a common one in product liability cases. But it was unclear in a situation like this, in which a fourteen-year-old got his hands on a gun that was unsafe for consumers.

The word *ordinary* was a nightmare. Some jurors thought, "Well, Mark *shouldn't* have had access to the gun, so it wasn't *ordinary*." Others thought, "Of course he *shouldn't*, but in the real world, lots of bad things *do* happen quite ordinarily. Since unsafe gun storage is so common, every day fourteen-year-olds *do* get their hands on their fathers' guns, so those teenagers are *ordinary* consumers, too."

The word *consumer* was a nightmare, as well. To some it meant the person who *buys* the product; to others, it meant the person who *uses* the product. How do you "consume" a gun except by pulling the trigger?

This is what Mark did, *after* he thought he'd unloaded it by taking the loaded magazine out. The gun had clearly failed to demonstrate to him—as well as it could have—that he still hadn't completely unloaded it.

*Ordinary* is not the same as *ideal*, however much we might wish it were.

Many jurors were disheartened that they had not reached a consensus.

A woman in the corner piped up. "If there had not been so many changes to the jury, things would have been different." Looking at Lynn and me, she repeated what another juror had said: "You almost won."

Eventually our discussion wound down, and I thanked them.

In the elevator on our way out, Daralyn Durie explained to me how two people who could not understand English had gotten on the jury. The judge had told the lawyers how very suspicious he was of people trying to get out of jury duty by saying that their English was not good enough.

As Daralyn and I mulled over what we had just heard, she said to me ominously, "Livingston learned more than we did."

It was a revelation to me, and not a compliment. This trial had been finished when the lawyers went into that room to talk with the jurors. I hadn't said much, but when I did, I had foolishly still been trying to convince them—too late. I had enjoyed listening to the drubbing Livingston took from jurors who saw through his expert witnesses. But I had been "fighting the last war."

Having never been in an after-trial discussion between jurors and lawyers, I had not fully understood its real purpose. Now it dawned on me: It was to help the lawyers prepare for the next trial, and Livingston had gotten a lot of useful information from these jurors. Later, reflecting on it further, I became uncomfortable thinking about Livingston pumping the naive jurors for information to help him deceive the future batch of jurors he would face in the next trial.

We had come very close to winning, even though our best juror had suddenly gotten sick and been replaced by a staunchly pro-Beretta alternate who was unable to understand English well. Then another pro-plaintiff juror had left during deliberations after she found it too emotionally difficult. Another pro-Beretta juror replaced her. After the judge had instructed them to start over, discussing all of the evidence and the law, from the beginning, they simply could not. By then their positions were set; they were angry at each other, emotionally spent, and frustrated. They had tried hard and had come very close to reaching a verdict but had ultimately *deadlocked*.

Never had the term seemed more appropriate.

## *Immunity II*

After the hung jury, we had the right to a new trial. But soon it looked like we might not get one. An increasing number of cities and individuals were suing gun makers, and some of the lawsuits had succeeded. The gun industry knew—from our lawsuit and others—that more lawsuits were likely to win. So, after failing in October 2002 to pass its bill granting gun makers and gun dealers special immunity from civil lawsuits, the gun lobby didn't wait long before going back to Congress to try again. The new bill still included a provision that could potentially throw our case and others like it out of court, even though judges had already ruled they were legitimate, and they were already being tried in the courts.[30]

In April 2003, the Republican-dominated US House passed the gun-industry-immunity bill, 285 to 140. GOP legislators seemed to believe the public had forgotten that granting the gun industry immunity from civil lawsuits would help arm criminals like the DC snipers by enabling the negligence of companies like Bull's Eye and Bushmaster.

But we were not defeated yet. In February 2003 a top gun-industry lobbyist had turned whistleblower. Robert Ricker explained in detail why the industry did not deserve immunity. As the NRA's assistant general counsel, he had represented it in its political and legislative efforts in Washington, DC. But recently he had signed a declaration in support of the *plaintiffs* in a lawsuit brought by twelve California cities and counties against many gun makers. "Leaders in the gun industry have long known that greater industry action to prevent illegal transactions is possible and would curb the supply of firearms to the illegal market," Ricker said.[31] But, he continued, they have resisted taking voluntary action to prevent firearms from ending up in the illegal gun market until faced with the threat of civil liability.

The leaders in the industry have consistently sought to silence others in the industry who advocated reform.[32]

Ricker pointed out that firearms are diverted from legal channels of commerce to the illegal market primarily at the distributor/dealer level. If dealers trained their salesmen, they could prevent many straw purchases and other illegal sales. But gun industry executives "adopt a 'see-no-evil, speak-no-evil' approach."[33] Ricker praised the lawsuits against the gun industry that Congress was trying to forbid.[34]

In May 2003, on *60 Minutes,* Ricker got into a set-to with our courtroom opponent, Larry Keane, of the National Shooting Sports Foundation. Ricker explained how Bushmaster could have helped to prevent the DC snipers from getting their assault rifle illegally by monitoring the dealers who sell its guns. If people at Bull's Eye selling Bushmaster guns were not reputable, Bushmaster should have known it, and said "We're not going to ship you any more guns."[35]

Keane offered an excuse: "It would be inappropriate for manufacturers to become a private police force and attempt to ferret out and identify on their own, as untrained civilians, who the corrupt dealers are."

Ricker countered: "This is spin. This is what I did for the industry."[36] But for him, this had become personal: "I don't want to have to come home some night from the office and have my wife tell me, 'Your son was shot in a drive-by shooting,' or, 'The neighbors' kids were killed.' That's what gets me."

Ricker's testimony gave me plenty of fodder for op-eds and *Chapter Chat* newsletters to Million Mom March leaders. And one day in Sacramento, after Ricker testified *in favor* of one of our bills in the California legislature, he and I and Nick Wilcox, our California Brady Chapters' co-legislative director, had a friendly chat. Things might have gone badly between us, since, as the NRA's top California lobbyist, Ricker had been responsible for passing the state's gun-industry-immunity law, which, in 2002, many of us had worked hard to repeal. But he had switched sides.[37] He told us that the leaders of the industry know that about 20 percent of gun sales go to the illegal market, and these leaders do not want those profits reduced.

Also in 2003, the Brady Center had published *Smoking Guns: Exposing the Gun Industry's Complicity in the Illegal Gun Market*. The report describes how the gun industry orchestrated an attack on Ed Shultz, CEO of Smith & Wesson, after he signed the agreement with the Clinton administration to implement a code of ethics. It involved refusing to allow dealers to sell the company's guns unless the dealers took steps to reduce illegal activity. For example, since they could identify many straw purchases, they would block those sales. S&W also agreed to design safer guns and improve distribution practices.[38]

The NRA and others directed their wrath toward S&W. The NSSF campaigned against the company.[39] Large firearm distributors refused to distribute its guns to dealers, so customers couldn't purchase them even if they wanted to. Soon S&W was sold to a company led by one of its former executives, Robert Scott, who derailed the agreement. "The firearms industry is a family," Scott said at the time. "We want to be part of family decision-making." Shortly thereafter, the National Shooting Sports Foundation gave Scott its "Man of the Year" Award.

The Brady chapters and allied groups all publicized how outrageous it would be if lawsuits like the one against Bull's Eye and Bushmaster led by Jon Lowy were to be thrown out of court.[40] Activists set up appointments with legislators in swing districts across the nation and got police chiefs to oppose the bill. The Brady organization sent senators a letter signed by those chiefs and by national police organizations, saying the bill would "strip away the legal rights of gun violence victims, including law enforcement officers and their families, to seek redress."[41] But it still looked like the bill would pass.

Then Senator Mike DeWine, a highly respected Ohio Republican, spoke against the bill on the Senate floor. "It singles out one particular group of victims and treats them differently than all other victims in this country," he pointed out. "It denies them their access to court." This bill would overturn "over 200 years of civil law, 200 years of tort law, 200 years of common law," he added. Civil liability law is about deterring irresponsible behavior by making sure there are incentives that encourage people to behave responsibly. DeWine asked, "Why not trust the good judges we trust in every other civil suit in this country to make the decision to throw out frivolous lawsuits?"[42]

A Brady press release listed Legal Action Project lawsuits—including *Dix v. Beretta USA*—that judges might have to throw out if the immunity bill became law.

On March 2, 2004, as I waited anxiously for news, an e-mail from Jon Lowy popped into my in-box: "Three remarkable victories today." Our side had passed amendments to the immunity bill that would reauthorize the assault weapons ban and close the "gun show loophole" by requiring background checks on all gun sales at gun shows. After those victories, the immunity bill had suddenly been defeated, 90 to 8. "I've been around here eighteen years and I've never seen anything quite as bizarre as this," said Senator John McCain, a chief sponsor of closing the gun show loophole.

What had happened?

NRA president Wayne LaPierre had e-mailed senators urging them to *defeat* the immunity bill. The amendments would have cut into profits from two prized markets: military-style assault weapons originally designed for war, and gun sales to criminals and other "prohibited persons" who can't pass background checks. So it was more palatable (and profitable) for them to forgo immunity.

The amendments led to the defeat of the gun-industry-immunity bill. Jon said it was a remarkable victory for all the activists and we should celebrate. We did.

## *Trial, Trial Again*

In 2004, our third trial took place. We lost.

As I expected, the Beretta USA lawyers displayed numerous precision engineering drawings, which the jurors in the discussion after the previous trial had said were impressive, even though they had nothing to do with the need for a prominent chamber-loaded indicator on the Beretta pistol. Nothing Beretta's expert witnesses said involved an understanding of American consumers or their home environments. We had never contended that the Beretta was a poorly made gun—only that it lacked safety features needed on handguns brought into consumer homes, features that could have saved Kenzo's life.

This time, more than before, Craig Livingston emphasized the declaration that the Beretta lawyers seemed to me to have written and had gotten Clifford to sign. It said everything their lawyers wanted, even things that contradicted what Clifford had said previously. In it, Clifford said he believed Mark was familiar enough with the Beretta to retrieve it from the camera bag in his bedroom, take the manual safety lever off "Safe," and fire it, if he needed to protect himself or any other family member in a life-threatening situation.

But previously, when asked if he'd wanted Mark to have access to the gun, he had responded with a definitive "No," because Mark "didn't have enough experience to handle the weapon." He'd said he wanted Mark to be able to access the gun only "eventually." Beretta's lawyers tried to have it both ways: blame Mark for violating his father's rule not to touch his gun, but also argue that Mark was an authorized user.

Our lawyers argued that, instead of believing this new declaration, the jurors should believe Clifford's depositions taken far closer to the time of Kenzo's death. In his first deposition, Clifford had said that if a safer gun had been available, he would have purchased it. By a "safer" gun, he'd explained that he'd meant a gun with "a safety device that you wear like a ring on your finger" that you could use to activate the gun. Clearly, he had wanted to prevent his children from accessing his gun. But now, he testified in support of the new declaration.

During the trial, the Beretta lawyers enumerated at length the many grievous errors made by Clifford and Mark, diverting attention from the times when a prominent chamber-loaded indicator could have prevented Kenzo's death, if the gun had had one.

When Lynn and I testified, what we said may have appeared rehearsed. In fact, it had been—in two previous trials. These jurors didn't know about those trials. As witnesses, we were supposed to once again make the jurors understand our loss. We had lost Kenzo ten years before and still missed him deeply. But we were not professional witnesses and could not deliver emotional performances for an audience.

The ground rules for all three trials had been set by Judge Hodge's ruling in the first trial: The case must be argued under comparative fault. He said it had to be applied, even though he did not agree with this California standard for product liability cases. The argument in the courtroom was presented to jurors as essentially an either/or choice: the mistakes of Clifford and Mark *versus* the mistakes of Beretta. But that didn't seem right to me, because they had *all* made grievous errors that led to Kenzo's death—errors that should not be set *in opposition to* each other, since they did not cancel each other out.

Throughout the trial the lawyers on each side talked past each other, emphasizing the doctrine favorable to them. Our lawyers talked about foreseeable misuse; Beretta's spoke of the either/or choice of comparative fault, pointing out the mistakes made by Clifford and Mark, as if those somehow proved that the design of the gun was not at fault.

Since the court was presenting jurors with contradictory instructions, the question became: Which side of the conversation would they listen to? By the logic of California's foreseeable misuse law, the *more foreseeable* the misuse, the *more* the manufacturer may be blamed for not recognizing an *obvious* danger, and for not designing a product that reduces that risk. That was the law.

In contrast, by the logic of comparative fault and the rules allowing testimony relevant to it, when a *misuse* occurs, because it is a *misuse,* the *less* the manufacturer may be blamed—no matter *whether the misuse is foreseeable or not*. At least, that is the way it worked out.

There was another problem with comparative fault. There were injured *third parties*: Kenzo, me, Lynn, and our son Kalani. No one was arguing *we* were at fault. How do the not-at-fault third parties get justice if the faulty (but *foreseeable*) misuse of the gun owner and his son *cancels out* the substantial fault of Beretta USA?

The manufacturer/distributor should have anticipated that its products would be in an environment where they were likely to be misused in exactly these ways. The manufacturer/distributor should have designed and sold a product that *minimized* the likelihood of harm. But when comparative fault sets the rules for evidence and argument, the injured third parties, the plaintiffs, got squeezed out. So, the incentive of the manufacturer/distributor to make a safe product was eliminated.

I thought Clifford and Mark needed all the help they could get from Beretta. Lynn and I were on the side of gun owners and their children in wanting them to get more support from gun makers, so they wouldn't have to go through what Clifford and Mark—gun owners and children who make mistakes—go through. We wanted them to get the help that would be prevention; Beretta wanted to sell more guns, and seemed to think that drawing attention to safety features would reduce sales.

In all three trials, some jurors saw that there were times in the fatal sequence of events when a safer design would likely have prevented the tragedy. They believed that a prominent chamber-loaded indicator could have made Clifford's and Mark's many mistakes irrelevant, because with a better gun design, Mark would have recognized that the Beretta in his hand still had a bullet in the chamber, and Kenzo would not have died. So those jurors voted with the plaintiffs. But there were not enough of those jurors for us to win the case.

The jury instructions were needlessly complex and confusing, with test after test the jurors had to apply. The wording was often ambiguous; the juries needed guidance, but the judges refused the jurors' requests for it. The judges told the jurors just to use their common sense. So, California's strong product liability laws were not applied.

Beretta's lawyers told the jurors they should "hold Clifford and Mark accountable"—in essence, "punish" them—for their obvious irresponsibility. But there was no way this trial could "punish" Clifford and Mark; the defendant Beretta USA was the only party that could have been "punished" in this trial. The errors of Beretta were no less lethal for being mainly errors of omission rather than commission.

So, after ten years of fighting, we lost. But I learned that with three trials, in many ways, we had won. Our lawsuit had argued that the Beretta handgun was unreasonably dangerous for use in a family setting in three ways: 1) It did not adequately tell people whether there was a bullet in the chamber; 2) there was no built-in way to lock the gun; and 3) Its manual did not adequately instruct and warn the user.

Although Beretta had mocked the idea of putting integral locks in guns, by the end of the trial, Beretta was advertising handguns with built-in locks. At least eight manufacturers had begun making guns with integral locks. That was a breakthrough.[43]

Before Lynn and I heard the jury's verdict, Jon Lowy told us, "Your case was the first to be tried on the theory that guns should be made to prevent unauthorized use." He said that our lawsuit had been a road map to several important cases that won.[44] It had also played a key role in several important legislative victories. Maryland had begun to require all handguns sold in the state to have built-in locks.

We had accomplished some of our objectives. And as our lawsuit had bumped along from trial to trial, I had been actively working with the coalition that had originally led me and Lynn to Jon Lowy. Many other parents in that coalition had gotten involved after they had received phone calls or knocks on their doors telling them that their child had been shot. These advocates had developed stronger organizations that had blocked repeated gun lobby attempts to enact federal bills granting gun makers and gun dealers special immunity from civil lawsuits.

But we were about to be challenged again.

# 16

## The Protection of Lawful Commerce in Arms Act

Our third trial ended in July 2004. Three months later, I was elected president of the California Brady Chapters. Amanda and Nick Wilcox had become our California Brady legislative advocates and my role was mainly to support their work passing gun laws in the state. The Wilcoxes' bright and beautiful daughter, Laura, had been murdered in December of 2001 while home from college on Christmas break, filling in as a receptionist at a health clinic in Nevada City, California. A paranoid patient had come there, shot her, and then killed two others. The Wilcoxes became very effective leaders for improving mental health treatment and gun laws.

In 2004 and 2005, once again the entire national gun violence prevention movement was strategizing to block the Protection of Lawful Commerce in Arms Act (PLCAA), a gun-industry-immunity bill.

I had not been the only one to learn by observing our courtroom battle against Beretta USA. When Lawrence Keane, the ever-watchful VP of the National Shooting Sports Foundation (NSSF), had observed our first trial for the gun industry as a Beretta USA lawyer, he must have seen that the gun owner and his son had made many foreseeable mistakes that a safer gun design and a better manual could have helped them avoid. He probably heard from the Beretta lawyers in our second trial that we had nearly won. Because of what he and others observed in our case, and in the many others against gun makers, the gun industry leaders had to know that they would lose some of these cases.

So they revived their top priority: the bill granting their industry special immunity from civil lawsuits. Their goal was to prevent juries from ever seeing these cases. And in the rare instance when one of these cases went to a jury, the gun industry apparently did not want jurors to see all the relevant evidence about the various causes of the injury. They wanted the verdicts to be only about the "sole proximate cause," even though, in the real world, injuries often have several important causes. Juries would be forced into a world in which injuries can have only one cause. But that would exclude many other causes of death or injury, leaving those other causes—like a hard-to-see indicator—to kill or injure again, over and over.

This time we were unable to block the gun-industry-immunity bill, which felt to me like an injustice with immense consequences. The September 11, 2001, terrorist attacks on the World Trade Center in New York had stirred up powerful emotions. President George W. Bush had been reelected in 2004. Republicans had increased their majority in the House and won a majority in the Senate. Larry Keane called the lawsuits against the gun maker and dealers "misguided efforts [that] attempted to blame firearm companies for the illegal actions of criminals."

Phyllis Segal, the chair of the Brady Campaign Board, replied in an op-ed, "What's actually at issue here is whether or not a gun dealer, distributor, or manufacturer should be responsible for its own actions—not the actions of others." Her analogy was, "If a drunk, barely able to stand, walked into a car dealership and demanded to buy a car and drove it off the lot in his inebriated condition, should the dealer who handed him the keys be held accountable?" Of course he should, she said.

But in October 2005, under the eyes of the NSSF's Larry Keane, Beretta USA's Jeffrey Reh, and the NRA's Wayne LaPierre, President George W. Bush sign the Protection of Lawful Commerce in Arms Act.

Virtually no other industry had been given such federal immunity from legal accountability. The law's repercussions—though not widely understood—would be deadly and long-lasting. David Kairys of Temple University wrote that with this law, "Congress and the president had violated the most fundamental tenets of constitutional separation of powers, in which government fashions rules of general application, avoids singling out powerful friends to be above the law, and leaves the outcome of pending lawsuits to the courts."[45]

Kairys refuted the gun industry's key points. The legislation was not really about frivolous lawsuits, which the courts quickly dismiss. It was about making one industry exempt from the laws that apply to all others. Normally, he said, when someone is responsible for interfering with public health or safety, local authorities or victims bring lawsuits to stop the nuisance and recover the costs of cleaning it up. But this law permitted gun dealers to create public safety problems with impunity.

Kairys noted that gun industry insiders themselves had explained why the industry was so adamant about being able to feed the criminal and youth gun market. "The large self-defense market is driven by fear....The steady source for the fear that drives the handgun market is crime, particularly crimes committed with guns." Anything that increases fear, he said, increases the demand for guns. What he said was true of Clifford, who bought the Beretta because he heard shooting in his neighborhood.

The gun industry insisted that their rights were based on the Constitution. Gun-industry-immunity did raise a constitutional issue, Kairys said, but the lawsuits did not interfere with gun ownership or the Second Amendment. The constitutional issue that PLCAA raised had greatly troubled the Framers of the Constitution—but it was not the one the gun-rights people talked about. The Framers were worried about the practice of legislatures intervening in pending lawsuits. James Madison had called this "legislative usurpation...[that] must lead to tyranny."[46] To help limit this abuse, the Constitution established separation of powers, with the legislature making laws of general application, the executive enforcing the laws, and the courts deciding cases based on the laws. Regarding tort liability law, the states determined the rules. But PLCAA violated this by limiting the traditional state authority.[47]

To this day, PLCAA still grants immunity from civil lawsuits to gun manufacturers and gun dealers. It shields the makers of defective guns from civil lawsuits if, for example, the trigger was intentionally pulled. That may seem reasonable, but it is too broad. In Kenzo's case, Mark pulled the trigger in part because the Beretta lacked a prominent chamber-loaded indicator to show him that a bullet was still hidden in the chamber. The boy's actions and the gun's design were both at fault.

The law does not allow lawsuits to be brought where the discharge "was caused by a volitional act that constituted a criminal offense." That also sounds reasonable. But again, it is too broad. A child who makes a fatal mistake with a gun that lacks safety features that would have prevented him from making it is deemed a "criminal," having committed involuntary manslaughter. But the design of the gun may

286

have been a significant cause of the death. Judges and juries should get to see the facts of the case.

The PLCAA grants six narrow exceptions for civil lawsuits. For example, a lawsuit can be brought by a victim against someone who has been convicted of knowingly transferring a firearm, if the seller knows "that such firearm will be used to commit a crime of violence." The victim has to have evidence that the person he is suing transferred a gun to someone that he absolutely *knew* would commit a crime with it. In other words, to sue, you need a great deal of evidence about what was going on inside the seller's head. Such knowledge is extremely rare.

Another exemption in PLCAA is for "negligent entrustment or negligence per se." Negligent entrustment occurs when a seller supplies a gun to someone that he knows, or should know, is likely to cause injury to that person or others.

The case of *Delana v. Odessa Gun & Pawn* is an example of negligent entrustment. Janet Delana's daughter, Colby, suffered from paranoid schizophrenia and depression. After Colby bought a handgun from Odessa Gun & Pawn in 2012, in Odessa, Missouri, her mother took the gun from her. Later, when Colby was about to receive a paycheck, her mother called the pawnshop and pleaded with them not to sell her daughter a gun. But a few days later, they sold her one anyway, and she killed her father with it. Jon Lowy and other attorneys won a settlement of $2.2 million for Janet Delana using the negligent entrustment exemption. Even a few cases like this can force rogue gun dealers to think twice, so these lawsuits are important for public safety.[48]

The gun industry was so eager to get special immunity from civil lawsuits in part because it was facing considerable liability. It had been settling lawsuits or losing them when juries saw the facts.[49] So the industry knew it needed its own special protection to keep juries from hearing the facts. It needed to put itself above the law.

Meanwhile, the industry was arguing that litigation that seeks to reform the industry should be attempted *only* by public debate and legislation, instead of by lawsuits. But that was hypocrisy. The industry knew it could prevent important information from becoming public. It even stopped government funding of legitimate research on how to prevent gun deaths and injuries. That deficit in research seriously hampered the possibility of legislative remedies.

After the PLCAA became law, not many lawsuits against the gun industry survived pretrial arguments to dismiss them.[50] Often valid cases were dismissed with no evidence heard. Yet, almost three-fourths of Americans—including two-thirds of gun owners—support allowing cities to sue gun dealers when there is strong evidence that their careless sales practices allow criminals to obtain guns, according to a national survey by the Center for American Progress.[51]

When the gun industry finally passed their gun-industry-immunity law, I wasn't surprised. I knew they needed it desperately. I had reason to be angry that they had been able to protect their marketing and sales of guns that were unsafe in design. But I realized that remaining angry about this could be harmful to my health.

Fortunately, I had started a book group of friends: four women, four men, all single and in the midst of transitions. We met each month to talk about books we read—mostly good fiction. (I was surprised how many plots turned on gun violence.) We became good friends, laughing with each other about the dating horror stories we shared. We went on hikes and bike rides together all over the Bay Area.

This small group of friends became a great source of comfort, entertainment, and stability during a troubled period of my life.

# 17

## Who Killed Kenzo?

The juries in the *Dix v. Beretta USA* trials were asked, in essence, who was responsible for Kenzo's death.

After he died, Lynn and I at first thought his death had been caused only by the mistakes made by his friend, Mark, and Mark's father, Clifford. But we soon learned there was more to it than that—much more. For me, those courtrooms were classrooms. Lessons about responsibility saturated the testimony of every witness.

But I also began to realize that many of the causes of Kenzo's death were excluded from the trials, or not discussed. Also, as time passed, new research and events revealed additional answers. This is not a murder mystery, but something close. It's a manslaughter mystery—a prevention mystery.

Before turning to what we—the coalition I joined—did to help prevent deaths like Kenzo's, now would be a good time to present the conclusions we came to about who killed Kenzo. Who was responsible for his death, and, since this type of tragedy is still common, who is to this day responsible for many deaths like his?

———

**Some decisions made by Mark's father, Clifford, killed Kenzo.** Clifford made the mistake of buying and bringing into his home a handgun that was unsafe in its design. He stored his Beretta unlocked, where his young son could get it. And he kept a loaded magazine in it, with a round in the chamber. Clifford also failed to train his son adequately in gun safety.[52]

Storing his gun loaded and unlocked was one of Clifford's worst mistakes—one that led to Kenzo's death. But this mistake is also remarkably common. At least one gun is found in about 35 to 40 percent of US homes with children eighteen or younger. And in her April 2018 *American Journal of Public Health* study, "Storage Practices of US Gun Owners in 2016," Cassandra Crifasi and colleagues found that only slightly more than half (55 percent) of gun owners with children under eighteen reported storing all their guns safely, i.e., locked, or in a way that reduces the risk of unauthorized use.[53] The study revealed that 4.6 million children live in homes with an unlocked or unsupervised gun,[54] and unfortunately, unsafe gun storage also seems to be increasing.[55]

———

**Mark killed Kenzo.** Mark went to retrieve the gun he had been told not to touch. He forgot that a round could still be in the chamber even when the magazine containing bullets has been removed. He put an empty magazine back in the pistol when he entered the room where Kenzo was, and pulled the trigger of the gun that he thought he'd unloaded.

He was playing with a death machine.

Unfortunately, children make mistakes. I believe it is up to adults—all of us—to see that the mistakes children make do not cause deaths, injuries, or lasting trauma. In their testimony, at least, Mark and his father admitted their responsibility for Kenzo's death. And later, Mark would join Kalani to speak on the radio about preventing deaths like this.

———

**Beretta in Italy and Beretta USA killed Kenzo.** The defective design of the Beretta semiautomatic handgun marketed by Beretta USA defied the gun lobby's absurd false assertion that "Guns don't kill people, people kill people." The Beretta should have had a prominent chamber-loaded indicator. The gun had been designed for highly trained law enforcement and the military, not for the general public. Its extractor, which removes the spent cartridge casing, was supposed to do double duty as a tiny chamber-loaded indicator. When a round was in the chamber, the indicator stuck out just slightly more on the side of the gun, for trained police to feel at night. It was so inadequate as a chamber-loaded indicator that neither Mark nor his father ever noticed it, and Beretta never presented the results of any tests about its effectiveness as an indicator.[56]

The manual that came with the Beretta, to my eye, was woefully inadequate for teaching Clifford about this tiny extractor, or about the dangers of storing a gun that was loaded where a young person could access it. The manual did not have prominent, explicit warnings that demand attention, and it contained conflicting and confusing safety instructions.

Unlike Clifford and Mark, Beretta USA never admitted its responsibility. It escaped liability, but in my opinion it was far from faultless.

——

**The gun industry also killed Kenzo.** Its propaganda stoked fear of violent intruders in order to sell more guns. Those messages must have resonated with Clifford, who read many gun magazines. Along with the tales of violent home invasions in many gun magazines came—and still come—stories of how guns are used for self-defense. But self-defense uses of guns are rare.[57] The gun lobby, the gun industry, and their publications spread extreme exaggerations of the number of self-defensive gun uses, relying on the bogus research of Gary Kleck and his colleagues.[58]

Dr. David Hemenway, in Public Health at Harvard, says that in Gary Kleck's 1991 book, *Point Blank: Guns and Violence in America*, Kleck asserted that guns were used in self-defense 700,000 times per year. The other eight studies he cited in support of his estimate suffered from many of the same errors as Kleck's. They typically had samples too small to make an accurate estimate of such a rare event. They did not clearly define what "use" of a gun for "self-defense" means. They failed to clearly delineate a time frame that could be remembered accurately by the respondents. They lacked follow-up questions to discover the nature of the incident. They were generally not based on a truly representative national sample. They often failed to distinguish civilian gun use from military or police use and did not distinguish using a gun for self-defense against a person rather than an animal, or, for that matter, a suspicious sound in the night, said Hemenway.

Then, in 1992, Gary Kleck and Marc Gertz did a national survey of 5,000 households. Now their estimate suddenly jumped from the original 700,000 to anywhere from 1 million to 2.5 million defensive gun uses. They said they thought 2.5 million was the most accurate, which would mean that the study Kleck defended just a year earlier, was off by a huge amount. Oops!

Kleck said that 1.33 percent of respondents to his 1992 study indicated they had used a gun in self-defense. That was only sixty-six respondents of the 5,000. Based on those few responses, he attempted to accurately estimate the incidence in the entire population of an extremely rare event. Hemenway explained that Kleck was committing a methodological error that is well-known, one that produces wildly inaccurate results.

In a lecture I attended, Hemenway said that every methodologically sound attempt to find external validation for Kleck's assertion found it to be a very large overestimate. For example, at about the time of Kleck's survey, his estimate of the use of guns to protect against offenders was thirty-eight times higher than that of the National Crime Victimization Survey, which used a carefully tested research design with a randomly selected sample of 50,000 American households. But the results of his research were—*and still are*—often quoted by the gun industry and gun lobby and their friends, including in magazines and other media.

The gun industry's dissemination of the false idea that firearms in the home are a good means of protection is one of the great con jobs of American history. This idea—so often in conservative media, and even repeated regularly in mainstream media, is generally voiced without rebuttal. But a review of sixteen cohort or case control research studies to understand the association between firearm availability in homes and suicide and homicide found that rates of homicide double in homes where there are guns, and rates of suicide more than triple.[59] Women who live with a gun owner are especially at risk of death by homicide or suicide.[60]

To sell more guns for self-defense, the gun industry also actually encouraged unsafe gun storage with a blizzard of conflicting messages. Beretta's ads, for example, were like those of other gun makers in promoting guns as a good means of protection and suggesting that these guns can be stored unsafely. And at gun shows, one can obtain NRA instructor's manuals or NRA home-protection course manuals with contradictory instructions that include advising the *unsafe* storage of guns kept for "protection." One of them says that guns kept for home protection are "always in use," "must be ready for immediate use," and "may be kept loaded."

———

**Congress also played a role in Kenzo's death, and in others like his.** Congress protected the gun industry's greed and negligence with a series of specific laws, loopholes, and exemptions that made it easy for the gun industry to continue to sell dangerously designed firearms and, more recently, for people to illegally traffic them into states that have enacted strong gun laws. The irresponsibility of Congress, the gun industry, and the gun lobby were, and still are, hidden behind a carefully constructed set of misleading justifications, false dichotomies, myths, and diversions, all maintained by money and political power. The jurors never heard about many of the laws, loopholes, and exemptions that contributed to Kenzo's death.

Here is a brief summary of some of them:

The gun industry was the only US industry that Congress made exempt from federal product-safety oversight when it created the Consumer Product Safety Commission in 1972.[61] Before the CPSC was established, Congress—the entire legislative body—had to discover that a particular product was poorly designed and harmful. This usually came to Congress's attention only after some horrendous series of injuries got major media coverage. The CPSC set up a more systematic method for making products safer, and American consumers benefited. The approximately 15,000 consumer products around us generally became more safely designed.

However, in our country, because of the political power of the gun lobby, firearms were given an exemption. Gun manufacturers have no requirement and no incentive to design them as safely as reasonably possible. As a result of this 1972 exemption, many of the firearms sold to Americans today are needlessly unsafe in a variety of ways.

In addition, the failure of Congress to require background checks for all gun sales is a loophole linked to Kenzo's death, and continues to be a cause of many other deaths and crimes. It is the essence of being "soft on crime."[62] Congress has not passed a federal law requiring background checks on all gun sales. Consequently, inter-state gun trafficking makes it easy for young people like those who Clifford feared in his neighborhood to obtain firearms that are illegal under state law.

But state gun laws are effective. Despite the problem of inter-state gun trafficking, the seven states that have had laws for five years or more requiring universal background checks had a 35 percent lower rate of firearm mortality among people age twenty-one and younger, "even after adjustment for socioeconomic factors and gun ownership," according to a 2019 study.[63]

Politicians in Congress complain about "crime." But by failing to pass a universal background check law, they are enabling violent crime. Then they continue to complain about the problem that they are helping create.

Congress also cut the CDC's budget for research on gun violence, causing Americans—including me—to remain ignorant about major risks to themselves and their children. Finally, in 2019, Congress appropriated $25 million for gun violence research. But more is needed to understand this complex set of problems. The information gap from the decades-long lack of federal research remains.

Steven Teret of the Johns Hopkins Center for Gun Policy and Research told the jurors that information on the make and model of guns used in accidental gun deaths is not collected. The studies did not indicate whether Beretta guns were involved. Funding for that research was scarce because Congress had cut the CDC's research budget for studying gun violence by the exact amount it had requested for that research, and the CDC was afraid that Congress would limit its budget more if it funded research on gun violence.[64]

Because Congress cut the budget, data about unintentional gun deaths is also not as accurate as it should be. In our trials, the jurors did not get the facts they needed, and did not hear anything about this political interference with the CDC's ability to conduct research. Parents, like Clifford and me, were kept from fully understanding the risks of firearms to our children.

The deceptively named Protection of Lawful Commerce in Arms Act (PLCAA), which Republicans passed in 2005, singles out people harmed by the misconduct of gun makers and gun dealers as a special class, and denies them equal justice under the law. Police officers, ordinary gun owners, or any other victims who are killed or injured by this misconduct, or their family members, cannot file most types of civil lawsuits.

This set of laws and loopholes makes up a unique history of irresponsibility that causes many American deaths. Congress should require companies that make and sell firearms to take reasonable care to prevent the deaths and injuries that result from foreseeable misuse. But instead, Congress helps the gun industry put unsafe guns into the hands of dangerous people by failing to pass the laws this nation needs.

———

**Who else killed Kenzo? I did.** I didn't ask if there were guns in the homes where my children play. It never occurred to me. But I learned the hard way, and now I speak about what happened to Kenzo at Brady End Family Fire[65] press conferences and elsewhere in hopes that others will learn from my experience. I love doing this because I meet some great people this way. Our coalition, which includes the Brady United chapters, the Giffords Law Center to Prevent Gun Violence, Moms Demand Action, and many other groups, encourages safe gun storage and advises parents to ask if there are guns in the homes where their kids play.

PART V

# The Long Game

# 18

## Safety Standards

When Lynn and I originally sued Beretta USA, our goal was to persuade the company to sell safer handguns to consumers in order to prevent others from suffering the loss of their child in the way we had lost ours. We met the victims of the 101 California Street massacre and other activists, and learned that our goal could be achieved through legislation as well as litigation. Observing some leaders of the gun industry in the first trial had increased our desire to have an impact on the industry, so we tried to help change the gun industry with legislation while we were fighting in court to change it.

Fortunately, Andrew and Kae McGuire, founders of the Trauma Foundation, had put together a coalition of remarkable leaders and organizations to pass regulations.[66] We had joined it within a year after Kenzo's death, in May of 1994. The coalition included Deane

Calhoun, founder of Youth Alive, a violence prevention nonprofit based primarily in Oakland; the Legal Community Against Violence in San Francisco (now the Giffords Law Center to Prevent Gun Violence); and many other organizations.

Mary Leigh Blek and Charlie Blek, Republican members from conservative Orange County, California, would soon be national leaders of our movement. The issue they came to care the most about was the same as the one I cared most about: setting safety standards for handguns.

### Junk Guns

In 1994, Mary Leigh and Charlie Blek's son, Matthew, was a twenty-one-year-old college student with a summer job in New York City. One night, as he was walking a girl home, three fifteen-year-old boys with two handguns approached him and demanded money. As he reached for his wallet, one of them shot him in the head. Matthew staggered to a gas station, where the attendant called 911. By the time the emergency medical team got him to an operating room, he'd lost too much blood to survive.

The police caught the boys. The shooter was sentenced to twenty-five years to life. Matthew's mother, Mary Leigh Blek, wrote to him and was surprised when he wrote back and told her he had two babies. She had asked him how he got the gun, and he told her that guns are easily available; people get them in the South and bring them to New York in the trunks of their cars to sell. Mary Leigh was amazed. "These kids were dirt poor, but they could toss the gun because they knew they could get another one," she told me. The police had told her the gun was a .380, made by Davis Industries, in Mira Loma, California. "They are only about fifty miles from where Matthew grew up," she said.

I had met Mary Leigh Blek in the mid-1990s, when we joined the coalition we called the firearms strategy group. She is a conservative dresser who seldom speaks in meetings, but when she does, everyone listens, because they know what she says will be wise and to the point. Charlie Blek is a lawyer with a booming voice. He too is often quiet, yet when he speaks, he is persuasive. The two are a study in contrasts—Charlie, outgoing, with a wicked sense of humor; Mary Leigh, soft-spoken, eminently rational, and unashamed to express her emotions.

There were essentially no laws setting handgun product safety standards when our coalition started. Although the 1968 Gun Control Act had made it illegal to import unsafe handguns with no sporting purpose, in order to protect the US gun industry, Congress did allow unsafe handguns to be manufactured domestically. Consequently, in the 1990s many people in California—and in the rest of the U.S.—were dying from homicides committed with domestically manufactured, poorly designed, easily concealable junk guns, also called Saturday Night Specials. Our coalition began to focus on these guns and unsafe handgun design.

In 1992, the *Wall Street Journal* had published a series of investigative articles about junk guns by Pulitzer Prize–winning journalist Alix Freedman. She wrote that a man named George Jennings, after graduating from high school in Kansas in the late 1960s, had transformed his small machine shop into a gun manufacturing company, Raven Arms, which "all but created the high-volume market for cheap handguns."[67] It took advantage of the loophole in the 1968 Gun Control Act that allowed unsafe handguns to be domestically manufactured.[68] Jennings designed a cheap .25 caliber pistol, the Raven, and invested $50,000 to manufacture it in large quantities. By the late 1980s his brochures boasted total sales of 1.8 million pistols.

Soon other family members created similar companies that went on to make the Jennings .22, the Davis .380, and Bryco guns.

Freedman called Jennings "the patriarch of a secretive clan in Southern California," and said he had "made his fortune from a market of misery: the surprisingly cheap small-caliber pistols that sell by the thousands, largely in America's inner cities." Every year, these companies pumped out 400,000 Saturday Night Specials, sold mostly in America's enclaves of poverty and crime.

The junk guns made by all the Jennings companies had virtually no safety features, and they were very cheap to make. The average retail price of other guns was around $600; the price for a Raven .25 caliber pistol was about $79. Profits were high. Criminals frequently used them, and they were especially likely to get into kids' hands. They often jammed and harmed their owners.[69]

On the "Saturday Night Special" junk guns that led to the very high rate of gun homicide in the U.S. in the 1990s and the reasons for the rise of the movement to prevent gun violence, see: *Ring of Fire: The Handgun Makers of Southern California, GJ Wintemute, Violence Prevention Research Program, 1994:* https://health.ucdavis.edu/vprp/pdf/RingofFire1994.pdf

### *Courageous Leadership*

With the backing of our coalition, the Bleks initiated California Senate Bill 15, establishing safety standards for handguns sold in the state. It included a procedure for testing handguns to block the sale of junk guns. The state would maintain a roster of the handgun models that were deemed safe enough to sell.

We found an exceptional resource in emergency physician Dr. Garen Wintemute.[70] He told me that Alix Freedman's *Wall Street Journal* article had blown him away.[71] "Behind the mayhem," he said, "are ill-bred, immoral, greedy men and women whose companies are responsible for products frequently involved in crime and not useful for defense."[72]

Soon the Bleks, the coalition, and our Brady members were handing out copies of Wintemute's book, *Ring of Fire: The Handgun Makers of Southern California*, to legislators. Wintemute, who had also studied public health, argued that the most effective interventions control the "point source" of hazards, rather than letting them get dispersed and then having to deal with the scattered problems they create.[73]

*Ring of Fire* explained that most junk guns were made from cheap, die-cast zinc alloy—metal so soft you could shave it with a knife. That's why these guns could not withstand heavy use and tended to misfire or jam. If dropped, they often discharged and killed or injured people, such as the gun owner or someone in his family.

When the Bleks began flying frequently to Sacramento to discuss their bill, the legislators didn't want to listen.[74] The various gun lobby groups had fourteen well-funded lobbyists.[75] Our chances looked bleak. To break the logjam, attorney Julie Leftwich thought we could pass the state law by first getting activists to persuade their city councils to pass local ordinances banning the manufacture and sale of junk guns. If enough cities did that, state legislators would have to take notice.[76] But then Eric Gorovitz, working as an intern in the Brady DC office, had found that the California preemption law did not totally prevent local ordinances; it only limited the state legislature's jurisdiction to *licensing and registration* of guns.

Leftwich, the smart and gracious legal director of the Legal Community Against Violence, wrote model local ordinances that could withstand the inevitable gun lobby lawsuits. All over the state, Brady leaders and coalition partners began trying to convince city councils to pass the ordinances.[77] This gave activists important local work to do. For the first time, hundreds of victims of gun violence and concerned parents matched the gun lobby's arguments with accurate facts and with the emotional intensity that parents feel for their children.

I spoke at several city council hearings in Northern California. In huge city hearing rooms, impassioned speakers from each side waited hours for their three minutes to plead before the city councils. The opposing sides contrasted dramatically. The parents supporting the ordinances were mostly professionals who told their stories, said their statistics, politely answered council members' questions, and sat down. The gun crowd sat across from us in their hunting shirts. Many were ordinary hunters who I thought had been misled. Some argued that the Second Amendment prevented regulating junk guns, and spoke as if banning guns that failed to meet safety standards was a ban on all guns. They didn't realize that we were trying to make handguns safer.

Some of them sitting across from us were scruffy and unruly. A few appeared to be downright unbalanced. When they spoke into the microphone, what they said had little to do with the ordinance. They repeated the same bizarre, apocalyptic phrases. If they didn't like what the government was doing and couldn't change it through the ballot box, they seemed to think that in the name of "freedom," they had the right to overthrow a democratically elected government by force and install their own rulers. They didn't seem to realize that the Constitution states that the militia's purpose is to "suppress Insurrections," not to lead them.[78]

They were their own worst enemies. But they were organized, and always had someone stalking around our group holding a little video camera to his eye, filming each of us with the implied threat that someday, they would be coming after us.

By mid-1999, forty-five California cities and counties had passed ordinances prohibiting junk guns. With news coverage, the pressure on state legislators mounted. Finally, in August 1999, Governor Gray Davis signed SB 15. Its author, Senator Richard Polanco (D-LA), dedicated it to Matthew Blek, and the California Senate honored Mary Leigh and Charlie Blek for their courageous leadership.[79]

306

It had taken five years of relentless effort for our coalition to build our grassroots capacity and establish an innovative California procedure for requiring that handguns meet safety standards. That drove the junk gun manufacturers out of California.[80] Our coalition also saw this law as a crucial step toward requiring that handguns meet additional safety standards.

# 19

## Progress

### *"Associate with People Whom You Enjoy"*

By the time the new millennium rolled around, I was still trying to put my life back together. Lynn and I had divorced in 1995. Kalani had been back from college, living with me, but had moved out to San Francisco when he got a job and started going to college there.

To try to cope with my oddly solitary new life, I took classes. In my old files there is a handout from one class I took: "Strategies for Stress Management." I can see underlined in red the items that struck me as the most promising ones to try:

1. Associate with people whom you enjoy and who support you.
5. View life as challenges to seek, not obstacles to avoid.
6. Take responsibility for your life and your feelings, but never blame yourself.
15. Open yourself to new experiences. Try new things, new food, new places.

Frankly, some of these sounded like torture. I liked staying home, reading books. But I did sign up for a dating website, then asked out a few women whose profiles seemed promising. When I forced myself to meet them, I knew within minutes whether I was interested. But, even when I wasn't, I often found our conversations worthwhile. The anthropologist in me would kick in. After brief initial banter, we would tell each other our life stories, our dreams, and how our lives had been battered by a tough world and by certain choices we had made. It seemed that everyone my age came with loads of baggage. I was no different. Some of my baggage was on that double-edged poster Kenzo had stuck on his bedroom wall: No Justice, No Peace.

As I sought relationships that met my needs, I found that working with other activists was most meaningful to me. I felt a bond with some of the others whose child had been shot, and who were struggling with the same feelings I was: grief, loneliness, anger, regrets; the desire to make people safe and not remain a helpless "victim," but also to get back to a normal life. I admired many of the activists and enjoyed collaborating. I became secretary/treasurer of the California Million Mom March / Brady State Council for three years, starting in 2001, often writing newsletters and op-eds about our gun bills.

After our California coalition passed the law prohibiting junk guns in the state, I hoped that next we would make it a priority to fix the problem that had killed Kenzo, by requiring chamber-loaded indicators on semiautomatic handguns. But for three years the group chose other important laws.

Finally, in 2002, at one of our meetings, when the Bleks and I championed it, our coalition made this our priority.

### *Whiz-Bang Technology*

We began working with Senator Jack Scott on California Senate Bill 489. Scott was a highly respected legislator whose son had been killed in an unintentional shooting. SB 489 would require models of semiautomatic handguns not already on the roster—the list—of handguns that could be sold in the state to have either a chamber-loaded indicator or a magazine-disconnect safety device, and, a year after the law went into effect, to have both devices. Unfortunately, Senator Scott, who represented the Pasadena area, insisted on a provision that grandfathered in unsafe handgun models like the Beretta 92, which had already been approved.

On March 18, 2003, Luis Tolley (from Brady), Eric Gorovitz (with the Coalition to Stop Gun Violence), and I waited hours in a crowded hearing room in Sacramento to testify for SB 489 before the state Senate Public Safety Committee. Along with the Brady organization, the Coalition to Stop Gun Violence, led by Josh Horwitz, had been the bill's sponsors.

When the bill finally came up, NRA lobbyist Ed Worley testified to the senators. He said that supporters of the bill couldn't even define what a chamber-loaded indicator is, and that it might be something with flashing red diodes that would dangerously attract the attention of curious children, who'd think the gun was talking to them. This was the usual NRA attempt to distract; the bill said nothing about flashing red diodes.

Worley also griped that magazine-disconnect safety devices are "passive safety mechanisms" that make people complacent. He said he couldn't even put his four-year-old in the front seat of his car because the airbag—a passive device—might kill her. "You don't save lives with whiz-bang technology," he grumbled. "You have to teach children not to touch a gun."[81]

Senator Scott replied, "So-called 'whiz-bang technology' put seat belts in cars—airbags as well. These safety devices have saved far more lives than they cost....Sure, I'm for teaching kids not to touch guns; but it's not an either/or choice. *Do both.*" He reminded the legislators that a General Accounting Office study had found that chamber-loaded indicators could have prevented 23 percent of accidental shootings.

Finally, I got to testify. I pointed out that semiautomatics without magazine-disconnect safety devices often deceive people. They think the pistol can't fire if they have removed the magazine with bullets in it.[82] Of course, they should know better; but many don't.

We know that safer designs would prevent many unintentional shootings, I said, yet no other state required both devices. I told them a prominent chamber-loaded indicator would likely have prevented Kenzo's death. Finally, I put this in context. "In the past ten years in California alone, 3,300 young people were killed or injured in unintentional shootings."[83]

With the strong leadership of the Coalition to Stop Gun Violence, the bill passed the legislature. In September 2003, Governor Davis signed it.

### *The Regulations*

Gun industry lawyers tried to undermine the law by influencing the way its "regulations" were written by the California Department of Justice (CalDOJ). The wording of a law cannot specify all the details about how it should be implemented. The DOJ's regulations do that. But weak or ambiguously worded regulations can prevent a law from being fully enforced by government officials or in courts, and gun lobby lawyers had succeeded before at manipulating the language that regulates a law.

On the DOJ's list of stakeholders commenting, there were four gun-violence-prevention people—including volunteers like me—opposed by nineteen gun lobbyists. Their lobbyists were led by Larry Keane of the National Shooting Sports Foundation and Jeffrey Reh, VP of Beretta USA—our two nemeses from court.

Fortunately, the law was strong and explicit. It said that for a chamber-loaded indicator to be acceptable, it had to "plainly" indicate that a round is in the chamber; it had to be readily visible; and it had to incorporate explanatory text or graphics, or both. These should indicate to a foreseeable adult user of the pistol, without requiring the user to refer to the user's manual, whether a cartridge is in the firing chamber.

Exchanges of comments on new DOJ-proposed regulations continued for several years. Our coalition demanded that the regs hold to the intent and letter of the law. The gun lobbyists argued for "latitude to develop innovative devices." Senator Scott replied that for decades, gun manufacturers had the ability to develop effective chamber-loaded indicators, but they had chosen not to.

Every time new proposed regulations arrived in the mail from CalDOJ, I pored over it to detect how gun lobbyists had inserted attempts to undo the law. And they were always there, often cleverly hidden. I had listened to Larry Keane for hours at our trials and knew he would not miss an opportunity to try to weaken the law in ways that might appear innocuous but were not.

Still, I was amazed at the lengths to which the gun industry would go to resist designs that would make their customers safer. In one of the letters Keane sent back to CalDOJ in response to their proposed regulations, he tried to make acceptable the design of the Beretta's extractor, which pulls out spent casings and tries to do double duty as a chamber-loaded indicator.[84] Keane argued that indicators often provide users with "a tactile and/or visual indication of the presence (or absence) of a cartridge in the chamber."

This was the design that had failed to prevent Kenzo's death.

I felt desperate to prevent Keane and his clients from getting away with this defective design. My comments on the DOJ's proposed regulations quoted the law, and argued that an acceptable indicator must be very visible, not just something tactile for highly trained police to feel at night (if they could).

I wrote, "Please understand that my dear, dear son was killed because an extractor they called a 'chamber load indicator' on the Beretta 92 was so tiny that neither my son's friend's father (who was into 'practical shooting,' and had cleaned the gun over 500 times), nor my son's friend (who had fired this gun at a shooting range with his father), ever even saw it, or knew it was there. It was hardly capable of indicating 'to a reasonably foreseeable adult user of the pistol, without requiring the user to refer to the manual or any other resource other than the pistol itself, whether a cartridge is in the firing chamber.' "

Each member of our coalition sent letters.

In 2006, the DOJ published the final regulations. To my great relief, they turned down many of the gun lobby's arguments, including most of Keane's.[85] But it was not a complete victory. In 2004, grandfathering in pistols previously approved would allow Beretta 92s—the type that had killed Kenzo—to continue to be sold.

I was disappointed. Nonetheless, we had accomplished most of what we hadn't been able to do in court. We had passed a law and ensured that it could be enforced with reasonably tight regulations.

But the gun industry continued to resist. For five years after 2003, when we had passed SB 489, and even after the 2006 regulations were published, no gun maker submitted pistols to CalDOJ with safety devices that met California's standards.

314

As the entire hierarchical gun industry boycotted California, its spokesmen were claiming that the state's handgun safety standards were unreasonable and could not be met. They were hoping that their boycott "proved" that. Larry Keane had already been complaining to the media that California would become like Cuba, with its old cars, because Californians would only be able to get old models of handguns. But it wasn't our fault if the gun industry was choosing not to meet California's safety standards. Their boycott hurt their sales and endangered their customers.

### At Last, Change

In 2008, Sturm, Ruger & Company, Inc., better known by the shortened name, Ruger, broke the gun industry's boycott. It submitted a pistol that met California's standards, and by the end of the year, the pistol was added to California's roster of handguns approved for sale. Then other gun makers submitted models that were approved for sale. The basic design of the chamber-loaded indicator on these pistols was the one that our coalition had laboriously passed, then defended as the regulations were written. It was also the design that Lynn, I, Jon Lowy, and our expert witnesses had argued for in our lawsuit against Beretta USA.

It was no coincidence that Ruger was the gun company to break the boycott. Since it is a publicly traded company, stockholders can potentially have some influence over it. Ruger began advertising the *safety features* of its handgun. This was virtually unprecedented in the gun industry. To advertise safety features would suggest to potential gun buyers that handguns are dangerous without them.[86]

But the gamble paid off. In April 2012, after the CalDOJ Firearms Bureau Chief told me that Ruger's stock price had risen, I looked it up and saw that it was near its high. "Outgunned! Sturm Ruger Says It Can't Keep Up with Orders, Shares Surge," said FOXBusiness.[87]

Apparently, many gun buyers like being able to easily see when a round is chambered. Later, in 2012, I happened to google "chamber-loaded indicator." Up popped a Google Images link. Dozens of pictures appeared.

I scrolled through screen after screen of close-ups of them on the pistols of major gun makers. They clearly showed when a round was chambered. Many seemed to meet California's standards. They had indicators on their top or back that protruded, and probably showed red only when a round was chambered. Many included clearly visible engraved text, such as LOADED WHEN UP, so users could understand their operation without referring to a manual, as we had required. Most seemed to utilize the design that our expert Les Roane had argued for in court.

Our coalition had fixed the problem that had killed Kenzo by requiring prominent chamber-loaded indicators on new models of semiautomatic handguns. We had also required magazine-disconnect safety devices.[88]

### Did the Handgun Safety Standard Laws Save Lives?

For decades our coalition had helped to pass dozens of California laws regulating firearms. For years, when new CDC data was released, I updated my annual report, which the Brady organization disseminated. The brief report documented the fact that as California's laws were enacted, the state's firearm mortality rate had declined by far more than the decline in "the rest of the country" (i.e., the US population, excluding California).

At a California Brady conference, I met Loren Lieb, an epidemiologist whose son had been badly wounded by white supremacist Buford Furrow in 1999, when he fired seventy rounds at children and staff at the North Valley Jewish Community Center in Granada Hills.[89] I asked her to collaborate with me on the annual reports.

Our report analyzing 2020 data, showed that from the peak gun death rate of 1993 in California and the rest of the nation, California had reduced its gun death rate by 51 percent, while the rest of the nation had reduced its rate by only 3 percent. California's reduction was seventeen times greater.

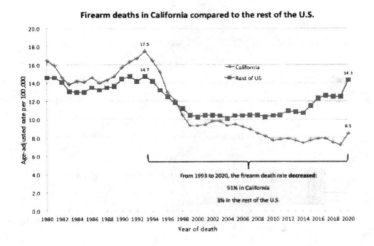

The gun laws our coalition had passed had indeed saved many lives.[90]

But how about *unintentional* gun deaths in California and the rest of the nation? I wondered: Did the handgun safety standard laws help prevent those?

The initial provisions of SB 15, the Unsafe Handgun Act, went into effect on January 1, 2001. From that point on, some models of unsafe handguns were no longer sold.

The bill requiring prominent chamber-loaded indicators and magazine-disconnect safety devices (SB 489) was passed in 2003. But no pistols with those two safety devices were sold in California until after November 2008, when Ruger broke the gun industry's boycott of the state's safety standards. Then, even though other gun makers' pistols with the safety devices were approved by CalDOJ, progress was slow because many unsafe pistols had been grandfathered in.[91]

By 2012 and 2013, over one-third of the pistols being sold in California had chamber-loaded indicators and magazine-disconnect safety devices. And the pistol safety standards laws appear to have helped save many lives. From the five-year period before California's handgun safety standard laws went into effect (1996–2000), to the period after both laws were in effect (2014–2018), the state's rate of unintentional gun death declined by two-thirds (66 percent).[92]

The unintentional gun death rate also declined in the rest of the nation—by 54 percent—12 percentage points *less* than California's decline.[93] The decline in the rest of the country probably occurred in part because gun makers were designing handguns to meet the safety standards of the large California handgun market and selling these safer handguns nationwide, along with their other unsafe handguns.[94]

Semiautomatic handguns with chamber-loaded indicators designed like the ones our expert witness exhibited at the trials were popular with gun buyers. They didn't blow up in shooters' faces, as Beretta's experts claimed they would.

Our coalition's "gun control" laws made semiautomatic handguns safer, and the people these laws made safer were probably mostly gun owners, their families, and people who visit their homes—like Kenzo. However, the semiautomatic handguns that meet the new safety standards are *only somewhat safer*. Homes without guns are still safer than homes with guns. Even if handgun designs are safer, places with higher rates of gun ownership—nations, states, homes—have higher rates of homicide and suicide, and higher rates of *gun* homicide, *gun* suicide, and unintentional gun death.[95]

As of this writing, Kenzo has been dead for twenty-eight years. During that time, more than 1,500 Californians have died in unintentional shootings. But it gives me some solace to know that our work is decreasing that risk.

No one knows whether the lower rate of unintentional gun death or of total gun death can be maintained in the face of the numerous ways it is currently being subverted by the gun industry, small-time operators, and gun traffickers, all of whom are eager to profit by selling unsafe firearms.

# 20

## Meditations

In addition to working on gun violence prevention, I had been attempting to rebuild my life. I had dabbled in Buddhist meditation, and in the early 2000s I had sporadically joined a Buddhist group connected to the Spirit Rock Meditation Center in Marin County. It met in a Chinese Buddhist monastery in Berkeley. The group, led by James Baraz, meditated together, then had thoughtful, sometimes profound, dharma talks and group discussions that were often about social issues. After I got to know James a little and he heard Kenzo's story, he asked me to lead a dharma talk, even though I had no knowledge of Buddhist teachings.

On the evening of my talk, I entered the Buddhist hall and took off my shoes, feeling more than a little nervous. But the large room where the sangha met was soothing. Incense in urns offered a sweet, slightly bitter, but pleasing aroma. Glass cases on the sides of the room held tiny clay figures of monks with contorted faces in various states of suffering, which Buddhists say is the condition of human life.

First, we meditated. But soon the gentle ringing of a sonorous bowl interrupted my attempts at letting go of my jabbering thoughts.

James invited me to sit cross-legged next to him in front of the group of sixty or so.

Mine was not the usual Buddhist dharma talk; instead, I spoke about what had happened to Kenzo, passionately explained some of the outrageous facts I had learned from our trials, and what could be done about gun violence. I also said something about suffering and trying to gently let go of troublesome thoughts.

When James asked the group for comments, most people agreed with me about ways to prevent gun violence; several related how gun crimes, gun suicides, and other gun violence had affected them and their families. Some spoke of their fears.

But then one elderly woman said thoughtfully, "I don't think we should take guns away from citizens. If the government turns corrupt, people may need them."

"I'm not for taking people's guns away," I said. Where did she get the idea that "gun control" really meant taking away people's guns? She was no NRA supporter. But like most of the pro-gun people I had debated, she had not acknowledged the specific policy suggestions I had explained, which were not about taking people's guns away, but only about keeping dangerous weapons out of the hands of dangerous people.

I realized anew the power of the gun lobby's framing of gun violence prevention as "gun control," a term which the media unfortunately continued to use.

A little later she said the same thing. No matter what I said, I could not disabuse her of the idea that I was a "gun grabber."

Worse yet, my talk had gone off track. The people there that evening wanted to discuss Buddhist practice. I had planned to talk about the inner turmoil of being an activist while trying to cope with disruptive feelings, like anger. But even when I went to a place of mindfulness and meditation, I ended up talking about gun policy, and not just my attempt to come to a sense of peace about what had happened to Kenzo.

I could not get away from the gun issue, nor did I want to. I had found that generally people *were* interested in the subject. Many of the people there were well-informed, but many others actually knew very little. I had been given my "calling" and would stick with it, but I had to learn not to let it eat me alive. I also had to learn to understand what the people listening to me wanted to discuss.

A different attempt to "get a life" proved to be a great deal more successful.

In January 2005, a friend in my book group asked me if I'd like to go with her to the home of some people she knew who got together to see films and discuss them. We went and watched *The Manchurian Candidate* with about twelve others, then had a lively discussion about it.

A woman named Marilyn was one of the most interesting and knowledgeable people there, and I noticed she wasn't wearing a wedding ring. During the discussion, she mentioned that she taught a class in film studies at UC Berkeley, not only for students, but also for members of the community. I sat in on her next class. After she showed a film, she led a discussion by posing questions and calling on students, or the (mostly retired) people who came. The diversity of opinions and experiences fascinated me.

That afternoon, a student happened to ask her what she thought of *The Aviator*, a movie in theaters then. She replied that she hadn't seen it yet, but wanted to.

Back home, I thought of calling her, and looked her up in the phone book. She lived on the same street I did. After carefully rehearsing to myself what I'd say, I dialed and asked her if she wanted to go see the movie. She said yes, and we set a date.

When we got to the theater, there was an awkward moment. Tickets for seniors age sixty-two and over were discounted. Marilyn, who was sixty-two, wondered whether to admit her age and pay the discounted price for her ticket, or accept my offer to pay full price for both tickets? Being a feminist, she told the clerk she was sixty-two, and paid for her ticket. I was sixty-one, so I had to pay full price. We laughed at the little moment of sexual politics.

We found we had a lot to talk about beyond sexual politics, and she lived so close that it was easy to just walk over. We would sit at her dining room table with a view of the San Francisco Bay, eat meals together, and talk for hours about our families, where we grew up, and the joys and sorrows of our lives.

Marilyn was born in Cincinnati, Ohio, into a close-knit Jewish family. Her father, with whom she was especially close, had owned a successful furniture store. Her mother, although a math major in college, had stayed home while her two daughters were growing up. When Marilyn was a sophomore in college, her father died due to a surgical error by a novice doctor. She was devastated by the tragic loss.

As we got to know each other, I could feel that she understood the depths of my own loss. We discussed my trials and her tribulations for hours. She was interested to hear about Kenzo, our lawsuit against Beretta USA, and my interest in gun violence prevention. Marilyn helped me find balance, and escape my consuming focus on gun violence prevention. She introduced me to films from all over the world, which we enjoyed discussing in detail. She could make me laugh, which I realized I hadn't been doing much of for some time, and we both loved to travel.

I enjoyed the delight she took in my son, Kalani—the way they would laugh together. He had struggled to find his way after Kenzo's death. But by the time they met, he had completed his college degree in information tech management at the University of San Francisco night school, while working in the IT department of UC San Francisco Hospital. One day he met an interesting premed intern while fixing her computer. They began seeing each other, and fell in love.

Years slipped by. Marilyn moved in with me, and, at the end of 2008, we got married. With Marilyn's help, I continued to publish op-eds in newspapers around the country, where they could make a difference. See my website: https://griffindix.com/ She joined the protests for stronger gun laws that I helped organize. I saw the infrastructure of our movement grow, and admired the Marjory Stoneman Douglas High School students from Parkland, Florida, who become incredibly effective organizers after the mass murder there.

Lynn also remarried. After an eight-year courtship, Kalani and his girlfriend got married, too. When she finished med school, her internship, and her residency, she and Kalani moved to Washington State, where she had gotten a job in her specialty. Soon they had a baby boy, and a few years later, a daughter.

For me, an unanticipated delight came with Marilyn's son and his wife, and their two daughters, who all live nearby. The two girls, now ages eleven and nine, bring us joy with their energy, enthusiasm, and curiosity.

I feel deeply grateful for the joys of having four grandkids. But, in a state of wonder, occasionally tinged with regret, I find myself reflecting on what it would have been like to play with Kenzo's kids, if only he had lived.

Children are precious.

They should always be kept safe.

# APPENDICES

# APPENDIX A

## "The Ambulance in the Valley"

'Twas a dangerous cliff, as they freely confessed,
Though to walk near its crest was so pleasant;
But over its terrible edge there had slipped
A duke, and full many a peasant.

The people said something would have to be done,
But their projects did not at all tally.
Some said "Put a fence 'round the edge of the cliff,"
Some, "An ambulance down in the valley."

The lament of the crowd was profound and was loud,
As their tears overflowed with their pity;
But the cry for the ambulance carried the day
As it spread through the neighboring city....

"For the cliff is all right if you're careful," they said;
"And, if folks ever slip and are dropping,
It isn't the slipping that hurts them so much
As the shock down below—when they're stopping."

So for years (we have heard), as these mishaps occurred
Quick forth would the rescuers sally,
To pick up the victim who fell from the cliff,
With the ambulance down in the valley.

Said one in a plea, "It's a marvel to me

That you'd give so much greater attention
To repairing results than to curing the cause;
You had much better aim at prevention.

For the mischief, of course, should be stopped at its source;
Come, neighbors and friends, let us rally.
It is far better sense to rely on a fence
Than an ambulance down in the valley."

From: "The Ambulance in the Valley" by Joseph Malins, 1895,
quoted in *While We Were Sleeping: Success Stories in Injury and
Violence Prevention*, by David Hemenway (Berkeley and Los Angeles: University of California Press, 2009), p. 5.

# APPENDIX B

## Did California's Handgun Safety Standard Laws Save Lives?

California's average rate of unintentional gun death declined by two-thirds from the five-year period of 1996 through 2000, which was before the handgun product safety laws began to be enforced, to 2014–2018, the period after they were both being enforced. In 1996–2000 the average rate of unintentional gun death was 0.24, and the five-year average rate from 2014–2018 was 0.08.

The CDC's data on unintentional firearm deaths undercounts those involving children and overcounts those involving adults. The decentralized system of coding death certificates by medical examiners and coroners doesn't seem to have fixed these problems during the period under study. Several research sources on this national problem say that the number reported by the CDC of children killed in unintentional shootings should be approximately doubled.[96]

I believe that California's handgun product safety laws were responsible for much of the state's reduction in unintentional gun deaths. Various factors convince me:

1) The reduction occurred more in California than in the rest of the nation. California's reduction was 66 percent; the reduction in the United States, excluding California, was 54 percent. Much of this reduction was probably because California prohibited unsafe junk guns. The state also began requiring chamber-loaded indicators and magazine-disconnect safety devices, and from November 2008, gun makers began selling pistols with the two safety devices.

2) California's reduction occurred in unintentional *firearm* deaths but did not occur in unintentional *non-firearm* deaths. This helps to

show that these handgun product safety laws made the difference, rather than other factors.

3) The time of the reduction matches the time when the two handgun product safety laws were enforced.

4) SB 489 appears to have helped reduce *nonfatal* unintentional firearm injuries in California. A comparison of the state's pre–SB 489 period (2000–2004) with the post–SB 489 period (2010–2014) shows a reduction of 18.8 percent in the rate of nonfatal hospitalizations for unintentional firearm injuries.

5) Other research indicates that these types of safety devices prevent gun deaths. One such study, "Unintentional and Undetermined Firearm Related Deaths: A Preventable Death Analysis for Three Safety Devices" (by J. S. Vernick, M. O'Brien, L. M. Hepburn, S. B. Johnson, D. W. Webster, and S. W. Hargarten, *Injury Prevention*, vol. 9, 2003: 307–11), analyzed the effect of three safety devices (personalization, chamber-loaded indicators, and magazine-disconnect safety devices on the preventability of unintentional or "intent undetermined" gun deaths. Of the deaths studied, 44 percent could potentially have been prevented by at least one of the safety devices. The use of personalization was associated with the highest preventability (37 percent), followed by chamber-loaded indicators (20 percent) and magazine safeties (4 percent).

Data from the National Violent Death Reporting System (NVDRS) indicates that handguns are involved in many of the unintentional firearm deaths. The 2014 data used here are from hospitals in eighteen states.

Hunting accidents account for only 8 percent of the unintentional gun deaths, and hunting is done with rifles or shotguns. *Handguns* are involved in approximately six in ten of the unintentional gun deaths, and we know that most handguns being sold by gun dealers are semiautomatic pistols. More than three-fourths of unintentional gun deaths occur in homes or apartments. The gun industry could do much more to help prevent these deaths.

The NVDRS reports the "context of injury" of unintentional firearm deaths: playing with a gun (40.9 percent); cleaning a gun (12.9 percent); showing a gun to others (9.8 percent); and the loading/unloading of a gun (6.8 percent). These activities are all likely to involve unsafe gun design or foreseeable misuse, *or both*.

The NVDRS also reports the "circumstances of injury." Laws requiring prominent chamber-loaded indicators and magazine-disconnect safety devices on semiautomatic handguns could help to prevent the deaths that occurred when someone "thought the gun was unloaded" (15.2 percent of the deaths), and when someone "thought the gun was unloaded because the magazine was disengaged."

After the two California handgun product safety laws passed, there were improvements in gun design; in the instruction manuals that come with the gun; and in firearm safety training. California laws our coalition passed could have helped to prevent the deaths that are due to unintentionally pulled triggers (26.5 percent of the deaths). Nationally, too many pistols have short and light trigger pulls. (Source: Box 3, definitions, National Violent Death Reporting System, 2014 data, 18 states, CDC Morbidity and Mortality Weekly Report, February 2, 2018 / 67(2) lines 1–36), Katherine A. Fowler et al., Surveillance Summary.)

Other products are recalled if their unsafe designs lead to injuries or deaths. But there are virtually no recalls of unsafely designed firearms. Gun makers could choose to design and sell only handguns with prominent chamber-loaded indicators and magazine-disconnect safety devices. Instead, the gun industry still designs and sells many unsafe handguns and other unsafe firearms.

# Acknowledgments

Not long after Kenzo was shot, I was shocked to discover that there were many others who shared similar tragedies due to the loopholes in our nation's gun laws. I thought: People should know about this. And thus began my project of putting what I learned into a book.

I gratefully acknowledge the many people whose support, activism and research helped me fulfill my goal. First, I want to thank my then-wife, Lynn Tsumoto, who led me to Andrew and Kae McGuire at the Trauma Foundation. The McGuires introduced me to the public health approach to gun violence prevention and directed me to a Coalition to Stop Gun Violence conference, where I met Josh Horwitz, its Executive Director, and heard presentations by Dr. Stephen Teret, Dr. Daniel Webster and others. Their information and insights provided me with much of the framework necessary for me to begin writing this book. I'd like to thank the many researchers like them whose work I have relied on, including other scholars at the Johns Hopkins Bloomberg School of Public Health, as well as Dr. Garen Wintemute, Director of the U.C. Davis Violence Prevention Research Program.

I am also deeply indebted to the founders of the Giffords Law Center to Prevent Gun Violence: Steve Sposato, Barrie Becker, Julie Leftwich, and many others. This book would not have been possible without their evidence-based advocacy.

I especially want to thank Tina Johnstone and Ellen Freudenheim, who taught me about the pitfalls and exhilaration of being an activist when I joined them to organize the 1996 Silent March. I also want to thank the many parents who lost a child, and who generously talked with me at the Silent March and elsewhere about their activism. I learned a lot from them and admire their dedication.

I am grateful to Dennis Henigan who, when he was the legal director of the Brady Center to Prevent Gun Violence, introduced me to Jon Lowy. Jon not only argued our case against Beretta USA in court, but also continued to be a mentor and inspiration for the book. Elliot Peters, of the law firm Keker, Van Nest & Peters, carried our case forward brilliantly and helped me understand legal strategies. Professor David Hemenway at Harvard patiently took the time to discuss many aspects of our case with me.

I also benefitted from the wisdom of Christian Heyne, Mary Leigh and Charlie Blek, Brian Malte, Deane Calhoun, Mattie Scott, Ruth Borenstein and Amanda Wilcox, leaders of our state gun violence prevention coalition. This book is in part the story of some of their successes.

When I started writing, I got expert help from the Community of Writers Conference (formerly the Squaw Valley Writers Conference), Linda Watanabe McFerrin, Adair Lara, and Jane Anne Staw. Elizabeth Bernstein and Connie Hale provided excellent editorial advice. I am grateful for their generosity toward me, as well as for their dedication to making us safer.

I'd like to thank my great agent, Delia Berrigan at Martin Literary Management for finding David LeGere and Miranda Heyman at Woodhall Press who believed in the importance of my book. I also want to thank Melissa Hayes for her meticulous editing.

Finally, most of all, I want to thank my wife, Marilyn Fabe, for carefully reading and commenting on draft after draft of my book chapters. This book wouldn't exist without her belief, encouragement, and enthusiastic engagement with my story.

# ABOUT THE AUTHOR

Griffin Dix has a Ph.D. in cultural anthropology from the University of California, San Diego, is a former college professor at Santa Clara University, and was Research Director at MacWEEK. He is a nationally known activist in gun violence prevention who has led the Oakland, California Brady chapter for many years, and was elected nationally by the chapters to represent them on the Brady Board. He has received many awards for his work and his op-eds have been published in more than twenty newspapers and media. See: https://griffindix.com/

# ENDNOTES

1   The California legislature strengthened child access prevention laws. In 2006 researchers at the Harvard School of Public Health published a study concluding, "States that allowed felony prosecution of offenders [Florida and California] experienced a greater effect of CAP laws than states that did not" (L. Hepburn, D. Azrael, M. Miller, and D. Hemenway, "The Effect of Child Access Prevention Laws on Unintentional Child Firearm Fatalities, 1979–2000," *Journal of Trauma*, vol. 61, no. 2, August 2006: 423–28). Also, a study found that CAP laws appear to reduce suicide rates by 8.3 percent among young people ages 14 through 20. (Daniel Webster, et al., "Association Between Youth-Focused Firearm Laws and Youth Suicides," *Journal of the American Medical Association* [hereafter, *JAMA*], vol. 292, 2004: 594–601).

2   For example, a woman told me that while visiting her brother in Georgia, she put her infant to sleep in his bedroom. When she went in to check on him, he was examining a loaded handgun he'd found in the headboard. Her brother had forgotten to remove it when she and her child came to visit. Almost every time I told someone about what happened to Kenzo, they had a story.

3   When the gun lobby runs "issue ads," they often go after a candidate's greatest weakness, real or made up. Frequently the ads do not even mention guns, or that the gun lobby paid for them.

4   During our lawsuit against Beretta USA, neither side ever told jurors about our settlement with Clifford. I always wondered if they should have, but they might not have been allowed to.

5   *The Economist* mentioned our lawsuit, and said legislatures, not courts, should decide issues of product safety. But courts often ruled on such issues, and their rulings have the force of law.

6   California Civil Code 1714.4, the gun industry legal immunity law, prevented the victims of the 101 California Street massacre, from getting their day in court. We overturned that law.

7   In 1999, Tom Diaz published *Making a Killing: The Business of Guns in America* (New York: The New Press, 1999). He pointed out that the men who "make, import and sell guns often wrap themselves in ideological and nostalgic symbols of early America." But they are not founding fathers; their goal is to make as much money as they possibly can (p. 3). They don't reveal information about product defects, the injuries they cause, and what, if anything, they have done to correct the design defects. Diaz showed that "Gun manufacturers, firearms industry associations, lobbyists, the gun press, gun importers, wholesalers, and dealers are all entwined in an interlocking network of mutual promotion." He concluded that rather than incorporating safety mechanisms into firearms, "the gun industry has deliberately enhanced its profits by increasing the lethality—the killing power—of its products." (p. 15).

8   In 1986, California voters passed Proposition 51, a ballot initiative heavily influenced by insurance industry spending for ads in favor of reducing large punitive damage claims, which they said were hurting city and county governments. Since its passage, the appeals courts—now filled with activist judges appointed by conservative Republican governors—have reduced the damages that guilty corporations have to pay.

9   Another of our *motions in limine* was to exclude any reference made by Beretta to the fact that the model of the gun that killed Kenzo had passed a safety test when it was imported from Italy. If Keane and Beretta's lawyers could convince the jury that Beretta's handgun had passed a comprehensive review

337

of firearms safety features, the jurors might not know that this regulation was not a comprehensive review of the safety design for imported firearms.

After the assassinations of President John F. Kennedy, Martin Luther King, and Robert Kennedy, Congress passed the 1968 Gun Control Act. It included a ban on importing "junk guns," inexpensive, short-barreled, easily concealable handguns made from inferior metal. They have few if any safety features and frequently misfire when dropped. Their short barrel makes them so inaccurate that they have no sporting purposes; they are too inaccurate for self-defense. However, they are well suited for close-up use by criminals in robberies and murders, and they are so cheap that after use in a crime, they can be disposed of and another one purchased.

But, when Congress banned importing them, it still allowed domestic manufacture of junk guns, and they inundated American cities. In 1993, the number of American civilians killed by guns reached its peak, of 39,595. See: G. J. Wintemute, *Ring of Fire: The Handgun Makers of Southern California*, Sacramento, CA: Violence Prevention Research Program, 1994.

10  Before the Consumer Product Safety Commission (CPSC) was established, Congress—the entire legislative body—had to discover that a particular product was poorly designed and harmful. This usually came to Congress's attention only after some horrendous series of injuries got major media coverage. The CPSC set up a more-systematic method for making products safer—and American consumers benefited.

We assume that the approximately 15,000 consumer products around us are generally safely designed. In the U. S., we rely on a safety net of consumer product safety regulation. If we lived in a third world country, we could not assume that. However, in our country, one consumer product—firearms—was made exempt because of the political power of the gun lobby.

11  The NRA was afraid that regulation of firearms by the Consumer Product Safety Commission could be a back door for "gun control." However, when the CPSC was established, legislative language to limit the regulatory

authority just to firearms product safety standards could have been agreed upon. But the NRA prevented any compromise.

There are many examples of injury prevention through product design changes. For example, eight deaths over several years caused the CPSC to recall hundreds of thousands of baby cribs that had bolts sticking out. Eight babies had hung themselves when the string tied around their necks to hold their pacifiers caught on the bolts. The CPSC knew you couldn't train all parents not to hang a pacifier on their child's neck. Safer product design was the answer.

In contrast, Congress forbids the CPSC from collecting data on firearms that are defective in design or manufacture. But private organizations have published studies of defectively designed firearms that continue to be sold due to lack of consumer product safety regulation. See: *Buyer Beware: Defective Firearms and America's Unregulated Gun Industry*, Consumer Federation of America, February 2005; and see: *Misfire: The Gun Industry's Lack of Accountability for Defective Firearms*, The Violence Policy Center, March 2021.

12 As in the news media, people seem to search for "the criminal," focusing on what public health researchers call "the portrait" (in this case, Clifford and Mark), and not on "the landscape," the context which influences people to make (unfortunate) decisions over and over. See: Lori Dorfman and Lawrence Wallack, *Moving from Them to Us: Challenges in Reframing Violence Among Youth* (Berkeley Media Studies Group, August 2009), p. 4 ff.

13 The NRA's Eddie Eagle training program is for K through third-grade kids, and is very brief. It teaches kids who see a gun to "Stop, Don't touch, Leave the area, and Tell an adult." No one could disagree, but there is no evidence that the Eddie Eagle training, which the NRA promotes to schools but refuses to test, actually works, and a lot of evidence that such programs do *not* work. (*Private Guns; Public Health*, Ann Arbor: University of Michigan Press, 2004, p. 84). "[P]rograms [like the Eddie Eagle] place the onus of responsibility on the children themselves."

14 The NRA forced Dr. Mark Rosenberg, director of the CDC's National Center for Injury Prevention and Control, out of his job. He was the leading researcher advocating the study of firearm injuries as a public health problem. See: David Hemenway, "Risks and Benefits of a Gun in the Home," *American Journal of Lifestyle Medicine*, accepted November 8, 2010.

15 In 2013, the *New York Times* found that among children under age 15, "accidental shootings occurred roughly twice as often as the [CDC's] records indicate, because of idiosyncrasies in how such deaths are classified by the authorities" ("Children and Guns: The Hidden Toll," *New York Times*, September 28, 2013). The study looked at accidental shooting deaths of children under age 15 identified by the *Times* in the eight states where records were available.

16 The following article summarizes the cuts in the CDC's funding and the attempts to revive the CDC's research (http://www.propublica.org/article/republicans-say-no-to-cdc-gun-violence-research). Finally, some federal funding began, but it is still not adequate. (Also see: https://www.nytimes.com/2019/04/17/upshot/gun-research-is-suddenly-hot.html).

17 "Self-defense gun use is a rare event. Results from the NCVS [National Crime Victimization Survey] find that guns are used by victims in less than 1 percent of crimes in which there is personal contact between the perpetrator and victim, and about 1 percent in cases of robbery and [non-sexual] assault." (David Hemenway and Sara J. Solnick, "The Epidemiology of Self-Defense Gun Use: Evidence from the National Crime Victimization Surveys 2007–2011," *Preventive Medicine*, vol. 79, 2015: 22–27.)

18 D. Weil and D. Hemenway, "Loaded Guns in the Home," *JAMA*, vol. 267, no. 22, 1992. A study by Matthew Miller and Deborah Azrael, published in 2022, found that in April 2021 of the adults with children, 40 percent lived in households with firearms. Of the firearm owners with children in the household, 36.1 percent had unlocked firearms and 37.1 percent had loaded firearms.

The percentage who stored at least one gun both loaded and unlocked was 15.0. Although firearms storage had gotten somewhat safer than their earlier 2015 study, many more U.S. households had guns. So, a similar number of children (4.6 million) lived in homes with loaded and unlocked firearms. See: https://jamanetwork.com/journals/jamanetworkopen/fullarticle/2789269

19 On the first page of the Beretta 92 manual, there was a picture of a Beretta series 92 gun with labels such as F7 and D3, then, after a long section in Italian, on page 17, came an English-language section with a list of labelled items like D1, F1, etc. Adams said that nothing in the English section referred back to the picture of the gun in the first section and told you that the letters and numbers in the English section corresponded with the numbers in the Italian section. The only way for English speakers to identify the parts was to fold out the picture of the gun and match up each letter and number on the picture with the same letters and numbers on the English-language page. "They are not really numbered consecutively," said Adams.

20 Before Adams testified, our lawyers had read portions of the depositions of several Beretta employees to the jury. Gabriele de Plano was a Beretta USA product engineering manager whose job involved establishing new products or modifications. He was not aware of any efforts by Beretta to determine how gun owners store their guns, or whether they keep them unlocked and loaded. He had never tried to find out. He had never investigated safety devices, such as lockable devices, and had not been asked to.

Rafael Aguirre-Secasa had been the marketing director for Beretta USA since about 1990. He assumed Beretta USA's customers stored their guns locked, but he'd never attempted to find out. As far as he knew, Beretta had none of the published information about accident rates or shootings by children.

21 Later I learned the history of the Springfield Armory and Colt's. Their work during the mid-1960s on the M-16 used by soldiers in the Vietnam War was less than stellar, to put it mildly. The M16 was developed (in part by the

organizations he worked for) and used by soldiers in the Vietnam War, many of whom died because it frequently jammed. I have no way of knowing of any involvement Mr. Bredbury had in those problems. But the story provides insight into military contracts, the gun lobby, and the gun industry.

Seth Bredbury testified that he'd worked at the Springfield Armory for two years, after he graduated from college in 1964. When he worked for the Springfield Armory, it *"had the responsibility for doing research and development work for the military small arms."* He was testing military rifles and machine guns and did some design work. The Springfield Armory was the military's primary facility for manufacturing military small arms, until Secretary of Defense Robert McNamara closed it in 1968. At the Armory, he had been, of course, merely a young engineer fresh out of college.

Bredbury said that after the Armory, he worked at Colt's from 1968 to 1978, testing military rifles as head of Colt's Test and Analytic Group. Colt's was the company shipping M-16s off to Vietnam for use by American soldiers, on whom they often jammed in battle. They may not have been properly tested for the conditions in which they would be used. I do not know if he played any part in that problem, however.

Here is a brief summary of the tragic story. In 1959 Colt's Firearms Division had purchased the manufacturing rights to the AR-15 (which the military renamed the M-16). By the early 1960s the military services had begun to search for a high-powered assault rifle. "Just about everything happened except what should have happened..." (C. J. Chivers, *The Gun*, New York: Simon & Schuster, 2010, p. 292).

The military services and a special committee set up by Defense Secretary Robert McNamara, with representatives from all the services "working through the government's arsenal and Colt's," made many changes to the AR-15 and its .223 round, with much infighting and inter-service positioning. "Throughout it all, as the [committee] members maneuvered and quarreled, the committee missed a basic step—ensuring that the rifle was resistant to corrosion.... Colt's...insisted that the barrel was made of a superior alloy, moly-vanadium, and would stand up to the elements without further protective steps. This was not the case. But the program rolled on, its momentum assured" (pp. 291–2). Because of a change from one type of powder (IMR 4475) to a dirtier one (WC 846, or "ball powder"), the moving parts were exposed to more heat and fouling. The rifle also became six times more likely to misfeed.

Officials from Colt's were working their contacts on Capitol Hill. Through what Chivers calls a naked political threat, Colt's profits were preserved. "General Westmoreland would get his guns ... troops in Vietnam would receive their weapons, including the unready M-16s soon to be put into the hands [of soldiers who lost their lives when the guns jammed]" (p. 296).

Chivers says, "Gun companies and gun magazines have long had relationships beyond cozy." And in 1966, "when gun journalism was needed, *Shooting Times* failed" (p. 297). The editors were mostly interested in the gun's accuracy and ease of use. Even in firing a relatively small number of rounds, however, they malfunctioned frequently. *Shooting Times* assured readers that before any gun is accepted by Army inspectors, it must pass extensive firing tests. But "[i]n fact, each rifle at Colt's factory had to fire only thirty-three rounds to pass its acceptance test..." And Colt's was allowed to use powder that gave it a lower rate of malfunctions than the ball powder soldiers would be using in Vietnam.

The NRA printed an article in *American Rifleman* praising the M16, saying it "bears up well under harsh field conditions," and that "dust, dirt and rain do not make the M-16A1 less functional, provided minimal care is exercised." According to Chivers, "The *American Rifleman* concluded, without offering evidence, that the rifle 'is proving itself in Vietnam' " (p. 298).

These early versions of M16s were indeed proving themselves—proving that they rusted easily, and that a recessed area on the bolt was difficult to clean. During firing, trigger pins and hammer pins often worked their way out of the receiver, and cartridges often ruptured, etc. When a technician was sent to investigate, his report blamed the marines for not keeping their weapons ready. "There was no mention of what was known in the Pentagon and at Colt's: the tendency of the rifles to corrode, the need for a new buffer, the problems with failure to extract" (p. 307).

343

In 1967 in the monsoon season, troops had rifles prone to failure, with a bureaucracy that blamed them when their rifles jammed. Soldiers developed a difficult and dangerous procedure called "punching a bore" to clear their jammed rifles. In battle the riflemen were unable to defend themselves or their fellow soldiers. (Ironically, this may have played into the gun industry's fear-mongering that added safety mechanisms would compromise a gun's reliability.)

In battle, says Chivers, when a second lieutenant ordered his men to fix bayonets, "He was effectively telling his men to fight to the death, hand to hand." (p. 312). Army troops began sending letters home, including to their congressmen. One survivor of a horrendously bloody battle wrote in the *Asbury Park Evening Press*, "Believe it or not, you know what killed most of us? Our own rifle. Before we left Okinawa, we were all issued the new rifle, the M-16. Practically every one of our dead was found with his rifle tore down next to him where he had been trying to fix it." (quoted by Chivers p. 313.) See chapter 7, "The Accidental Rifle," in C. J. Chivers's *The Gun* (New York: Simon & Schuster, 2010). This story shows how the political power of the gun industry and its lobby is detrimental to American military preparedness and has cost the lives of many American soldiers.

22 To improve my writing skills, I took a class from well-known *San Francisco Chronicle* columnist, Adair Lara. When we wrote essays, my first ones were so hopelessly filled with anger that she wrote in one of her columns about a father whose son was shot: "As his teacher, my job is to urge him not to be so angry. He can't describe the downtown office of a handgun-control organization without adding, 'The bare-bones decor of an office like this makes you realize there's not much money to be made in public safety. We know there's a lot to be made in selling guns.'...[T]his mild man sits before hearings in Sacramento, trembling with anger, trying to help get laws passed. 'In a society that values its children, says Griffin, 'an angry kid should not be able to buy a gun on the street for $50.'...[Griffin] can tell you that in California your child is more likely to die from being shot than from anything else" (Adair Lara, "Why Kenzo's Dad Is Angry," *San Francisco Chronicle*, November 19, 1998).

Her subtext was that I had something to be legitimately angry about. She got hundreds of angry letters in response, some with incorrect suppositions, others, with outright falsehoods. One guy, for example, said, "to blame an inanimate object (even a firearm) is ludicrous."

I had to respond. In my letter to the editor, I said I understood that it was hard for people to see that guns could be made safer. Concerning the 1,200 to 1,500 annual *unintentional* gun deaths (according to CDC data at the time), I wrote, "It is not effective just to blame the irresponsible parents again and again after all these deaths year after year. I'm for personal responsibility *and* corporate responsibility. Why should it be either/or? Makes no sense." And, "People will keep dying needlessly until gun makers are forced to make their products safer for consumers" (Griffin Dix, "Letters," *San Francisco Chronicle*, December 1, 1998).

I had taken the writing class hoping to distract me from the anger I was feeling. Well, that didn't exactly work out. The reactions I saw in the letters to the editor were so boneheaded, they made me even angrier. So, I had to re-argue our lawsuit in the press against a slew of preconceived biases. This only added new stress. Yet, I felt this was a discussion we should have in our media, and that I *should* share my experiences and the facts I had learned. I wasn't going to change the minds of the guys who wrote those letters. But I might change the minds of a few others, or make them more active on the issue. And a few more people might store their guns safely. So, even though it was stressful, I knew I was doing the right thing.

23 When the Great Recession hit, I took a job with Physicians for a Violence-free Society, a small nonprofit helping doctors assess, treat, and prevent domestic violence. That, too, was gun violence prevention. About two-thirds of the women who die from domestic violence are shot.

24 Because Tina Johnstone had organized the Silent Marches, she was able to identify plaintiffs for the *Hamilton v. Accu-Tek* case that lawyer Elisa Barnes had filed in 1995. The Castano Safe Gun Litigation Group persuaded

thirty-seven law firms to join it for gun industry reform. See: "Private Lawyers, Public Lawsuits: Plaintiffs' Attorneys in Municipal Gun Litigation," Howard M. Erichson, in *Suing the Gun Industry: A Battle at the Crossroad of Gun Control and Mass Torts*, Timothy D. Lytton, ed., (Ann Arbor: University of Michigan Press, 2005).

25 The gun industry knew the benefits of legal immunity. In California, because of a state law granting the gun industry legal immunity, a court had thrown out the lawsuit that my friends, the victims of the 101 California Street massacre, had filed against the maker of the guns used there.

After the 1996 Silent March, organized by Tina Johnstone, Ellen Freudenheim, and me, Tina, and many of the gun victims she had met in the march had initiated the *Hamilton v. Accu-Tek* lawsuit. And in February 1999, the jury had found that fifteen gun manufacturers were guilty of saturating states that had lax gun laws with far more firearms than markets in those states could purchase. The jury's decision was later overturned by an appeals court. Analysts predicted that the *Hamilton v. Accu-Tek* case would lead to similar suits. This case was another important reason that in 2002, gun-industry-immunity bills (H.R. 2037 and S. 2268) were working their way through Congress ("June Hellraiser Tina Johnstone," *Mother Jones*, May/June 1999 issue).

26 Buford Furrow had scouted the Los Angeles area looking for defenseless Jewish targets, then attacked the North Valley Jewish Community Center day-care facility in Granada Hills, firing more than seventy bullets from a Glock, and wounding three kids, their sixteen-year-old counselor, and a sixty-eight-year-old receptionist. After he fled, he murdered a Filipino-American postal carrier. Furrow had been prohibited from possessing firearms because he'd attacked a social worker and the director of a hospital psychiatric facility in Washington State. While he was still on probation, he had easily obtained the Glock at a gun show.

27 Colt's had used the marketing plan of selling at cost to the military and law enforcement in order to penetrate the consumer market long before. Glock had also, from the mid-1980s on, reached the consumer market by first winning police contracts. It had cleverly melded police training and supposedly "independent" consulting on departmental gun choice with marketing by people who were in fact on Glock's payroll—in a "built-in conflict of interest" (Barrett, *Glock: The Rise of America's Gun*, p. 58. And see: "Glock Pistol Used by Police Raised Safety Issues," Paul Barrett and Brian Grow, *Bloomberg Businessweek*, September 9, 2009.)

28 *NRA Home Firearm Safety Course: Course Outline and Lesson Plans*, 1990, National Rifle Association, Fairfax, Virginia, 1990, pp. II-22, II-41 (emphasis added).

29 In an earlier deposition, Clifford had been asked to recall when Nancy Hersh had asked him if there had been a safer gun, would he have purchased it. "I told her I would have." he'd said. When he was asked what a safer gun would be, he'd said, "I believe she described a safety device that you wear like a ring on your finger that had to be worn to be able to activate the gun." No gun like that was for sale. (The gun industry resisted it.)

30 If the bill became law, we'd argue that that provision did not apply in our case.

31 Ricker's issue had already been raised by Bill Bridgewater, executive director of the National Alliance of Stocking Gun Dealers (NASGD), the gun dealers' trade association. In his 1994 editorial in *The Alliance Voice*, the official NASGD publication, Bridgewater had said that gun dealers knew "full well that there are felons hidden among us." And he had told the gun dealers, "Let us quit pretending that we don't know that a big chunk of the 'FFL-holders [federal firearms licensees] have the licenses in their pocket as

nothing more than access to firearms at quantities and prices tha will allow them to be successful in the firearms black market."

32 Declaration of Robert A. Ricker filed in the *California Firearm Cases*, p. 8. Quoted in *Smoking Guns: Exposing the Gun Industry's Complicity in the Illegal Gun Market,* The Legal Action Project, Brady Center to Prevent Gun Violence, 2003, p. 15.

33 Robert Ricker said, "Firearm manufacturers and dealers have long known that the current firearm distribution system encourages and rewards illegal activity by a few corrupt dealers and distributors." He also said the firearms industry knows that ATF "is hampered in its enforcement efforts by inadequate resources and constraints in federal law on its ability to crack down on corrupt dealers....The industry asserts that curbing sales of guns to the illegal market is ATF's responsibility; at the same time, the industry knows that ATF cannot do this job effectively."

34 Robert Ricker said, "Until faced with a serious threat of civil liability for past conduct, leaders in the industry have consistently resisted taking constructive voluntary action to prevent firearms from ending up in the illegal gun market, and have sought to silence others within the industry who have advocated reform."

35 Rebecca Leung, "Firing Back," *60 Minutes*, CBSnews.com, May 9, 2003.

36 On *60 Minutes*, Robert Ricker said, "The National Rifle Association, every year, is before the appropriations committees of Capitol Hill advocating that ATF's budget be cut. They know that ATF does not have the manpower or the money to do an adequate job enforcing our gun laws."

37 I mentioned to Ricker that when I was a teenager my father bought me a rifle, taught me how to use it safely, and took me hunting, and that, in fact,

as kids, Nick Wilcox and I both had set up rudimentary "shooting ranges" in our basements, with targets for our BB guns. Nick and I wanted him to know that we did not advocate preventing law-abiding citizens from owning guns.

38 Smith & Wesson terminated sales to some dealers in the program who violated the Code's terms and developed a sales training syllabus for the sales associates of the retail outlets that it owned (*Smoking Guns: Exposing the Gun Industry's Complicity in the Illegal Gun Market*, Legal Action Project, Brady Center to Prevent Gun Violence, 2003, p. 25). The gun maker would, for example, sell guns only through authorized dealers who would:

- provide annual training to employees and require that they pass an exam on how to spot suspect sales and promote safe handling and storage;
- sell guns only to people who pass a certified firearms safety course or exam;
- carry out specific security procedures to prevent theft; and
- keep electronic records of crime gun traces and report them monthly to the manufacturer.

Authorized dealers would also *not*:

- sell any firearm until the background check had been completed, even if that took longer than the three days that dealers are required by law to wait;
- sell more than a single gun at a time to a customer;
- sell at gun shows, unless every seller there (including unlicensed private sellers) conducts background checks on every sale; and
- sell firearms especially attractive to criminals, such as guns with large-capacity magazines or semiautomatic assault weapons, even if they are legal.
- Smith & Wesson also agreed to do something that meant a lot to me: make design changes, such as introducing integral locks and other safety features.

349

39 When the NSSF commissioned a nationwide telephone survey to see what the public thought, it found that many knew of the S&W settlement, and that 79 percent of respondents favored it, while only 15 percent opposed it (documents produced by Sturm, Ruger & Company in the *California Firearms Case* [SR 20910-69]). It was more evidence of the great divide between the public—even NRA members—and the leadership of the gun industry.

40 The Brady Campaign and its allies ran TV and print ads, which quoted the NRA's top leaders. Soon, a *New York Times* article said, "A large number of police chiefs and other law enforcement officials have joined gun control advocates in the campaign" to block the bill.

41 The letter referred to a Brady Center lawsuit against a West Virginia pawnshop by two former Orange, New Jersey, cops, Ken McGuire and David Lemongello, who had been severely wounded by an armed robber whose gun was one of twelve handguns sold in a single transaction by the pawnshop to a drug-addicted, suspicious "straw purchaser." After purchase, the guns had quickly been trafficked to the streets. Judges in the case had already upheld the right of the lawsuit to be tried in court; in other words, the court had ruled this was not a frivolous lawsuit. (The case proceeded, and the officers won a $1 million settlement.)

42 *Congressional Record*, speech, Senate floor, on February 25, 2004.

43 Perhaps participating in the first trial influenced Larry Keane. After that trial, in 1999 the National Shooting Sports Foundation developed a program called Project HomeSafe, supposedly to "educate gun owners about their responsibilities to safely handle and properly store firearms in the home, with the goal of preventing tragic accidents among children" (Project ChildSafe web page, NSSF). This was all to the good, if it prevented injuries, but I worried it was merely a public relations stunt to be trotted out at the next trial.

Then, in 2003, not long after many police chiefs had joined us to defeat NSSF's and the NRA's gun-industry-immunity bill, the Bush administration granted the NSSF $50 million of taxpayer money for the NSSF's Project ChildSafe, which involved passing out free cable locks. Instead of giving them to gun buyers primarily at gun shops—where people buy guns—the NSSF offered them to police officers, to hand out at police stations. It seemed to me that the NSSF was trying to shore up its relations with police chiefs by aiding them in their community relations . NSSF seemed to be trying to rebuild its political power to block gun laws by regaining the support of law enforcement—at taxpayer expense, no less.

44 Jon Lowy told me that our case was "the first to be tried on the theory that guns should be made to prevent unauthorized use." He said that the Barry Grunow case was the second. This Florida case involved a student who got angry at his teacher, got a gun from home, and killed him. Apparently, the jury was angry that, like most guns, this cheap Saturday Night Special lacked a mechanism to prevent access by unauthorized users, such as the locks on automobiles, so it awarded the Grunow family $1.2 million. Unfortunately, a Florida higher court later overturned the jury's decision. But the Grunow family won favorable settlements against the gun owner and the gun dealer. "Your case was a road map for Grunow," Jon Lowy told me.

Later Jon also told me that our trial had strongly influenced the *Maxfield v. Bryco* case at which Beretta's expert witnesses, Seth Bredbury and Michael Lane, testified. After our first trial, lawyer Richard Ruggieri had sought out Jon to learn about our case, and in *Maxfield v. Bryco*, he used many of the same arguments to win.

This case, described earlier, involved the Bryco Model 38 that originally had warned users to unload the gun only on "Safe." But when the gun frequently jammed, Bryco changed it to require the safety to be placed on "Fire" during unloading, and deleted the written warning. This defect and negligence made Brandon Maxfield a paraplegic. (See http://www.brandonsarms.org/selling.php).

351

On denying victims of negligence justice in civil courts, see: Stephanie Mencimer, *Blocking the Courthouse Door: How the Republican Party and Its Corporate Allies Are Taking Away Your Right to Sue* (New York: The Free Press, 2006).

45 David Kairys, "Jurisprudence Fire Sale: How the Gun Industry Bought Itself Immunity from the Rule of Law," *Slate.com*, November 7, 2005.

David Kairys noted, "The gun-industry immunity act was a direct response to lawsuits filed in the last several years by more than 30 cities—including all the major cities in the country…and individuals harmed by gun violence… The suits primarily used a traditional public-nuisance approach based on the theory that some (not all) within the industry are knowingly supplying and marketing handguns through distribution outlets—such as particular distributors and dealers and gun shows—that provide youths and criminals that easy access." Kairys said that if the cities and individual plaintiffs had been given the opportunity to prove their allegations in court, "the industry would have been in trouble—as well it should be for such reckless conduct."

The Pentagon interfered in domestic politics. Its top lawyer, Daniel Dell'Orto, said the bill was needed to "help safeguard our national security." ("The Pentagon's Unholy Alliance: How Chuck Hagel Could Single-hand-edly Do More to Advance Gun Control than Almost Anyone Else," *Slate. com*, January 29, 2013).

The lawsuits could have been settled in ways that did not bankrupt the gun industry. The Pentagon's interference brought to mind President Eisen-hower's 1961 farewell speech, warning the nation to "guard against the acquisition of unwarranted influence, whether sought or unsought, by the military industrial complex."

46 Thomas Jefferson complained about this legislative usurpation becoming "habitual." The Federalist Papers denounced it.

47 Kairys foresaw that when they are sued for wrongdoing, other industries would also seek to suspend the rule of law for themselves, and would make large campaign contributions to get it, "since the rule of law appears to be suddenly up for sale." His prediction proved to be accurate. In 2010, with the Citizens United decision, the Supreme Court ruled that corporations were people and were entitled to First Amendment free speech rights. Their money could drown out the speech of folks who lacked the financial resources of corporations.

Unprecedented sums of money flowed into races for elective offices. The Citizens United decision also increasingly influenced the choice of judges in the 87 percent of state judgeships chosen by elections. (Robert Reich, *Saving Capitalism for the Many, Not the Few*, New York: Alfred A. Knopf, 2015, p. 78).

48 See:

https://www.bradyunited.org/legal-case/delana-v-odessa-gun-pawn

49 Here is an example of a settlement. In 2001 two police officers were shot in Orange, New Jersey, with a Ruger pistol that was part of a multiple-gun sale in a straw purchase in West Virginia. The Ruger was later transferred to a felon in New Jersey. Brady lawyers joined Scott Segal of the Segal Law Firm in Charleston against the gun dealers, and it settled for $1 million ("Brady Legal Action Project, Current Cases: Past Cases Involving Negligent Gun Distribution," p. 25, *Lemongello and McGuire v. Will Jewelry and Loan, Sturm Ruger & Co.*)

50 "Immunizing the Gun Industry: The Harmful Effect of the Protection of Lawful Commerce in Arms Act," Center for American Progress, January 15, 2016, p. 2.

51 See the Center for American Progress report: https://www.amer-icanprogress.org/issues/guns-crime/reports/2016/01/15/128949/immunizing-the-gun-industry-the-harmful-effect-of-the-protection-of-

lawful-commerce-in-arms-act/, p. 2. Data from: Colleen L. Barry, et al., "Two Years after Newtown: Public Opinion on Gun Policy Revisited," *Preventive Medicine*, vol. 79 (2005): 55–58. Valid cases that were dismissed include, for example, the unintentional shooting of Josh Adames by his friend Billy Swan in 2009 with his father's Beretta handgun that lacked a magazine-disconnect safety device. Another dismissed case was the 2012 shooting death of the daughter of Lonnie and Sandy Phillips in an Aurora, Colorado, theater. They sued the online retail company that sold the shooter thousands of rounds of ammunition and the 100-round magazine used to kill eleven people.

52  As mentioned, when Mark's father Clifford was asked if, aside from at the shooting range, he'd demonstrated anything to Mark about the Beretta, he'd replied that he'd done so once, when cleaning his gun at home: "I was trying to get his attention, but I think I was competing with the television." I think this kind of "training" of teenagers is common.

53  Cassandra Crifasi, et al, "Storage Practices of US Gun Owners in 2016," *American Journal of Public Health*, April 2018, https://ajph.aphapublications. org/doi/10.2105/AJPH.2017.304262. Also: Deborah Azrael, et al., "Firearm Storage in Gun-Owning Households with Children: Results of a 2015 National Survey," online, May 10, 2018, *Journal of Urban Health*, vol. 95, no. 3. And see: https://www.bradyunited.org/program/end-family-fire

54  https://www.bradyunited.org/program/end-family-fire; and Azrael, et al., "Firearm Storage in Gun-Owning Households with Children."

55  The estimate that seven percent of American children live in homes with a gun kept both loaded and unlocked is more than double an estimate made in 2002. (Azrael, et al., "Firearm Storage in Gun-Owning Households with Children").

56 Beretta's marketing plan had been to win the US military contract, selling its handguns at close to production cost in order to penetrate the much larger consumer market. See: Tom Diaz on Beretta USA's marketing plan and the 1993 interview Robert Bonaventure, head of Beretta USA Corp., gave, describing the plan, in Diaz, *Making a Killing*, p. 82. (The footnote for Bonaventure's interview referred to should be number 47, not 46.)

The marketing plan had worked in Clifford's case. He had been impressed when a friend told him the Beretta had passed a lot of tests for the military and police, so he felt it was reliable. During our trial, the Beretta lawyers boasted about the Beretta being subjected to the sandbox and mud tests, and yet still firing. But they presented no evidence about tests for consumer households with children.

57 On Gary Kleck's overestimates of self-defense uses of guns, see: David Hemenway, "Survey Research and Self-Defense Gun Use: An Explanation of Extreme Overestimates," *Journal of Criminal Law and Criminology*, vol. 87 (Northwestern University, 1997), 1430, available online. And: Hemenway, *Private Guns, Public Health*, p. 66ff. And see: https://www.hsph.harvard.edu/hicrc/bad-science-3/. According to *Discover* magazine, "Most other criminologists are critical of Kleck's methods, and almost all of them are incredulous at the results." See Hemenway, "Survey Research and Self-Defense Gun Use," 1430–45.

58 See: Hemenway, *Private Guns, Public Health,* p. 72; Hemenway, "Survey Research and Self-Defense Gun Use," 1430–45. And these: https://pubmed.ncbi.nlm.nih.gov/?linkname=pubmed_pubmed&from_uid=11200101

59 Andrew Anglemyer, Tara Horvath, George Rutherford, "The Accessibility of Firearms and Risk for Suicide and Homicide Victimization among Household Members," *Annals of Internal Medicine*, vol. 160 (2014): 101–10.

60 David M. Studdert, et al, "Homicide Deaths among Adult Cohabitants of Handgun Owners in California, 2004 to 2016," *Annals of Internal Medicine*, vol. 175 (April 2022), https://fsi.stanford.edu/news/californians-living-handgun-owners-twice-likely-die-homicide. Matthew Miller, et al., "Suicide Deaths among Women in California Living with Handgun Owners vs. Those Living with Other Adults in Handgun-Free Homes, 2004–2016," *JAMA Psychiatry*, April 27, 2022, https://news.northeastern.edu/2022/04/27/women-living-with-guns/.

61 https://www.thetrace.org/2016/01/gun-safety-standards/. And: *Buyer Beware: Defective Firearms and America's Unregulated Gun Industry*, Consumer Federation of America, Feb. 2005.

62 In 1993, Congress passed the Brady Law, which was soon strengthened to require that licensed gun dealers conduct background checks on people who buy guns of any type from them. But unfortunately, federal law left gun sellers a gaping loophole. As of this writing, Congress still has not required private, unlicensed gun sellers to have background checks conducted by licensed dealers on firearm sales made between individuals, including online, or at gun shows.

A national survey in 2017 on gun sales and transactions found that 22 percent are conducted without a background check. The gun lobby opposes requiring background checks on all gun sales, because with the "private sales loophole," gun makers can sell more guns. Criminals and other "prohibited persons," are especially likely to purchase firearms without background checks. See my op-ed (https://thehill.com/opinion/healthcare/439461-senate-should-hold-hearings-on-background-checks).

Years ago, Congress also passed a law forbidding ATF from investigating licensed gun dealers more than once a year. No other industry is protected in this way.

The gun lobby also doesn't want the public to understand gun violence or how to prevent it. For decades since 1996, Congress has passed budget appropriations stipulating that the CDC could not use funds "to advocate or promote gun control." It had cut the CDC's budget by the amount it had spent on gun violence research, and later extended the restriction to other agencies, such as the National Institutes of Health. These agencies were so cowed that they did not want to test what the boundaries of that restriction were for their budgets.

As a result, research about gun violence became severely underfunded. Compared with the rates of mortality due to other leading causes of death, gun violence received only 1.6 percent of the funding and 4.6 percent of the volume of publications. In comparison to mortality rates, "gun violence research was the least-researched cause of death." (David E. Stark and Nigam H. Shah, "Funding and Publication of Research on Gun Violence and Other Leading Causes of Death," *JAMA Research Letter*, vol. 317, no. 1, January 3, 2017.)

63 Monika K. Goyal, et al., "State Gun Laws and Pediatric Firearm-Related Mortality," *Pediatrics*, July 2019, https://pediatrics.aappublications.org/content/130/5/e1416.full

64 The following article provides a summary of the cut in the CDC's funding for research on gun violence: http://www.propublica.org/article/republicans-say-no-to-cdc-gun-violence-research.

65 https://www.bradyunited.org/program/end-family-fire.

66 In the early 1990s, when a large California, tax-free, health maintenance organization switched to for-profit status, it had been required by law to contribute funds to improve the health of Californians. That established the California Wellness Foundation. Firearms were the number-one killer of young Californians, and in 1993, the Trauma Foundation became the policy center for the Wellness Foundation's ten-year statewide Violence Prevention

Initiative. Andrew and Kae McGuire's informal coalition that my wife, Lynn, and I joined spearheaded that effort.

Andrew McGuire had spent many years working to prevent traumatic injury. He was also a victim of gun violence; his favorite cousin was killed with a gun. As a child he had been burned badly in an Oakland fire. He went on to campaign for fire-retardant children's pajamas and other measures to prevent trauma. He won a MacArthur Fellowship "Genius Grant."

67 *Wall Street Journal*, February 28, 1992, p. A1
See Dr. Garen Wintemute's summary of Alix M. Freedman's reporting on the Jennings family and it "Saturday Night Special" gun dynasty, on pp. 4-9 of his book *The Ring of Fire: The Handgun Makers of Southern California*: https://health.ucdavis.edu/vprp/pdf/RingofFire1994.pdf

68 The 1968 Gun Control Act established factoring criteria to determine if a handgun is deemed a "nonsporting handgun" and unsafe to import. No such standards apply to guns made in the United States. See: https://giffords. org/lawcenter/gun-laws/policy-areas/child-consumer-safety/design-safe- ty-standards/ Also see: Tom Diaz, *Making a Killing: The Business of Guns in America, The New Press, 1999*, p. 81.

69 It may seem odd that the Bleks' interests and mine coincided so closely. The Bleks and I were very different. The Bleks' son Matthew had been murdered with one of the poorly made junk guns. Kenzo had been killed unintentionally with a well-manufactured, expensive handgun designed for the military and bought legally. But both types of guns were exempt from consumer product safety regulation. And the Bleks—Republicans from conservative Orange County—and I—a Democrat from Berkeley—wanted a law establishing safety standards for handguns. Although the Bleks and I may have originally disagreed on some things, when it came to preventing gun violence, we didn't need political ideology; we knew what needed to be done.

I collaborated with them when Ellen Freudenheim, Tina Johnstone, and I initiated the 1996 Silent March. The Bleks were organizing groups in Southern California, asking people to contribute pairs of shoes with notes telling how gun violence had affected them. At California's capitol in Sacramento, we displayed the 5,500 pairs of shoes representing Californians who had died by gunfire in 1993. Then Mary Leigh's son, Timothy, trucked the California shoes, including a pair of his murdered brother Matthew's shoes, across the country, where we laid out all 39,595 pairs, which came from almost all of the states and represented US gun deaths.

70 Dr. Garen Wintemute's research had already led to AB 497, the 1990 California law that required background checks on all firearm sales, and denied the sale of handguns to persons guilty of certain violent *misdemeanors*—not just felonies. Subsequent research proved the law was effective. (Garen J. Wintemute, et al., "Subsequent Criminal Activity among Violent Misdemeanants Who Seek to Purchase Handguns," *JAMA*, vol. 285, 2001:1019–26). See: http://www.ucdmc.ucdavis.edu/vprp/publications/.

When I interviewed Dr. Garen Wintemute, he told me that during his residency at the UC Davis hospital, he began to think, "There must be something better than sewing up injured drunks at 3:00 a.m. [and] sending them back out, and [then] seeing the same person come back again and again." So he had studied public health as science in the public interest with Professor Stephen Teret at Johns Hopkins.

Dr. Wintemute found he could make a difference by researching a national problem that few had the chance—or the guts—to study. Many stay away from researching controversial, hard-to-study issues like gun trafficking. There is personal risk involved. He's been threatened many times, but likes the controversy, and the fact that few researchers work in the field.

71 On how gun-related terms permeate American English, see Tom Mauser's book, *Walking in Daniel's Shoes* (Littleton, CO: Ocean Star Publishing, 2012), p. 286.

72 Like a film noir detective, on a weekend in the spring of 1994, Wintemute went to Southern California to find the junk gun makers' plants and take pictures. He chose a weekend "to minimize the chance of a hostile encounter," and was astonished that so many guns could come from such small, humdrum sites that had so little security. As he drove from plant to plant around East Los Angeles, he thought of the title "Ring of Fire," like volcanoes spewing forth death. The media picked up the metaphor when he used it as the title of his report.

73 In this case, because California is such a large state, state-level legislation to deal with junk guns at their origin could benefit the entire country.

Some states have banned junk guns. In 1988 Maryland established a Handgun Roster Board whose job is to prohibit the manufacture and sale of handguns judged not "useful for legitimate sporting, self-protection or law enforcement purposes." The NRA tried to overturn that law. Although it spent nearly $7 million, the NRA was defeated in a state referendum.

Later research showed that Maryland's junk gun ban was associated with an 8.6 percent decrease in firearm homicides in the state "during the post–Saturday Night Special ban period than would have been expected without the ban" (D. W. Webster, J. S. Vernick, and L. M. Hepburn, "Effects of Maryland's Law Banning 'Saturday Night Special' Handguns on Homicides," *American Journal of Epidemiology*, vol. 155, no. 5, March 2002, p. 406).

74 "It's hard," she said. "I'm a Republican. The Republicans used to be good on public safety. They'd work with the police. But now the Republican legislators are against them, even though the California Police Chiefs Association made this gun legislation their priority."

75 During their years going to Sacramento, Mary Leigh and Charlie Blek learned that politicians would listen to people connected to organized groups in their district, especially ones that could get media attention and cause a

stir. To mobilize people, martial the facts, and shepherd a bill through the legislative process, they created an organization with a paid staff.

76 The NRA's money is most effective when it does not have to fight public opinion in local jurisdictions and can focus on influencing key state legislators. So, in four-fifths of the states, it had legislated "preemption" laws forbidding cities from passing gun laws stricter than state law. That amazed me. While conservatives were touting local control, they made cities and counties powerless to protect their citizens, just as junk guns were flooding their streets and gun death rates were soaring.

Once in control, state legislatures did little to prevent junk gun makers from arming criminals and kids. In fact, aided by the repeatedly disproven research of John Lott, state legislatures passed laws that required law enforcement officers to issue virtually anyone permits to carry concealed weapons. The gun industry saw profit in selling gun owners new models of small, easily concealed guns. John Lott said that in the ten states that had originally passed such laws, violent crime was reduced. But research by John Donohue and colleagues found that so called "right-to-carry" laws are associated with 13-15 percent *higher* aggregate violent crime rates ten years after adoption. (Right-to-Carry Laws and Violent Crime: A Comprehensive Assessment Using Panel Data and a State-Level Synthetic Control Analysis, National Bureau of Economic Research Working Paper, John Dononue, Abhay Aneja, Kyle D. Weber, http://www.nber.org/papers/w23510 )

A review of Lott's book pointed out, "In at least six articles published elsewhere, ten academics found enough serious flaws in Lott's analysis to discount his findings completely (David Hemenway, *New England Journal of Medicine*, December 31, 1998). With help from the gun lobby's PR machine, Lott's study got lots of press, while the others got almost none. (On John Lott, also see: https://www.thetrace.org/2022/11/john-lott-gun-crime-research-criticism/ )

77 It was a tough job. City administrators are wary of getting their city sued. But if enough cities would ban the sale of Saturday Night Specials locally, eventually state legislators would be shamed into trying to make California safer. If the city councilmen are getting headlines for dealing with an issue the public sees as important, state legislators pay attention. City councils are the training ground for many challengers for state office in the next election.

78 As Joshua Horwitz and Casey Anderson point out in their book, *Guns, Democracy and the Insurrectionist Idea* (Ann Arbor: University of Michigan Press, 2009), the insurrectionist myth and the purported "defense of liberty" by the gun rights movement has "turned *freedom* into a code word understood by the initiated to imply a quite remarkable conception of the role of private violence in our political system, eliminating the need to spell out the idea in detail or confront its logical implications" (p. 4). Horwitz and Anderson explain what is implied by the ideas I heard at those city council meetings, and show that, "The Constitution was specifically framed to prevent individuals from using mob power as a fourth branch of government" (p. 6).

79 All new models of handguns manufactured in California had to be tested by independent laboratories certified by the state. See SB 15 signed by Governor Davis on August 27, 1999 (www.leginfo.ca.gov). Unfortunately, older models that had been selling in the state prior to the bill could continue to be sold. See: http://smartgunlaws.org/design-safety-standards-for-handguns-in-california/.

80 Loraine Taylor whose twin sons had been murdered, became president of our Oakland / Alameda County Brady Chapter. Together, as we developed our chapter, several of us held regular meetings with Marilyn Washington (Marilyn Harris when she remarried) and her Khadafy Foundation friends. Marilyn's son Khadafy had been shot and killed. After a period of deep grief, Marilyn devoted herself to helping mothers whose sons had been shot. We met with her in the public housing unit where she lived to organize rallies in Oakland that involved all the Black churches, and we went together to testify

in Sacramento for gun bills. When we met, we heard more stories about the deadly effects of the junk guns trafficked into her neighborhood.

81 This only got me more annoyed, because I knew the NRA's Eddy Eagle training for children attempts to transfer parental responsibility onto kids and to interest them in guns. The NRA resists evaluating Eddie Eagle. But two recent studies had found that children who'd been taught not to touch guns were just as likely to handle them as those who had not received the training.

We had pointed out in our Arguments in Support in the Senate Public Safety Committee's analysis that, "Study after study has shown that gun safety programs for children are ineffective and may even increase the risk of unintentional firearm injury to children." Two recent experiments in which guns had been hidden in rooms where children played had found that children who had been taught not to touch guns were just as likely to handle them as those who had not. (One study was done at the University of North Carolina, the other by ABC News.)

Worley said, "Lock up firearms." But the NRA's gun safety training course materials say to keep "protection" guns instantly at hand, ready for the home invasions that the NRA talks about. To my knowledge, the NRA does not advise that everyone should lock up *all* guns.

82 Over one-third of adults either do not know that when the magazine is removed a gun can still fire, or believe—incorrectly—that a gun cannot be fired (Jon S. Vernick, et al., " 'I Didn't Know the Gun Was Loaded': An Examination of Two Safety Devices that Can Reduce the Risk of Unintentional Firearm Injuries," *Journal of Public Health Policy*, vol. 20, no. 4 (1999), pp. 427).

83 "LCAV Case Study: Lending Expertise to Groundbreaking Legislation—Research in Support of California's Handgun Safety Law," Legal Community Against Violence, June, 2004. At the time, on average, eighty-three Californians died each year in unintentional shootings. (California reduced that number

by about two-thirds as of 2020.) Nationally, for every child who died from this type of shooting, an estimated ten were treated in hospitals for *nonfatal* unintentional gunshot wounds, many of them disabling for life (SB 190, Fact Sheet, March 5, 2003).

84 Ironically, John M. Browning, the original designer of the Colt 1911-pattern pistol, did patent an effective chamber-loaded indicator in 1910, but the US military turned it down. That mistake led to the deaths and injuries of many soldiers. The modern gun industry hides that history. See: http://www. icollector.com/Colt-1911-Prototype-w-Tansley-loaded-Chamber-Indicator-Device-No-serial-45acp-mfg-1912-Finishe_i8788115.

85 CalDOJ rejected Larry Keane's argument that chamber-loaded indicators should be allowed to provide users with "a tactile and/or visual" indication of the presence of a cartridge in the chamber. The law clearly stated the indication should be "readily visible." The "loaded" indication also had to be of a contrasting *color* that was visible *only* when a round is in the chamber. The DOJ also accepted our suggestion that the accompanying explanatory text and/or graphics must be of a certain minimum size, but required them to be only one-sixteenth of an inch. Keane objected, as usual. He said, "Some devices may require more text than others." The gun industry was hoping to sell lots of tiny guns for concealed carry in California. He argued it was best to allow manufacturers the maximum flexibility, so the DOJ should require only that each letter of explanatory text have an *average* minimum height of one-sixteenth of an inch.

Keane's suggestion made me think of a discussion we'd had with him and other Beretta lawyers one day in the hall during our first trial. When we said there should be text on the gun explaining the chamber-loaded indicator, they'd said that would be impossible because it would interfere with the *scrollwork*. Some models had fancy doodles; they thought those were more important than showing a clear explanation of the chamber-loaded indicator. They hated the idea of explanatory text interfering with the sleek black, fearsome look of their death machines. The DOJ replied that text any smaller than 1/16th of an inch would not be sufficiently visible.

86 Historically, if a gun company broke ranks and challenged the NRA, the NSSF, and the few dominant gun makers, it would be punished. Ruger's CEO, Mike Fifer, knew that. When Smith & Wesson had cooperated with the Clinton administration and announced it would design safer guns and take measures to help prevent dealers who sold its guns from making illegal straw sales, the gun industry had facilitated a boycott. Large distributors stopped distributing S&W guns to dealers. Mike Fifer also knew that after Colt's president, Ron Stewart, had complied with the Clinton administration's request to design safer guns and to train dealers on how to prevent illegal straw sales, the industry had gotten him removed, even though he had succeeded in bringing Colt's from bankruptcy to profitability. ("Colt's Chief Stands Up for Federal Gun Control: The Views of Ronald L. Stewart Have Made Him a Pariah in the Gun Community. His Critics Question His Motives," *Philadelphia Inquirer*, July 13, 1998; "Chief Executive to Leave Colt's," *Hartford Courant*, August 15, 1998).

But Mike Fifer also knew there was profit to be made in the large California handgun market. So, on April 1, 2011, Ruger announced its "One Million Gun Challenge to Benefit the NRA." In widely circulated promotions, Ruger explained that for every gun sold in the commercial market in 12-months, it would give $1 to the NRA-ILA, with the goal of donating $1 million. The payment to the NRA sounded like "protection money" to me. By pledging $1 for each gun it sold between the NRA's 2011 and 2012 annual meetings, was Ruger pleading with the NRA not to exact retribution, as it had against defiant S&W and Colt's?

When Ruger ended its challenge on March 31, 2012, sales had been so good that it renamed it the "1.2 Million Gun Challenge to Benefit the NRA." The NRA's Institute for Legislative Action probably used the funds, in part, to block expansion of background check laws, thus making sure that convicted felons and other dangerous "prohibited persons," can easily obtain guns with which they shoot Americans and commit crimes, in turn generating fear—much amplified by the NRA. Ruger was so pleased with its Gun Challenge to Benefit the NRA-ILA that it carried out similar but larger ones in subsequent years.

But by January 2021, the NRA had declared bankruptcy and was trying maneuvers to escape the lawsuit against it by the New York state attorney general for not fulfilling its obligations as a New York charity. LaPierre had been accused of widespread corruption.

87 In March 2012, after Ruger said its first-quarter orders were so strong that it couldn't keep up and had to temporarily stop accepting new orders, its stock price had soared. (Dunstan Prial, FOXBusiness, March 22, 2012). By the beginning of 2012, ten different Ruger pistol models had been added to California's roster. (Ruger was also selling lots of small guns for concealed carry, but so were other gun makers. The timing of this surge in its stock price seems related to the introduction of handgun models with chamber-loaded indicators, as the Firearms Bureau Chief suggested.) Many avid gun enthusiasts like guns with safer designs.

88 Eric Gorovitz, who had been instrumental in getting SB 489 passed, told me that Senator Jack Scott had been ready to drop the magazine-disconnect safety device from the bill to make it easier to pass. But Eric got him to speak with Jon Vernick, a professor at Johns Hopkins, who told him that this part of the bill might save even more lives than the chamber-loaded indicator part. Passive devices that do not require any knowledge by the user are often more effective at prevention than ones that require the user to have learned something, such as what the indicator means. So, Senator Scott had left the magazine-disconnect safety device in the bill.

89 After Buford Furrow attacked the North Valley Jewish Community Center in Granada Hills, California, the white supremacist murdered a Filipino-American postal worker.

90 The types of California laws we passed shown by research to be associated with lower rates of gun death or injury include, for example: state laws to maintain records of handgun ownership or purchasers; comprehensive background check laws and laws regulating gun dealers and gun shows; one-handgun-a-month laws; laws requiring safety devices; child access prevention laws; laws targeting illegal gun possession; laws about domestic violence and firearms; and others.

Fortunately, the Giffords Law Center publishes research summaries (see: Giffords Law Center to Prevent Gun Violence website: http://lawcenter.giffords.org/resources/publications/). And researchers at the Johns Hopkins Bloomberg School of Public Health publish careful summaries (see: Daniel W. Webster and Jon S. Vernick, eds., *Reducing Gun Violence in America: Informing Policy with Evidence and Analysis*, Baltimore, MD: Johns Hopkins University Press, 2013, and updated edition, 2014, https://www.jhsph.edu/research/centers-and-institutes/johns-hopkins-center-for-gun-policy-and-research/index.html). See also: Harvard Injury Control Research Center, https://www.hsph.harvard.edu/hicrc/. On the effectiveness of various types of gun laws, see: http://smartgunlaws.org/category/effectiveness-of-gun-laws/.

Gun lobby spokesmen sometimes say that firearm safety training or California's Three Strikes law caused the reduction. But there is no evidence that there was more gun safety training in California than in the rest of the nation, and if there was, it was due to our laws requiring it.

And California's Three Strikes law does not explain the state's reduction in crime or violent crime. UC Berkeley professor Franklin Zimring, and five other criminal-law professors who had studied Three Strikes, signed a report saying, "The great weight of empirical studies discounts the role of three strikes in reducing crime." That included the most serious crime: homicide. (See: Emily Bazelon, "Arguing Three Strikes," *New York Times Magazine*, May 21, 2010, http://www.nytimes.com/2010/05/23/magazine/23strikes-t.html).

91 Progress in getting more of the pistols that are sold in California to meet the state's handgun safety standards continued to be slow also because the gun

industry refused to equip pistols with microstamping technology. In 2007, our coalition had sponsored and helped pass a California law (AB 1471) requiring this technology on pistols sold in the state. Microstamping technology imprints tiny markings on the cartridge casings that are expelled from pistols when fired. The markings allow law enforcement to link the casings recovered at a crime to the crime gun that fired them. But the gun industry doesn't like this technology for solving gun crimes. Due to patent issues and lawsuits, the microstamping law did not go into effect until May 2013. The gun industry boycotted California and sold very few new models of pistols in the state. California and other states should end all exemptions for old models of pistols that lack safety features and microstamping. On microstamping, see: https://giffords.org/lawcenter/state-laws/microstamping-ballistics-in-california/

92 In 2021, California's rate of unintentional gun death had crept up to 0.085. More unsafe ghost guns were being made; more unsafe handguns were being trafficked in from other states; and the gun lobby and the rank-and-file police union had passed California laws expanding the exemptions that allow more government employees to use unsafe handguns. In the "rest of the U.S." the rate of unintentional gun death in 2021 had increased much more: 0.181.

93 San Joaquin County's 2005 data was so high, Loren Lieb and I called the county epidemiologist, who told us that because of an error we should not use their 2005 data, so I used an average of the previous and subsequent years.

94 On average, during the 2011–2015 period, when many of the pistols being sold in California had the required safety features, twenty-nine fewer Californians died per year in unintentional shootings than in 2003–2007. That was 145 lives in those five years in California alone.

95 D. Hemenway, "Does Owning a Gun Make You Safer?," *Los Angeles Times*, Aug. 4, 2015.

96 Catherine Barber, David Hemenway, "Too Many or Too Few Unintentional Firearm Deaths in Official U.S. Mortality Data?," *Accident Analysis and Prevention*, 43 (2011) 724–31.

# INDEX